STARTING A LIMITED LIABILITY COMPANY

STARTING A LIMITED LIABILITY COMPANY

Martin M. Shenkman
Samuel Weiner
Ivan Taback

John Wiley & Sons, Inc.
New York • Chichester • Brisbane • Toronto • Singapore

To my wife Shelly, and my three sons: Yoni, Dovi, and Daniel.

M.M.S.

To my wife, Sondra, my three children, Evonne, Alexis, and Nikki, and my parents, Paul and Evelyn Weiner.

S.W.

To my wonderful wife Sheri, who is my inspiration, my son Evan, and my parents, Joel and Evelyn Taback.

I.T.

This text is printed on acid-free paper.

Copyright © 1996 by Martin M. Shenkman, Samuel Weiner, and Ivan Taback.
Published by John Wiley & Sons, Inc.

Library of Congress Cataloging-in-Publication Data:

Shenkman, Martin M.
    Starting a limited liability company / Martin Shenkman.
      p.   cm.
    Includes index.
    ISBN 0-471-13357-4 (alk. paper). — ISBN 0-471-13365-5 (pbk. : alk. paper)
    1. Private companies—United States. I. Title.
KF1380.S53   1996
346.73'0668—dc20
[347.306668]   95-26492

Printed in the United States of America

10 9 8 7 6 5 4 3 2

ACKNOWLEDGMENTS

We would like to thank a number of people who were of considerable assistance in the preparation of this book. Michael Hamilton of John Wiley & Sons provided outstanding support and encouragement, as usual. Special thanks to Joshua Klavan for his research and drafting assistance. The book could not have been completed without his expertise. Michael R. Leighton, Eugene Gorrin, Scott Tayne, Lori I. Bornstein, and Gary A. Phillips also provided invaluable assistance to the completion of this book. We would also like to thank Howard Kaplan for several financial planning suggestions. Bud Picillo of the New Jersey Institute for Continuing Legal Education (ICLE) has always been helpful and encouraging in the development of numerous seminars, including "Limited Liability Companies—Made Easy," the preparation of which helped develop many of the ideas presented in this book.

Any errors or omissions are ours.

MARTIN M. SHENKMAN
SAMUEL WEINER
IVAN TABACK

March 1996

CONTENTS

Part One

INTRODUCTION

1 WHAT IS A LIMITED LIABILITY COMPANY?

The "Limited Liability Company," or "LLC," has become a popular new form for organizing business and investment activities. Presently, 48 states and the District of Columbia have passed laws authorizing LLCs; the remaining states (Vermont and Hawaii) have pending LLC legislation and are expected to enact LLC laws.

CAUTION: Because the LLC laws are so new, users of this form must exercise great caution. Even in those states that have had LLCs the longest, LLCs are still very new compared with the laws for other types of business entities, such as corporations. This means that there are likely to be changes as the state legislatures refine their laws. Also, the position of the Internal Revenue Service (IRS) toward LLCs has been evolving. As this book is written, the IRS has only just announced the possibility of a more lenient approach to LLCs. Finally, court cases interpreting both the tax and legal rules will take years to develop a thorough and consistent resource. The concepts explored throughout this book will not likely change, but the nuances, and in particular the specific rules applicable in your state, or for your tax situation, could change. Therefore, it is essential to consult competent legal, tax, and accounting advisers before making any commitment. While you see this caveat in most financial, tax, and legal books, the newness of LLCs makes this caution especially needful.

An LLC is a hybrid between a corporation and a partnership. The tax and legal advantages offered by the LLC may make it the preferred entity for new transactions. This book will guide you step by step through the process of forming and operating an LLC, and at the same time will describe the many benefits that make this new form of company organization a practical way of doing business.

THE HISTORY OF THE LLC

Limited liability companies have existed throughout Europe and Latin America for many decades. The origin of the first LLC was an 1892 German company law commonly known as the *Gesellschaft mit beschränkter Haftung* (GmbH). Although Germany was not the first country to enact legislation regarding an entity similar to an LLC, it became the focal point for the countries that eventually adopted this form of business organization. Once it was established in Germany, many countries in both Europe and Latin America adopted business forms similar to the LLC.

Subsequently, limited liability company statutes were enacted in Portugal (1901), Panama (1917), Brazil (1919), Chile (1923), France (1925), Turkey (1926), Cuba (1929), Argentina (1932), Uruguay (1933), Mexico (1934), Belgium (1935), Italy (1936), Peru (1936), Switzerland (1936), Colombia (1937), Guatemala (1942), Costa Rica (1942), and Honduras (1950).

The LLC laws in these countries have had the following five basic characteristics:

1. Limited liability.
2. Required use of the word "limited" in the entity's name.
3. Full juristic personality (the LLC can sue or be sued).
4. The partnership concept of "delectus personae" (permitting a member of an association to control admission of new members to the entity).
5. Dissolution of the LLC on the death of a member, unless specifically stated otherwise in the LLC's organizational documents (Articles of Organization) and/or Operating Agreement (the contract between the various owners or Members of the LLC).

Unlike other civil law countries, LLCs have only begun to surface in the United States over the past 5 to 10 years. In the early nineteenth century, five states allowed the use of "limited partnership associations" or "partnership associations." The purpose of those entities was to provide a form of limited liability combined with the beneficial characteristics of a partnership association. The legislation that allowed these forms of organization was restrictive, and because of their unattractiveness as business entities, these associations were not used extensively.

In 1977, Wyoming became the first state to enact true legislation regarding LLCs. The Wyoming Act came as a direct result of the efforts of the Hamilton Brothers Oil Company, a company involved in international oil and gas exploration using Panamanian limited liability companies. Hamilton Brothers was embarking on a joint venture for oil exploration in the United Kingdom sector of the North Sea but preferred to do it through a U.S. entity. The Peat, Marwick, Mitchell & Co. office in Dallas, Texas, drafted the terms of the original legislation; it was presented to the Wyoming Legislature and enacted with virtually no changes.

Five years after the adoption of this landmark legislation, Florida passed its own limited liability company act. Florida enacted its legislation to limit loss of investments to Panama and other countries having limited liability company laws. Due to the uncertainty of how an LLC would be classified by the IRS, very few states followed suit. In 1982, the IRS set up a study group on LLCs, and six years thereafter, the group's input resulted in the IRS issuing Revenue Ruling 88-76 (Rev. Rul. 88-76). This ruling held that a Wyoming LLC should be classified as a partnership, rather than a corporation, for federal income tax purposes. This ruling had a significant effect. Being taxed as a partnership means that the entity pays no entity level tax. All income flows through to the members to be reported on their tax returns. Corporations generally pay two levels of tax. The corporation itself pays tax on its income and the shareholders pay a second tax on the distribution of dividends.

NOTE: The recent date of this first IRS ruling shows how new the LLC entity is under U.S. law.

As a result of this ruling, over the past five years 48 states and the District of Columbia have passed legislation permitting LLCs as a form for transacting business. The final two—Vermont and Hawaii—have pending legislation.

To properly understand the nature of any LLC, it is essential to examine the state statute under which that particular LLC was organized. The law can differ greatly from state to state.

CAUTION: When retaining a lawyer to assist you in the organization of an LLC, be certain the lawyer has knowledge and experience with your particular state's LLC laws. Also, if the business your LLC will operate will extend beyond your state's boundaries, be certain your lawyer is familiar with the other state's LLC laws or hires special counsel with the requisite knowledge for LLCs in those states.

Most statutes, known as "flexible" statutes, permit members (who are the owners) of an LLC to enter into any agreement they desire to govern internal relationships within the LLC, and are only limited by broad public policy restrictions. Under these flexible statutes, depending on the terms of the contract between the parties, the LLC could be taxed as either a corporation or a partnership for federal income tax purposes. Other statutes, like Wyoming's statute, are known as "bulletproof" statutes. Bulletproof statutes limit the ability of Members to vary provisions that are considered essential to classification of the LLC as a partnership for federal tax purposes. In states with bulletproof statutes, the LLC will always be taxed as a partnership for federal tax purposes. Other states have statutes referred to as "flexible-bulletproof," which contain default rules that ordinarily result in the classification of an LLC as a partnership for federal tax purposes but can be modified by agreement of the Members.

Under this third type of statute, unless the Members agree or provide otherwise in the Operating Agreement or Articles of Organization, unanimous consent is required for the admission of an assignee of an existing Member as a new Member and for the continuance of the LLC after the occurrence of a specific event that causes dissolution of the LLC. As will be discussed in detail in this book, those provisions ensure that the LLC will be taxed as a partnership.

NOTE: As this book is being prepared, the IRS has begun to consider permitting LLCs to simply check off a box on a tax filing indicating whether they should be taxed as a partnership or corporation. While this may minimize the risk of an LLC that intends to be taxed as a partnership (which almost all will) being reclassified by the IRS as a corporation, this concept has not yet been finalized. If it is, it may not necessarily mean that the issues discussed here should be ignored. It may still be prudent to take the steps necessary to assure proper classification of your LLC even if the IRS accepts a box check-off. Be sure to consult with your attorney and accountant as to the current IRS position before filing any tax return.

The contract between the parties, known as an "Operating Agreement," must also be reviewed when analyzing an LLC. Many states provide substantial latitude in the provisions which can be included in such an agreement. Other states mandate certain provisions that cannot be modified by an Operating Agreement.

There has been a great deal of legislation, comment, and study about LLCs since the landmark Wyoming IRS Rev. Rul. 88-76. This ruling marked the shift of IRS policy toward entities that provide limited liability to their owners. Since 1988, the

IRS has ruled that LLCs formed under 4 bulletproof statutes and 10 flexible statutes would be classified as partnerships for federal income tax purposes.

To reduce the confusion regarding the classification of LLCs for federal tax purposes, the IRS recently issued Revenue Procedure 95-10 (Rev. Proc. 95-10), which sets forth guidelines to follow under which the IRS will rule that an LLC should be classified as a partnership for federal tax purposes. Rev. Proc. 95-10 applies to all LLCs formed under U.S. law, or any LLC formed under a foreign jurisdiction that provides limited liability for its members. The IRS also recently issued Notice 95-14, which suggests that the IRS is considering abolishing the four-factor rule that distinguishes a corporation from a partnership for LLCs and other unincorporated entities (discussed in detail in Chapter 18). In addition to the IRS, other organizations also have been trying to eliminate the confusion and differences between the various states' LLC legislation. The American Bar Association (ABA) has appointed two subcommittees to study LLCs, one of which is the subcommittee of the Partnerships and Unincorporated Business Organizations Committee of the Section of Business Law of the ABA.

The IRS has issued numerous rulings determining that limited liability companies formed in the following states will be taxed as partnerships, the following is a partial listing:

- Rev. Rul. 93-4 (Germany, a modification of Rev. Rul. 77-214).
- Rev. Rul. 93-5 (Virginia).
- Rev. Rul. 93-6 (Colorado).
- Rev. Rul. 93-30 (Nevada).
- Rev. Rul. 93-38 (Delaware).
- Rev. Rul. 93-49 (Illinois).
- Rev. Rul. 93-50 (West Virginia).
- Rev. Rul. 93-53 (Florida).
- Rev. Rul. 93-81 (Rhode Island).
- Rev. Rul. 93-91 (Utah).
- Rev. Rul. 93-92 (Oklahoma).
- Rev. Rul. 93-93 (Arizona).
- Rev. Rul. 94-5 (Louisiana).
- Rev. Rul. 94-6 (Alabama).
- Rev. Rul. 94-30 (Kansas).
- Rev. Rul. 94-51 (New Jersey).
- Rev. Rul. 94-79 (Connecticut).
- Rev. Rul. 95-9 (South Dakota).

NOTE: More rulings are possible. Check with your tax adviser as to the current status of any ruling affecting the state in which you wish to organize an LLC.

THE UNIFORM LIMITED LIABILITY COMPANY ACT

The National Conference of Commissioners on Uniform State Laws has recently drafted a uniform "model" LLC Act, known as the Uniform Limited Liability

Company Act (ULLCA), which would serve to limit the differences between the various states' LLC laws. The Conference on Uniform Law Commissioners reviewed and approved the draft in 1994. The purpose of the ULLCA is to simplify, modernize, and clarify the law as well as to make it uniform throughout the United States. The ULLCA is currently being fine-tuned and will soon be reviewed by the ABA.

CAUTION: Even with a uniform act, many state legislatures will put their own "spin" on the uniform act before adopting it. Be sure to consult your lawyer about the specific laws applicable in your state. Never assume that a uniform rule will apply.

Despite the tremendous benefits derived from utilizing limited liability companies, there are a wide diversity of LLC statutes throughout the United States. Multistate activities of businesses are extensive. The recognition of out-of-state LLCs varies. The lack of uniformity among the various states raises a multitude of basic questions: May an LLC be engaged in not-for-profit activities? Can a member withdraw from an LLC and mandate the payment of fair value for the member's interest? Are one-member LLCs permissible? Who can bind an LLC and are there any limits on this authority? What fiduciary obligations are imposed on owners and managers of an LLC to the entity and its members? Do the LLC members have the authority to sue the LLC on their own as well as on behalf of the LLC? Can general and limited partnerships be converted to LLCs and how is this accomplished? Which law governs out-of-state LLCs? How is the LLC managed?

The effect of the varying state laws has been a reluctance to utilize a limited liability company beyond one's own state for fear of lack of knowledge and potential pitfalls of the other states' LLCs statutes. There is virtually no interpretive case law regarding LLCs since they are relatively new. Furthermore, even when there is case law, it will be of little assistance in interpreting the laws of other states. Therefore, uniform legislation in this area is of heightened importance. Similar uniform laws govern limited partnerships and general partnerships. These statutes have been beneficial in allowing the use of these entities across state lines. A similar benefit would certainly be achieved by having a uniform limited liability company act.

As presently drafted, the ULLCA is a flexible statute containing numerous default provisions complying with the most recent IRS rulings. These default provisions take effect unless otherwise provided in the LLC's Operating Agreement or organizational documents. The ULLCA would apply to all LLCs formed in the United States in states that adopt the ULLCA. Generally, under the ULLCA, an LLC would have the right to choose its structure, the way it conducts business, and how it distributes profits and income. However, there are general provisions in the ULLCA that would apply to all LLCs. Those provisions include the following:

1. An LLC is a legal entity separate from its members. ULLCA Sec. 201.

2. An LLC may be for profit or nonprofit. ULLCA Sec. 112(a).

3. An LLC may have one member. ULLCA Sec. 202(a). (The tax treatment of one Member LLCs has not yet been addressed by the IRS. Until it is, a one-member LLC should probably be approached with considerable caution.)

NOTE: This differs from the laws in many states, which presently require at least two members for an LLC. If this becomes the norm, the one-member LLC will eliminate the need for using S corporations in these cases and thus further cement what will ultimately be the predominance of LLCs over other forms of business and investment operation.

4. No distributions to Members may be made if the LLC cannot pay its debts, or if the LLC's assets are less than its liabilities plus amounts necessary to satisfy preferential rights upon dissolution. ULLCA Sec. 406.

5. A Member has no transferrable interest in an LLC's property, but does have a transferrable interest in distributions from the LLC and return of capital. ULLCA Secs. 501(a) and (b).

In addition to the preceding provisions, the ULLCA establishes seven mandatory provisions that cannot be overridden by an LLC's Operating Agreement. Accordingly, an Operating Agreement may not:

1. Unreasonably restrict a Member's right to access the LLC's books and records.

2. Eliminate a Member or Manager's statutory duty of loyalty.

3. Unreasonably reduce a Member or Manager's statutory duty of care.

4. Eliminate a Member or Manager's obligation of good faith and fair dealing.

5. Restrict the rights of third parties.

6. Vary the statutory requirement to wind up an LLC in certain limited circumstances.

7. Vary the statutory right to expel a Member in the case of a judicial determination that such member (a) engaged in wrongful acts that adversely affected the LLC's business, (b) committed a material breach of the Operating Agreement, or (c) engaged in conduct that makes it impractical for the LLC to carry on any business with such Member.

The ULLCA is a voluminous document containing over 80 pages of default provisions. These provisions, however, may be modified in a particular LLC's Operating Agreement to meet the requirements of a particular business. Some examples of the default provisions are:

1. *Limited Liability.* Debts of an LLC are solely those of the LLC unless the Articles of Organization provide otherwise. An LLC is legally independent from its members who are not generally liable for the debts, obligations, and liabilities of the LLC. Accordingly, Members are generally not proper parties to lawsuits against the LLC. ULLCA Sec. 303(a).

2. *Agency of Members and Managers.* Members of a Member-managed and Managers of a Manager-managed LLC, serve as agents of the LLC and can therefore obligate the LLC to third parties. Members in a Manager-managed LLC are not agents and do not have the power to bind the LLC. Acts beyond the scope of the ULLCA can only bind the LLC if they are approved after the act. ULLCA Sec. 301. A Member or Manager, as agent of the LLC, is not liable for the debts, liabilities, and obligations of the LLC simply because of the agency relationship.

3. *Existence.* LLCs may have a specific term of years or be "at will." Members of an LLC must agree to remain as Members until the expiration of the term. ULLCA Sec. 101(a). An LLC which is to exist for a specific term of years will generally dissolve upon the expiration of that term of years unless the Articles of Organization are amended before the term expires providing for an additional specified term. Alternatively, the Members or Managers can simply continue the LLC as an "at-will" entity. Pre-existing operating agreement provisions will govern the relationship of the Members except to the extent inconsistent with rights and duties of Members of an at-will company with an Operating Agreement containing the same provisions.

4. *Transferees and Creditors of a Member.* Generally, Members have no property interest in property owned by an LLC. ULLCA Sec. 501(a). This interest may be evidenced by a certificate of the interest issued by the LLC and may also provide for the transfer of any interest represented by the certificate. ULLCA Sec. 501(c). The only interest a Member may freely transfer is the Member's rights to distributions from the LLC. A transferee may only acquire the remaining rights (e.g., to vote) by being admitted as a Member of the LLC by all of the remaining Members. A transferee who is not admitted as a Member is not entitled to participate in management, require acts as to information, or inspect a copy of the LLC records. The only rights of a transferee are to receive the distribution the transferor would otherwise be entitled, receive a limited statement of accounting, and seek a judicial dissolution under ULLCA Sec. 801(b)(6). A judgment creditor may only receive the Member's right to receive distributions from the LLC and seek judicial liquidation of the LLC. ULLCA Sec. 504.

5. *Dissolution.* An LLC is dissolved upon (i) the occurrence of a specific event described in the Operating Agreement, (ii) the consent of the number of Members specified in the Operating Agreement, or (iii) the dissociation of a Member-Manager, or if none, a Member of an at-will LLC for any reason. The term "dissociation" relates to the change in relationships among the dissociated member, the remaining Members, and the LLC. If the Member files a bankruptcy or the equivalent thereof, dies, or the Member is deemed mentally incompetent, the LLC will dissolve unless continued by a vote of a majority of the remaining Members. ULLCA Sec. 801.

Enactment of the ULLCA is already being considered by several states and is expected eventually to be passed by most states. It is hoped that providing for the consistent and uniform treatment of LLCs will diminish the differences currently present among the states' LLC legislation; therefore creating LLCs and transacting business in the LLC form will be easier and more efficient.

HOW CAN AN LLC BENEFIT YOU?

An LLC generally can be viewed as a hybrid entity combining the characteristics and, importantly, the benefits of a corporation and a partnership.

A properly structured LLC will be taxed as a partnership. This means there will only be one level of taxation, not the two layers of taxation that occur with a C, or regular, corporation, and this benefit can be obtained without the complexity and restriction of an S corporation.

With limited liability for its Members, an LLC resembles a corporation. The owners of an LLC, like shareholders of a corporation, are generally not responsible for the debts and obligations of the LLC beyond their contributions to the LLC. An LLC, however, if properly structured, is not taxed at the entity level like a corporation; instead, an LLC's profits are taxed on its owners' individual tax returns, like partners in a partnership.

A third and equally important benefit of an LLC is that all its Members can manage and control the business without causing the LLC to be taxed as a corporation. Members of an LLC can directly participate in the company's management or can elect Managers to manage the business. The Members' ability to participate in the LLC's management distinguishes LLCs from limited partnerships, where there is a risk of losing one's limited liability by managing the business. Many of an LLC's benefits are available without the various restrictions faced by corporations and partnerships.

NOTE: The ability of all Members to manage should be carefully addressed in the Operating Agreement. What Members can make what decisions? What about major decisions, such as selling the business; what portion of Members should be required for approval?

LLCs also address many practical concerns faced by closely held small businesses. These businesses uniformly wish to have limited liability for their owners. To accomplish this objective, they have had to organize either as a "C" corporation and face double taxation, or as an "S" corporation and face severe restrictions on the structure of equity interests and shareholder numbers and characteristics. At the state tax level, many states impose a corporate tax on the income of an S corporation, which reduces the attractiveness of this form of entity.

Partnerships could be used to achieve a single level of taxation. With a general partnership, however, there is personal liability for all partners. In a limited partnership, at least one partner must be liable for the business's debts. A solution is to use a limited partnership with a corporate general partner. In this scenario the partner that is liable is the corporation. Since corporations have limited liability, no individual owner is liable. For a limited partnership with a corporate general partner to be taxed as a partnership, the net worth of the corporate general partner (without regard to the general partner's interest in the limited partnership) must equal 10 percent of the total contributions of all limited partners. As a result, more assets become vulnerable to the liabilities of the limited partnership. Furthermore, this requires the formation of two entities (a corporation as a general partner and the limited partnership itself) and the resulting complications, multiple tax returns, and costs.

While the LLC can solve many of the problems associated with the aforementioned business entities, it does not eliminate all problems of business owners. For most closely held small businesses, the principal owners likely will be required to personally sign leases, bank loans, and other legal documents, and provide personal guarantees, no matter whether the business is a corporation, partnership, or LLC. Thus, an important practical limitation on achieving limited personal liability of a business's owners will remain despite using the LLC format. In addition, there are certain liabilities for which the members could still be liable such as the nonpayment of payroll taxes that have been withheld from employees' wages and not turned over to the IRS or the state taxing authorities. The same holds true for sales taxes and certain environmental liabilities.

This practical limitation, however, does not negate the importance to the owners of achieving limited liability for a business. The LLC, as a C corporation, S corporation, and limited partnership with a corporate general partner, provides limitations on nonmonetary liabilities such as a customer slipping and injuring himself or herself on the business premises. While a principal owner in any of these entities may have to personally guarantee a bank loan, the proper use of an entity to own and operate the business will provide limitations on an owner's liability from lawsuits and other claims such as environmental and tort liabilities. To the extent that an LLC can provide a simpler method of achieving limited liability, it will be more effective. The simplicity of an LLC will be attractive to and increase its use by business owners and investors.

SUMMARY

The LLC is a relatively new form of business entity that has come into existence in the United States largely in only the past five years. In a nutshell, the LLC is a hybrid with the best features of a partnership and a corporation. The LLC can provide the tax benefits traditionally associated with the partnership business entity and the limited lability protection for its owners traditionally associated with the corporate form of doing business.

TIP: These benefits can be tremendous. In time, the LLC is likely to become the favored form of operating most closely held businesses and investments. Whether you run a retail store, own a small rental property, operate a home-based business, or have a family manufacturing enterprise with $100 million in sales, it pays to at least consider the LLC.

Presently, almost all the states have enacted statutes authorizing the formation of limited liability companies. These statutes vary from state to state and each statute must be examined to determine the potential tax effects to a specific entity. The ULLCA is a model act that has been drafted with the hope of providing a uniform statute for forming LLCs so there can be consistency when analyzing a particular LLC. Furthermore, the ULLCA provides tremendous flexibility in structuring the LLC.

2 COMPARING LIMITED LIABILITY COMPANIES WITH OTHER BUSINESS ORGANIZATIONS

Perhaps the best way to understand an LLC and the advantages it can offer to you, is to compare it with the following traditional business organizations: "C" corporations, "S" corporations, limited partnerships, and general partnerships.

LLCs COMPARED WITH CORPORATIONS

The LLC versus a "C" Corporation

Any corporation (no matter what its classification for tax purposes) is a legal entity formed under the laws of a particular state. Although the names and procedures vary from state to state, a corporation is generally formed by a person, called the "Incorporator," who signs a brief several-page legal document called a "Certificate of Incorporation." This contains certain key facts about the soon-to-be-formed corporation such as the number of shares (certificates that prove ownership), number of directors, the name of the corporation, and the name of a person (called the "Registered Agent") to whom legal notices can be sent. The Incorporator files this Certificate of Incorporation with the Secretary of State, and the corporation is formed. Once formed, a key tax decision must be made: Should the corporation choose ("elect") to be taxed as an S corporation (discussed later in this chapter)? If no action is taken, the corporation will be a "C" or "regular" corporation for tax purposes.

A C corporation is a regular corporation, which must pay a corporate level tax. C corporations are subject to two layers of taxation. First, a corporate tax is imposed against the corporation's earnings and then, after the earnings are distributed to the shareholders as dividends, each shareholder must pay taxes separately on his or her share of the dividends. Since no tax deduction is allowed to the corporation for its distribution of dividends, there is no chance of lessening the overall tax liability.

NOTE: In a closely held corporation (one owned by a small number of owners or shareholders), the shareholders often are also employees of the corporation. In this capacity, they withdraw most or all earnings of the corporation as salary, leaving little or nothing to pay out as dividends. When this is done, the corporation claims a deduction for the salaries paid, and the shareholders report the salary received as income on their personal income tax returns. This eliminates the double taxation.

This strategy is not without risks. The IRS often challenges salary payments as being excessive compensation if they are larger than a nonowner normally would receive. If successful, the IRS would require the corporation to treat a portion of the "salary" as a dividend, thus forcing the corporation and its owners back to the unfavorable situation of double taxation.

One of the principal goals of an LLC is to be treated as a partnership, not as a corporation, for federal and state income tax purposes. A partnership is not subject to federal income tax; rather, it is an entity through which income or loss "flows through" to partners who are taxable in their individual capacities on their distributive shares of partnership taxable income. This means that all the LLC's income, deductions, gains, losses, and credits flow through to, and are reported on, the tax returns of its members. The LLC itself, if properly structured, pays no tax, which is similar to a partnership but unlike a C corporation.

The classification of an entity as a corporation or partnership for federal income tax purposes is governed by Section 7701 of the Internal Revenue Code of 1986, as amended (the "Code"), and the regulations promulgated thereunder. The regulations set forth six basic characteristics of a corporation. Two of the characteristics are common to both partnerships and corporations and are therefore not material in distinguishing a corporation from a partnership for federal tax classification. Those characteristics are (1) the presence of associates and (2) the objective of carrying on a business for profit. The remaining four characteristics, however, are relevant and decisive for tax treatment.

TAX TIP: The IRS has indicated that it may permit taxpayers to simply check a box on an LLC tax return to indicate that it wishes to be taxed as a partnership and not a corporation. Check with your tax adviser to see the status of this when setting up your LLC. Even if the IRS accepts this, still consider structuring your LLC to qualify as a partnership with consideration with the following requirements. For now, it's still better to play it safe.

For federal tax purposes, every corporation has the following four key characteristics:

1. *Limited Liability of Shareholders.* A corporation has limited liability if no shareholder is personally liable for the debts of, or claims against, the corporation.

CAUTION: Although limited liability may exist in the IRS's eyes, for most closely held businesses this is almost never a reality since lenders, landlords, and others often insist on a personal guarantee from the individual shareholders.

2. *Continuity of Life.* A corporation has perpetual duration and does not cease to exist if one or more shareholders dies, sells out, or becomes bankrupt.

NOTE: Most Certificates of Incorporation contain a provision stating that the corporation's existence is perpetual.

3. *Free Transferability of Shares.* A corporation's shareholders may transfer their shares to anyone without the consent of the other shareholders, unless there is an agreement among the shareholders to the contrary.

> **PLANNING TIP:** Every shareholders' agreement (and LLC Operating Agreement) should carefully address in detail what rights any particular shareholder has to sell shares. You wouldn't want a disgruntled shareholder (e.g., your just ex-brother-in-law) to sell shares to your biggest competitor!

4. *Centralized Management.* Corporations are managed by a board of directors who have the exclusive authority over business decisions and are elected by the shareholders.

> **NOTE:** The bylaws of the corporation often contain details as to the rights and powers of the board of directors. Bylaws are analogous to the "constitution" for a corporation and take the form of a legal document listing rules governing the operations of the corporation. Bylaws are usually adopted by the shareholders at their first meeting. A shareholders' agreement often includes provisions detailing the rights of the directors. An LLC Operating Agreement would include analogous provisions governing the operations and management of the LLC and the rights or powers of the LLC's Managers.

LLCs generally have one or two of the preceding corporate characteristics. Most state LLC statutes provide for limited liability of its Members and for centralization of management, and do not provide for an LLC's continuity of life or free transferability of interests. For a more detailed discussion on the classification of an LLC, see Chapter 18.

The IRS has issued pronouncements (Revenue Procedure 95-10 and Notice 95-14) addressing the classification of an LLC for federal tax purposes. The IRS has suggested that it may eliminate the complicated four-factor test, previously described, which decides whether an entity is taxed as a corporation or a partnership for federal tax purposes. This would mean that the IRS would permit any LLC to be taxed as a partnership or corporation.

Under the proposed new regulations, all the Members of an LLC would have to sign ("execute") a statement indicating their choice of tax status (an "election") to be taxed as a partnership. This election has been referred to as a "check-the-box" election. If a new entity fails to make an election, it is automatically classified as a partnership. Entities in existence when the rules take effect would continue with their current tax status, unless they change their status with an election.

> **CAUTION:** There are serious tax considerations which need to be contemplated before an existing entity changes the tax classification of its entity. No such conversion should transpire without the advice of tax counsel.

For a more detailed discussion regarding the classification of LLCs under these IRS announcements, see Chapter 18.

Advantages of an LLC Compared with C Corporations

From a tax perspective, if a substantial portion of a C corporation's income is to be distributed to its shareholders as dividends, the corporation will have to pay a corporate tax and the shareholders will be taxed on the distributed dividends, resulting in double taxation. Under this "double tax" scenario, it would be preferable to be an LLC where there will be only one level of tax, which is at the Members' level. An LLC is not subject to this "double" taxation on the sale of its assets and its subsequent liquidation, where a C corporation would be so subject.

EXAMPLE: You form a C corporation to manufacture widgets. Ten years later, you decide to end the corporation and sell out. The buyer does not wish to buy your stock because she is afraid of any liabilities that the corporation may have which she may not have been able to identify during the investigations she did before agreeing to purchase your business. So she insists on buying the assets of your corporation. To do this, you have to end (liquidate) your corporation and have the corporation distribute its assets to you personally as the shareholder. You will then sell the assets to the purchaser. On receiving the distribution of corporate assets, you will likely face a tax. The corporation may also have to pay a tax on the distribution. Thus, even in liquidation, you and your C corporation could face double taxation.

However, if the entity's income is not to be distributed to its owners, then it may be more advantageous to be a C corporation.

EXAMPLE: You are a successful businessperson and pay tax at the highest federal, state, and local rate of 48 percent. Your corporation earns so much money that you decide to leave funds accumulate in the corporation. In this situation, the corporation can be an advantageous form for your business since the corporation is in a lower tax bracket than you.

CAUTION: If your corporation accumulates too much money (beyond the reasonable needs of the business), the IRS may seek to apply a penalty tax called the accumulated earnings tax. The accumulated earnings tax is a penalty imposed on a C corporation that the IRS determines has retained too much earnings, rather than paying such earnings to the shareholders, with the purpose of avoiding taxes on shareholders. The rate of tax on improper accumulations, applicable to all corporations subject to the tax, is 39.6 percent of "accumulated taxable income."

Being an LLC avoids the risk of being subject to certain potential taxes applicable to C corporations.

The personal holding company (PHC) tax is a tax in addition to the regular tax on corporate income. It is a special 39.6 percent tax imposed on the "undistributed personal holding company income" of a personal holding company. The personal holding company tax is aimed at "incorporated pocketbooks" that the corporation has established to receive and hold investment income or compensation of their shareholders. The PHC tax is assessed on undistributed PHC income of a PHC. This is PHC income reduced by dividends paid and federal income tax. A PHC is a corporation with at least 60 percent of its adjusted ordinary gross income for the year consisting of PHC income; also, during the last half of the tax year more than half of the value of its stock is owned by five or fewer shareholders. PHC income consists of dividends; interest; royalties (excluding copyright and computer software royalties); annuities; rents (an exclusion is provided for real estate businesses where more than half of the adjusted ordinary gross income is rents); mineral, oil, and gas royalties (an exclusion is provided for corporations where royalties are more than half of the adjusted ordinary gross income); rents for film exhibition and distribution (an exclusion is provided for corporations where rents are more than half of the adjusted ordinary gross income); amounts received under contracts for personal services; and so on.

There is also the accumulated earnings tax mentioned earlier. An overview of how this accumulated earnings tax works can illustrate its severity. Where an accumulated earnings tax is assessed, it is charged at a flat 39.6 percent rate on accumulated taxable income, which for most corporations includes taxable income of the corporation subject to several special adjustments:

Taxable Income

- (−) Federal income taxes are deductible.

- (−) Charitable contributions which could not be deducted for purposes of the regular tax because of the limitation that contributions cannot exceed 10 percent of taxable income.

- (+) No deduction is allowed for dividends received. Most corporations can receive a deduction equal to a large portion of dividends they receive from other corporations. This special deduction is added back.

- (+) Capital loss carryovers are not permitted. These are amounts that are not deductible in certain years because of the limitation on capital losses, but they can be carried over to and perhaps deducted in other tax years.

- (−) A deduction is permitted for net capital gains and losses. However, this amount must be adjusted by a special factor.

- (−) The accumulated earnings credit is the amount of income that the corporation can retain for the reasonable needs of its business. A minimum amount is permitted to most corporations (other than personal service corporations) of $250,000 (from the combination of both past and current earnings). The courts will often consider whether the liquid assets of the corporation are excessive when compared with the reasonable business needs of the corporation. Reasonable business needs can include maintaining reasonable working capital, replacing plant and equipment, redeeming stock of a deceased shareholder, and amortizing debt.

The accumulated earnings tax is a particular concern for every closely held corporation. The corporation should document, such as in board of director minutes, the commercial business reasons for retaining funds. These could include working capital needs, proposed expansion plans, contingent liabilities, and so forth.

With a C corporation, one way to reduce the amount of income subject to corporate level tax would be to increase the compensation paid to employees and shareholders, rather than paying them dividends. This was noted briefly earlier. In this manner, the double taxation on the dividends the corporation pays to its shareholders is bypassed by way of distributions through salaries.

The IRS, however, may consider such compensation as excessive, and reclassify part of the compensation as a dividend. In this case, the corporation loses its deduction for the excessive amount of compensation, while the employee is required to include the payment and income as a dividend, resulting in two levels of taxation. A similar result can follow where inappropriate personal expenses are deducted.

Being an LLC avoids the personal holding company and accumulated earnings taxes as well as any unreasonable compensation issues. Also, if there is no double taxation, there is less incentive to claim inappropriate personal expenses as a business deduction.

Numerous employee fringe benefits enjoy tax-favored status. Employees of a C corporation may enjoy these fringe benefits without having them taxed as income. By contrast, fringe benefits provided to LLC members who own greater than 2 percent of the Membership interests in the LLC are taxable as income to the Members. An example of such fringe benefits are term life insurance and medical benefits.

There is also an alternative minimum tax that may be imposed on a C corporation. This is a tax designed to make sure that corporations taking substantial advantage of tax benefits provided under the Code still pay a minimum tax. An LLC would not be subject to this tax. However, the Members may be subject to a personal alternative minimum tax.

Another significant incentive to utilizing an LLC rather than a C corporation is the potential double taxation on the liquidation of a C corporation. Prior to 1986, if a C corporation was planning to liquidate and sold appreciated assets, it would not have to recognize a gain on such a sale and there would only be a subsequent gain or loss to the shareholders on liquidations of the corporation.

The Tax Reform Act of 1986 substantially modified this law and stated that there will be double taxation when the C corporation sells its assets and then liquidates. With an LLC, there is only one level of taxation on the sale of appreciated assets and subsequent liquidation.

The pass-through nature of LLCs can be a major advantage since losses, as well as gains, pass through the LLC to its Members. In this fashion, the Members are able to utilize losses of the LLC against other income they may have, depending on the character of such losses.

Under the current tax structure, there may be an incentive to utilizing a C corporation over an LLC. The Revenue Reconciliation Act of 1993 ("1993 Tax Act") sets the highest individual tax rate at 36 percent with an additional 10 percent surcharge on all taxable income in excess of $250,000. This creates an effective marginal tax bracket of 39.6 percent for individual taxpayers with taxable income in excess of $250,000.

Thus, as a result of the 1993 Tax Act, the highest C corporation tax rate is 34 percent for a C corporation with taxable income not exceeding $10 million. It is somewhat higher for taxable income in excess of that amount. Therefore, the highest federal individual tax rate is greater than the highest corporate tax rate.

EXAMPLE: Assume two 50 percent members (owners) of an LLC are in the highest marginal tax bracket (39.6 percent) for federal income tax purposes, and the LLC has $500,000 of taxable income in 1996. The owners combined will pay a total $198,000 of taxes on the $500,000 of income.

EXAMPLE: Use the same facts as in the preceding example, except now assume that the two "members" are instead 50 percent shareholders in a C corporation. The corporation will pay a 34 percent corporate level tax on the $500,000 of taxable income, which results in a $170,000 income tax liability. Thus, if the corporation in this example does not distribute its earnings to the shareholders, the total tax paid is greater using an LLC.

EXAMPLE: If the corporation, however, distributes all of its after-tax income to its shareholders, there will be a dividend of $330,000 ($500,000 income − $170,000 in corporate taxes calculated in the preceding example) payable to the shareholders. The shareholders would then pay federal income taxes on the $330,000 dividend they received of $130,680 (assuming again the 39.6 percent tax rate). The total amount of tax paid by the C corporation and the two shareholders in this example, where the C corporation distributes its after-tax income, is $300,680. Therefore, the total amount of tax paid would be significantly greater for the C corporation if its earnings are distributed to the shareholders than if it utilized an LLC.

Thus, the advantage of being a C corporation solely because corporate income tax rates are lower than individual rates may not be prudent if there is an intention of distributing the profits to the owners.

While there are many advantages of an LLC over a C corporation, certain tax incentives apply to a C corporation.

EXAMPLE: The 1993 Tax Act includes an incentive for individuals (investors other than corporations) who have held qualifying stock in a Qualifying Small Business (QSB) and have sold it at a profit. This new benefit applies whether the stock owned is common stock or preferred stock. If you meet the various requirements, you can exclude up to 50 percent of the taxable gain when you sell, or otherwise dispose of, the stock. The half of the gain that is not excluded is taxed at favorable capital gains rates (28 percent compared with individual tax rates of up to 39.6 percent), since under the 1993 Tax Act the stated maximum tax on capital gains is 28 percent. Therefore, if you can exclude one-half of the gain, the effective tax rate on the entire sale is only 14 percent. Be careful in evaluating the benefits of this special tax incentive because the tax benefit could be less than expected if you are subject to the alternative minimum tax. To qualify for this favorable benefit, the entity must be a C corporation. An S corporation, partnership, or LLC will not qualify. Thus, if this benefit could be important, choosing to organize the business as an LLC could be a mistake.

Another important advantage that a C corporation may have over an LLC is that it is relatively inexpensive to form because the filing fee is minimal and the documentation is pretty straightforward. LLCs, on the other hand, may have more significant start-up expenses.

EXAMPLE: Some states require that an LLC publish a notice in specified legal or other papers. This cost can exceed $1,000.

While LLCs have flow-through treatment for federal tax purposes (the members who own the LLC report the income—it flows through from the LLC to their personal tax returns), there may be state and other local taxes.

Also, the C corporation offers greater flexibility in selecting a fiscal year; generally, an LLC must use a calendar year. A fiscal year is a tax year for the corporation that ends at the end of any month other than December.

The LLC versus an "S" Corporation

Like C corporations, S corporations are entities formed under a state's laws by a person called an Incorporator filing a Certificate of Incorporation. The only difference between an S corporation and a C corporation is its tax status. This difference is vitally important.

S corporations are currently the most common type of organization for structuring a closely held business. These corporations are popular because they provide the limited liability associated with a corporation, and the flow-through tax treatment associated with a partnership. As such, the corporation may be held liable with its assets available to creditors of the corporation, but the personal assets of the shareholders will generally not be at risk. Only the amount invested by the shareholder in the corporation will be obtainable by the corporation's creditors.

S corporations have commonly been used as the general partner of a limited partnership that owns real estate or other family limited partnerships, to protect the general partner/family business owner from personal liability. Although limited liability is far from a fail-safe protection, it is almost always worth striving for.

The "S" designation in an S corporation refers to its special tax treatment. S corporations are taxed like partnerships for federal tax purposes, which means the income and deductions flow through to the shareholders and are reported on their personal tax returns. For legal purposes, however, the entity is treated like a regular corporation. Income earned from C corporations is subject to tax twice. As previously discussed, a regular C corporation pays tax on its income; then if it distributes a dividend, its shareholders must pay a second tax on this same income. This tax benefit of avoiding double taxation has made S corporations a common ownership form for many, if not most, small, family or closely held businesses.

A corporation must meet a number of requirements to obtain the benefits of S corporation status.

There Can Be Only One Class of Stock

This means that each share of stock must give the same rights as every other share when it comes to corporate profits and to corporate assets if the corporation is liquidated. The shares are allowed to differ with respect to voting rights and transfer, repurchase, and redemption rights. Therefore, if there is to be a distribution of profits to a shareholder, there must be a simultaneous proportionate distribution to all the other shareholders. For example, if there are equal shareholders A, B, and C and there is to be a $50,000 distribution to A, there must be a simultaneous $50,000 distribution to each of B and C.

There Can Be No More than 35 Shareholders

This limitation only applies to a single S corporation. If multiple S corporations are formed to hold interests in a partnership created to operate the business, there can be more than 35 shareholders. For this limitation, a husband and wife are treated as one shareholder.

Only Persons Who Are Individuals May Be Shareholders (with Certain Exceptions)

Most important, only certain trusts and estates are allowed to be shareholders.

For a trust to be a shareholder, it must be a special trust called a Qualified Subchapter S Trust (QSST). For a corporation to qualify as an S corporation, it must have only qualified shareholders including only certain types of trusts. The beneficiary must be treated as the owner of the portion of the trust that consists of S corporation stock. This means that you can have a trust with S corporation stock as an asset as well as other assets. In effect, such a trust will be treated as if it is two separate trusts: (1) a qualified S corporation trust (QSST) that meets all the requirements outlined here; and (2) a regular trust that can accumulate or sprinkle income in any manner. Your trust will qualify as a QSST if it meets the following four requirements:

1. If the trust terminates during the life of the person who is then receiving the trust's income, all the assets must then be distributed to that beneficiary.

2. During the life of the current income beneficiary, only that person can receive income from the trust. More specifically, all the trust's income must be distributed, or at least is required to be distributed currently to one and only one individual beneficiary. This beneficiary must be a citizen or resident of the United States.

This latter requirement helps assure that the beneficiary will be taxed by the United States. The IRS can forgo the corporate-level tax but cannot forgo the corporate level tax and then have to chase a foreign resident for taxes. These requirements can significantly infringe on your planning. For example, typical children's trusts where several children are beneficiaries of a single trust will not qualify. Charitable remainder trusts also cannot qualify as QSSTs.

A grantor trust qualifies since all income is taxed to the grantor. A trust over which a person other than the grantor is treated as the owner of the trust qualifies. This is a trust where such person (often the current beneficiary) has the sole power to vest the corpus or the income in him- or herself. These are trusts in which the income is taxable fully to that person. An example is the revocable living (loving) trust. The typical credit shelter or bypass trust used in many estate plans can create serious problems if the decedent owned shares in an S corporation.

3. If any principal of the trust is distributed while the current income beneficiary is alive, the income must be distributed to that beneficiary. This means the trustee cannot have the power to sprinkle trust income, or make discretionary principal distributions, to different beneficiaries, or to accumulate income that is not distributed (all income must be distributed currently).

CAUTION: The IRS has interpreted many of these provisions very strictly. A trust agreement permitted the trust to distribute principal to someone other then the current income beneficiary if the trust no longer held S corporation stock. In one case, the IRS held that this did not violate the QSST requirements since the trust provision was only effective where there was no S corporation stock. In a different, but similar situation, the IRS held that such a provision, when coupled with other deficiencies in the trust agreement, violated the S corporation/QSST requirements because there was a possibility that a distribution could be made to someone other than the current income beneficiary, while such beneficiary was alive.

---

4. The interest the current income beneficiary has in receiving his or her current income distributions from the trust must end on the earlier of the death of that beneficiary, or the termination of the trust. If the trust ends during his or her life, the trust assets must all be distributed to the current income beneficiary.

A trust to which S corporation stock is transferred pursuant to the terms of a will can only be an S corporation shareholder for 60 days, or the S corporation status will be lost.

CAUTION: S corporation shareholders must review their estate plans to avoid future problems. Representations should probably be obtained in the shareholders agreement stating that estate plans will be reviewed and changed if necessary.

It's not enough that your lawyer merely include the necessary provisions in your trust agreement for it to qualify to hold S corporation stock. There are several important filing requirements to be made with the IRS for your trust to qualify as a QSST and thus be able to own S corporation stock without tainting the tax status of the corporation. This election must be made separately by the current income beneficiary for each S corporation stock held by a trust. For example, a grandfather made gifts of S corporation stock to trusts for each of his grandchildren. Each grandchild, as the current income beneficiary of each trust, must make the required election with the IRS office where the S corporation files its income tax returns. Don't file such an election in the IRS where you happen to live or work, unless the S corporation files its tax return in the same IRS office.

The election must clearly indicate that it is an election under Internal Revenue Code of 1986, Section 1361(d)(2). The election should demonstrate that the beneficiary, or other person, making the election is in fact entitled to make the election.

CAUTION: The election must generally be made within 2½ months of the date on which the trust first becomes a shareholder. Also, the election must be filed before the QSST election is effective. While you should make every effort to file a timely and proper election, the IRS has shown compassion to some of those missing the deadline. This doesn't mean miss the deadline. It means, if you inadvertently do, try letting your tax adviser pursue the IRS's gratitude with a request for a waiver of the particular provision (whether it's the election or something else). You might just have some luck.

If there are successive income beneficiaries, there is no need to make a new election.

NOTE: Carefully review with your adviser whether to make the election. Once you have made the election, you cannot change it.

The beneficiary of a QSST should be given the necessary information for tax filing. This becomes somewhat confusing because of the various legal entities involved, and because the guidance from the IRS is a bit sparse. The S corporation must provide the trust (the QSST) with a Form 1120S, Schedule K-1, reflecting all income or loss to the trust from the S corporation for the year. The trust could then attach a copy of this form to the Form 1041, Schedule K-1, which the trust then gives the beneficiary.

A Nonresident Alien May Not Be a Shareholder

A nonresident is a person who lives outside the United States. An alien is a person who is not a U.S. citizen. Thus foreign persons cannot own an interest in an S corporation. For most businesses, this is not an issue. However caution must be exercised.

TIP: Have every shareholder represent in the S corporation shareholders agreement that they are not nonresident aliens and that they will not sell or transfer their stock to one.

NOTE: Congress has talked about liberalizing this requirement. If this happens, it will put S corporations on more even ground with LLCs in this regard. However, until they do, those businesses or investments with a nonresident alien owner (or that want the flexibility to admit one at a later date) should carefully weigh the benefits of using an LLC.

A Timely and Proper S Corporation Election Must Be Made

Tax choices must always be made with care. Anytime you form any entity, be certain to follow up immediately with your accountant to be sure any necessary tax elections are made and filed with the appropriate formality.

An S Corporation May Not Own 80 Percent or More of Another Corporation

This is a problem for holding company structures. If you require a more complex structure, the S corporation may not work. While an LLC has more flexibility in this regard, C corporations often seem the most common.

The S Corporation Must Be a Domestic Corporation

This means the S corporation must generally be organized under the laws of one of the states. For most people, this is not an issue.

CAUTION: Where a corporation will do business in more than one state, it will have to be qualified in that second state. This may require the formal filing of a certificate in that state.

TIP: An additional problem with using an LLC in more than one state is that the LLC laws are relatively new and differences exist from state to state.

Advantages of LLCs Compared with S Corporations

Unlike an S corporation, an LLC is not subject to restrictions on the number of owners (Members). This contrasts favorably with an S corporation, which may have no more than 35 shareholders. In addition, there are no restrictions on the nature and character of those who can be owners of an LLC, as opposed to an S corporation. S corporations are subject to substantial restrictions that can wreak havoc with the best of plans. For example, S corporation shareholders are limited to individuals, decedents' estates, bankruptcy estates, and only specific types of trusts; nonresident aliens are not permitted to be shareholders; and an estate can only hold stock in an S corporation for a limited time period.

NOTE: Many people desire to set up trusts for their children to be the owners of stock in an S corporation. These trusts must be specially tailored to be eligible for holding stock in an S corporation. They must require mandatory distributions of income to the child and the trust can only provide for distributions of principal to that same child. Therefore, if the trust involves a minor child, the parents would have no alternative but to distribute all the income to that child, which generally would be contrary to their objectives.

With an LLC, the trust can be structured in any fashion desired by the parents and still be permitted to be a Member in an LLC.

An S corporation requires an election to enjoy pass-through tax treatment. This election must be filed by the 15th day of the third month of its tax year for the election to be effective for that year. No such election is required of an LLC to enjoy pass-through tax treatment.

Any shareholder of an S corporation can cause a termination of the S corporation's "S" status by transferring stock to someone not permitted to hold stock in an S corporation. No such problem exists with an LLC.

An LLC can provide for almost any type of allocation of the structure of its cash flow, income, expense, and gains among the members. An S corporation, on the other hand, is inflexible; each share of stock must be entitled to identical distribution and liquidation rights. This can be an important drawback where owners make different contributions to the business. For example, it is common for the owners of a start-up company to desire different allocations of income among the owners when one owner contributes land, another a building, and another contributes other assets. This is almost impossible to do in an S corporation, and cumbersome efforts often cannot achieve the desired objectives. The LLC can provide tremendous flexibility in this regard.

EXAMPLE: If an S corporation is owned 50 percent by Parent and 25 percent each by child A and child B and the corporation makes a $50,000 cash distribution to the Parent, then the corporation must make a simultaneous distribution of $25,000 each to child A and child B. There is no flexibility for the Parent to receive the $50,000 distribution without corresponding distributions to the children. With an LLC, there is the flexibility to make a $50,000 distribution to Parent with no requirement to make distributions to the children.

PLANNING TIP: Consider using both an LLC and S corporation or two (or more) LLCs for the situations previously described. For example, if your business will own real estate and valuable equipment, have one LLC own the building and rent it to your business (which may be organized as an LLC or S corporation, or perhaps a C corporation to take advantage of one of the special tax benefits available to corporations), and a second LLC could own your equipment and rent it to the business. This is useful from an asset protection perspective. If the creditors, customers, or other plaintiffs sue the business entity, they should have no rights to reach the valuable real estate or equipment assets since the business does not own them.

In addition to the many other restrictions, the S corporation is subject to the following two statutory restrictions, neither of which apply to the LLC:

1. Shareholders may not include other corporations, nonresident aliens, partnerships, LLCs, trusts that distribute income to more than one beneficiary, pension funds, or charitable organizations.

2. It cannot have subsidiaries. Unlike an S corporation, an LLC may own any amount of the stock of a corporation, or interests in other entities (LLCs, partnerships, etc.).

PLANNING TIP: As illustrated in the preceding planning tip, it can be advantageous to have separate entities own different assets for liability protection purposes. When this is done, don't have any one entity own all or even part of the other entities (e.g., subsidiaries as in this discussion) since this could enable the creditors or claimants of one entity to reach the assets of the other entity.

Moreover, the treatment of deductible losses may be more advantageous to the LLC Member, compared with the S corporation shareholder. An S corporation shareholder's deductible losses are limited to the shareholder's basis in his or her stock plus any loans he or she has made to the corporation. In contrast, an LLC Member, like a partner in a partnership, can deduct losses in an amount up to the sum of his or her basis in his or her LLC Membership interest plus his or her allocable share of the LLC's debt.

EXAMPLE: Ten investors contribute $100,000 each to a newly formed entity to acquire an office building. The entity borrows an additional $500,000 as the balance of the building's purchase price. If the entity is taxed as an S corporation, each shareholder's deductible loss is limited to $100,000. However, if the entity is an LLC taxed as a partnership, each Member can deduct losses up to $150,000 ($100,000 basis plus $50,000 share of the entity's debt).

This distinction relating to the deductibility of the entity's losses is very important where a business will be financed with a loan. Even if the shareholders in the S corporation guarantee the corporation's debt, they cannot deduct losses against their share of the corporation's debt. The tax basis of the investors for purposes of determining deductible losses can differ substantially between an LLC and an S corporation and, more often than not, will benefit the LLC owners.

EXAMPLE: Assume two S corporation shareholders contributed $10,000 each in cash to the corporation, and the corporation borrowed $200,000. As S corporation shareholders, their basis, and thus their deductible losses, is limited to the $10,000 invested. LLC owners, however, will each have a basis of $110,000 because they can include in their basis their pro rata share of entity level debt ($100,000 each) plus their initial contributions ($10,000 each).

With an S corporation, if a purchaser purchases stock in an S corporation, the basis of the assets of the S corporation remain the same despite the purchase price paid by the purchaser. For example, assume an S corporation has two equal shareholders and the corporation's assets include a piece of machinery that has been depreciated to $10,000; if a purchaser buys the stock of one of the shareholders for a purchase price of $100,000, the corporation's basis in the machinery remains at $10,000.

With an LLC, the entity can make an election to adjust the basis of the LLC's assets attributable to the purchaser to correspond to the purchase price paid for Membership interests. Assuming the same example utilizing an LLC, the LLC's basis in the machinery would be increased to $105,000 (i.e., $100,000 for one-half of the machinery based on the purchase price of the Membership interests and one-half of the old basis in the machinery, which would equal $5,000).

It is also important to note that with all the S corporation rules, there is the risk of an untimely filing of an election, transfer to someone not permitted to hold stock in an S corporation, violation of the prohibition against two classes of stock, or any other rule that would have the effect of terminating the S election. This would result in the corporation being taxed as a C corporation. Once an S corporation's S election is terminated, then that corporation cannot reelect S status for five years. These potential problems are avoided by utilizing an LLC.

NOTE: While the IRS may permit the entity to immediately re-elect to be taxed as an S corporation on the basis that the event which caused the favorable S corporation status to terminate was "inadvertent," the IRS may require the payment of a significant tax cost to do so. Further, the IRS may decide not to accept the shareholder's excuse, in which case the five-year period would apply.

Finally, unlike an S corporation, there are no limitations on the ability of an LLC to have subsidiaries. Thus, an LLC can serve as a holding company for several investments.

LLCs COMPARED WITH GENERAL AND LIMITED PARTNERSHIPS

What Is a Partnership?

For federal income tax purposes, a partnership is a syndicate or group through which any business, financial operation, or venture is carried on. A partnership is an association of two or more people to carry on as coowners of a business for profit. This can be contrasted with the mere coownership of property which is rented or leased, which does not constitute a partnership. Similarly, a joint undertaking merely to share expenses may not be a partnership.

General and Limited Partnerships

The simplest and most common type of partnership is a general partnership. To form a general partnership, you and at least one other person file a certificate (statement) with the appropriate government agency, usually the clerk of the county where you reside. This certificate states that you and your partners are going to conduct business as partners, lists the name and address of the partnership, and so on. This filing is usually quite simple and inexpensive (fees can be $25 or less, but check with your county clerk).

A general partner is a partner in a general partnership and can be held personally liable on all partnership debts (even beyond his or her capital contributions). A general partner may actively participate in the management of the partnership's affairs. Thus, if the activities of the partnership constitute an active business, rather than a passive investment, and the partner "materially participates" in those activities, then the general partner will receive active income or loss for purposes of the passive loss rules.

A limited partnership is more complex and costly to establish and maintain. It offers, however, some valuable advantages over the general partnership form. A limited partnership has two types of partners. There must be at least one general partner who is personally liable for all partnership debts and is authorized to participate in the partnership's management. There must also be at least one limited partner who is not personally liable for partnership debts and, as a condition of remaining not liable, cannot participate in the active management of partnership activities. The limitation on the personal liability of a limited partner is a major factor encouraging the use of limited partnerships over general partnerships.

A limited partnership is formed by filing a certificate that states the name of the partners, which are limited and which are general, the name and business of the partnership, and other information required by the laws of your state. The certificate is more complex and expensive. Also, it is more common to have a detailed and often complex partnership agreement where a limited partnership is used. Some states may even require the formal publication of a summary of the limited partnership certificate in specified papers. This could cost $1,000 or more.

ADVANTAGES AND DISADVANTAGES OF PARTNERSHIPS

The most important aspect of a partnership structure, from a tax perspective, is that the partnership itself is not subject to taxation. All the income, deductions, credits, and so on flow through to the individual partners to be reported on their individual tax returns. This is advantageous for two reasons. First, there is no tax at the entity level. As a general rule, this compares favorably to a C corporation (S corporations generally have pass-through tax treatment similar to that of a partnership), which is taxed at the corporate level. Distributions from a C corporation are also taxed to the recipient shareholders, resulting in two layers of taxation. Partners and partnerships avoid two layers of taxation. This conduit character of a partnership has caused the partnership form of organization to be a preferred vehicle for structuring many business and real estate transactions.

NOTE: As previously discussed, corporate income tax rates are currently lower than individual rates. Therefore, to the extent income is not going to be distributed to the individual owners, overall taxes could be lower with a C corporation.

Second, the flow-through feature of partnership taxation may enable individual owners/partners to utilize the losses generated by the partnership to offset other income they may have. However, this ability to offset other income with partnership losses may be subject to the passive loss rules and other restrictions.

The passive loss rules generally treat any income or loss received by a limited partner in a limited partnership as passive income or loss. Thus, if an investor has passive losses that cannot be used to offset active income and is contemplating another income-producing investment, a limited partnership interest to produce passive income that can offset the investor's otherwise unusable passive losses would be preferable over a general partnership. Obviously, the investor's involvement in each situation must conform with the active or passive result desired.

LIMITATIONS AFFECT A PARTNER'S ABILITY TO DEDUCT PARTNERSHIP LOSSES

A number of restrictions affect a partner's ability to deduct his or her share of partnership losses. A partner, for example, cannot deduct a loss that exceeds his or her tax basis (roughly equal to investment, increased by income plus his or her pro rata share of the partnership's debt, reduced by distributions and losses) in his or her partnership interest.

Passive Loss Rules

The passive loss rules can limit a partner's ability to deduct certain partnership losses. The passive loss rules generally divide all activities (and the income or loss they generate) into three categories:

1. *Passive.* Activities in which the family business owner does not materially participate, such as a passive tax shelter investment. Income and loss allocated to a limited partner of a limited partnership are per se passive.
2. *Active.* Activities in which the family business owner materially participates, such as a full-time profession.
3. *Portfolio.* Interest, dividends, and so on.

Passive losses generally cannot offset income in the other two categories. Unused passive losses are carried over to future years until they offset other passive income or the family business owner's entire interest in the activity is sold. The passive loss rules may be important to choosing between various types of partnerships since general partners can earn active income; limited partners can only earn passive income because they cannot participate in the management of the partnership without risking the loss of their limited liability. The IRS has not stated whether, and to what extent, the passive loss rules apply to LLCs.

At-Risk Limitations

Partners can also be subject to another set of limitations known as the "At-Risk" rules. These rules can limit the amount of losses that a partner can deduct to the amount the partner is considered to have risked in his or her investment in the partnership. This can include cash and property invested in the partnership, and partnership debt on which the *partner* is liable.

FAMILY LIMITED PARTNERSHIPS

An overview is necessary to understand the use of partnerships by family businesses, and the taxation of partners and partnerships generally.

A family limited partnership, or "FLP," gives the partners more flexibility than a corporation provides to its shareholders. For example, the partners in a family limited partnership may want the personal use of tax benefits of the partnership, such as tax losses. This is permissible in a family limited partnership, whereas with a C corporation this is not available, and in an S corporation flexibility is significantly curtailed. Moreover, in a FLP, it is far easier from a tax perspective to distribute money or property from the partnership than it would be from a corporation.

EXAMPLE: Family limited partnerships are often used for asset protection and estate planning benefits. For example, instead of owning assets directly, you could transfer them to a family limited partnership and gift ownership interests to your children as limited partners. You would still control the entire partnership by serving as the general partner. The children would have some of the value of the partnership assets transferred to their names. This would remove the value of what you have given your children from your estate, even though you still control it. These gifts are often made at discounted values. Finally, the family limited partnership offers protective features that make it difficult for creditors to obtain rights to the assets and economic benefit of the partnership. An LLC can offer similar benefits in a more cost effective, simpler, and secure manner.

EXAMPLE: FLPs can be used as a substitute for trusts. Often, a parent will establish an irrevocable trust for the benefit of a minor child.

Trusts

The trust could own assets directly connected with the family which the parent gives to the trust as gifts for the benefit of the child. The trust is used to control the child's use of and access to the assets, protect the child's assets from a failed marriage or creditors, and to pass income to the child at a lower tax bracket (once the child has reached age 14 so that he or she is no longer subject to the "Kiddie Tax"). A FLP can also accomplish these goals, in some instances with greater flexibility. The child's interests are protected from divorce or creditors because of the restrictions on transfer of a partner's interest in the limited partnership agreement (see discussion of asset protection in Part Three). The parent, as general partner, has substantial control over the assets and, subject to certain tax restrictions, significant control over distributions out of the partnership.

Trusts and partnerships can be combined for even greater protection and control. By establishing a family partnership and gift partnership interests to a trust for a child, the parent will have a double element of control. The parent will select the trustee of the trust and the general partner of the partnership (or serve as the general partner himself or herself).

With the parent owning a general partner interest, the parent has control over the FLP (example, power to make management decisions, sell assets, and determine the time and amount of distributions to partners) regardless of the overall ownership percentage reflected by that interest. The general partner interest is usually small (e.g., 1 percent) because the objective is to transfer the value to younger generations.

Limited partnership interests usually are given to younger members of the family. In valuing those interests for gift tax purposes, discounts are generally available for lack of control (a limited partner is not entitled to participate in management) and lack of marketability. These discounts, which are discussed in greater detail in Chapter 19, usually range from 20 percent to 50 percent and create a leverage that allows the FLP technique to produce significant transfer tax savings.

If a trust is set up to own the limited partnership interest on behalf of a child, even greater control can be asserted by the parent. The parent could serve as the sole general partner of the partnership and control the partnership from that perspective, and the parent can then select the trustee to manage the trust thereby indirectly controlling the trust.

EXAMPLE: A husband and wife own $2 million of General Motors stock that they want to gift to their three children. The annual exclusion allows the parents to gift up to $20,000 per year to each child without having to pay a gift tax. This would allow the parents to gift an aggregate of $60,000 of stock each year (based on the New York Stock Exchange trading price) without gift tax consequences. If the parents decide to use a FLP, they can contribute the entire block of General Motors stock to the FLP (which would initially be established with each spouse owning a 1 percent general partnership interest and a 49 percent limited partnership interest) and give the children (or trust for their benefit) a limited partnership interest. That converts the gift from one of stock with a readily determinable value into a closely held business interest that can be discounted, thereby allowing more General Motors stock to be transferred to their children free of gift tax.

If a valuation discount of one-third can be justified for the limited partnership gifts, a 1.5 percent limited partnership interest could be gifted to each child (or their trust) each year. This results in a gift of an interest allocable to $30,000 of FLP assets (1.5% × $2 million) for a gift tax value of only $20,000 as a result of the discounting. Thus, gifts of interests allocable to $90,000 (rather than $60,000) of stock could be transferred, fully covered by the gift tax annual exclusion.

Lease

While a lease is not typically viewed as a method of structuring a business, it can be an important means of arranging transactions. Real estate or valuable tangible property (e.g., construction equipment, medical equipment) can be given as a gift, or part gift/part sale, to family members, children, or trusts for their benefit. These assets can then be leased back to assure the business the use of the assets. Lease arrangements can be structured as gift-leasebacks by the children, trusts, or others purchasing the assets directly.

License

Concepts similar to the lease arrangement in the preceding paragraph can be used to carve out the rights to important intangible assets, vest ownership in another person or entity, and then pay a license fee to obtain the use of these assets.

EXAMPLE: The name and logo for a restaurant or other business could be owned by a family trust or partnership. The restaurant can then license the right to use the name and logo. In the event of a suit or challenge to the restaurant business, these assets could have some measure of protection. This same technique can facilitate the transfer of income to lower tax bracket family members, remove assets from the estate of an older generation family member, and so forth. If the concept for the restaurant were to "take off," the children, through the family limited partnership or other entity would own the license to the name, logo, and related intangibles. These could be licensed to future restaurant locations. Thus, a future appreciation would be outside the business owner's estate.

PARTNERSHIPS AND LLCs

If the LLC is properly structured, partnerships and LLCs are treated the same way for federal tax purposes. Every partner in a general partnership, however, is personally liable for *all partnership debts*. This is a substantial disadvantage of a general partnership compared with either a corporation or an LLC.

A limited partnership can offer this benefit of limited liability to its limited partners. However, accomplishing this goal requires a more complex, expensive, and cumbersome organizational structure. The limited partnership requires at least one general partner meaning that at least one owner must agree to remain personally liable on all partnership debts. This is a major disadvantage of the limited partnership form and is frequently unacceptable.

In most instances, a limited partnership is structured with a corporation as general partner. This structure requires forming two entities and having legal documentation, tax returns, and fees for both. Not only is this approach costly, it may also create a potential tax problem in that the limited partnership could potentially be found by the IRS to be an association taxable as a corporation rather than a partnership. The tax consequences of such a finding could be a nightmare to the owners.

The utilization of a corporate general partner generally requires the corporation to have substantial assets that can be reached by creditors rather than having a new corporation serve as a "dummy" acting as an agent of the limited partners. The IRS has published certain guidelines in Revenue Procedure 89-12 ("Rev. Proc. 89-12") for the net worth standards the corporate general partner must have before the IRS will rule on the characterization of the entity as a corporation or a partnership.

If these tests are satisfied, it is a good indication, although not a certainty, that this corporate characteristic does not exist. The requirement is for the corporation to have a net worth equal to 10 percent of the total capital contributions of the limited partnership.

EXAMPLE: A limited partnership is set up with Newco as a 1 percent general partner and various limited partners owning 99 percent of the partnership. The total capital contributions to the limited partnership are $1 million. Newco must have a net worth of at least $100,000 to satisfy the IRS guidelines. Thus, if there is a large liability or judgment against the partnership, all the assets of the partnership plus the $100,000 net worth of Newco would be utilized to fund that judgment. Therefore, the use of the limited partnership, in this example, exposes another $100,000 of assets to the claims of creditors.

The LLC can offer the advantages of the limited liability of a limited partnership structure, for less cost, in a more simple manner, and with less tax risk. The LLC will minimize the amount of assets exposed to the liabilities of the entity.

An advantage of using a FLP over an LLC is that FLPs can do business in every jurisdiction. Only two states do not currently have LLC statutes, and the use of an LLC in those states is unclear. Furthermore, limited partners in a limited partnership enjoy limited liability in all states. It is unclear whether Members in an LLC are entitled to limited liability in those states that do not have an LLC statute. The strong likelihood is that those states that do not have LLC statutes would give full faith and credit to LLCs formed in other states with limited liability. However, the extremely cautious adviser may shy away from using an LLC to conduct any business that may take place in a state currently without an LLC statute. This risk is greatly diminished since only two states still do not have such statutes, and the likelihood is that this risk will be fully eliminated within the next year or two.

Finally, Members of an LLC have the right to participate in management, unless the Operating Agreement or Articles of Organization provide otherwise. The ability to limit a Member's participation in the LLC's management is only a contractual limitation. In contrast, limited partners in an FLP cannot participate in management without losing their liability shield. This is a statutory feature of limited partnerships, not merely a contractual restriction (although the FLP agreement may contain restrictions as well).

An LLC has some advantages not available to limited partnerships that are especially relevant to real estate investors. A limited partner always will be subject to passive loss limitations because he or she cannot participate in the active management of the partnership's business without losing his or her liability shield. However, a Member of an LLC who is actively involved in the management of the LLC's business will have an easier time satisfying the material participation rules and thus may be able to utilize LLC losses to offset other income. Effective January 1, 1994, the 1993 Tax Act granted some relief from treatment of rental activities as passive activities for certain taxpayers in a real property trade or business. This makes the benefit of using an LLC over a partnership even more attractive for these types of taxpayer.

FLPs AND LLCs

Every family business owner must become familiar with this newest form of business operation. An LLC can offer many of the same advantages as an FLP in a much more streamlined fashion without exposing additional assets to the liability of the enterprise. An LLC offers control because it can designate the person who is to be the Manager (analogous to the general partner in an FLP for control purposes), the interests of the other Members (analogous to the limited partners in an FLP) can be severely restricted, and limited liability of the owners can be achieved. This can be accomplished without the costs of forming yet a second entity (e.g., the corporation typically used as general partner of an FLP) and hence without the tax risk of the partnership being characterized as an association taxable as a corporation. An LLC deserves consideration in the appropriate circumstances.

(For a more detailed discussion regarding family businesses and LLCs see Chapter 12, "Family Businesses and LLCs"; Chapter 13, "Using LLCs in Estate Planning"; and Chapter 19, "Valuation, Minority Discounts, Lack of Marketability Discounts, and LLCs.")

SOLE PROPRIETORSHIPS AND LLCs

Generally, most states require an LLC have at least two Members. There are some states which permit one Member LLCs. Examples of such statutes include New York, Colorado, Texas, Indiana, Montana, and Idaho. The term "persons" generally includes individuals, partnerships, limited partnerships, trusts, LLCs, business trusts, estates, and other associations. The requirement of having two Members prevents the use of LLCs for sole proprietorships who want limited liability without having to set up multiple entities to become coowners. The IRS has not addressed the issue of one-Member LLCs and the manner in which they will be taxed. The primary reason for the LLC requirement of two Members is to allow the entity to be classified as a partnership for federal and state income tax purposes, which require two or more partners to have a partnership.

SUMMARY

To determine whether or not an LLC is the right entity for you, you must compare it with the traditional forms of doing business: the corporation (S and C corporations), the general partnership, or the limited partnership.

Compared with a C corporation, an LLC, if structured to be taxed as a partnership, has only one level of tax, which is at the Member's level, and no entity-level tax. Under the current rate tax structure, C corporations generally pay lower taxes than individuals and thus, to the extent income is not being distributed to the owners of the entity, a C corporation may be somewhat more advantageous than an LLC. However, to the extent income is to be distributed to the ultimate owners, then the LLC avoids double taxation and dramatically reduces the overall tax burden. Furthermore, the LLC avoids the accumulated earnings tax, the personal holding company tax and the unreasonable compensation issues. It also avoids a significant double taxation on the sale or liquidation of a business. The C corporation allows significant owners to receive fringe benefits and not have fringe benefits taxable as income to those owners.

S corporations offer the pass-through tax treatment of a partnership (like an LLC) but have severe restrictions on the type and number of shareholders and classes of ownership interests. S corporations are much less flexible than an LLC in the estate planning context. The limitation on the types of trusts that can be shareholders as well as the inability to make non pro rata distributions to its shareholders greatly impedes the attractiveness of this entity. Furthermore, the amount of losses that shareholders can deduct is subject to far greater limitations than required by an LLC.

Utilizing an LLC may allow the purchaser of an LLC interest to receive the benefits of increased basis for his or her allocable share of the assets of the LLC compared with an S corporation where there is no such increase.

Compared with a general partnership, an LLC offers identical tax benefits, if properly structured, but also offers limited liability protection to its owners. A major drawback to a general partnership is that the owners (partners) are each personally liable for the partnership's liabilities.

A limited partnership is an entity that has both limited partners who are not personally liable for the partnership's liabilities and at least one general partner who is personally liable for all the partnership's entities. Therefore, a limited partnership does not provide the true limited liability protections to all its owners as is provided by an LLC. Additionally, the limited partners may not participate in the partnership's management without risking that they will lose their limited liability, whereas Members of an LLC may participate in management without jeopardizing their limited liability protection. Compared with limited partnerships with corporate general partners, an LLC provides the advantages of avoiding the need to have two entities (a corporate general partner and the limited partnership) with its attendant additional costs, organizational documents, and tax returns. The corporate general partner would also need to be funded with an amount of assets equal to at least 10 percent of the total capital contributions of the total partnership in order to obtain an advance ruling from the IRS that the limited partnership will be taxed as a partnership. The result of these capital contributions is to expose more assets to the liabilities of the limited partnership. All these requirements are eliminated by using an LLC.

An extensive table appears in Appendix C, which sets forth many of the differences between LLCs and other business organizations.

Part Two

SETTING UP, OPERATING, AND DISSOLVING YOUR LIMITED LIABILITY COMPANY

3 HOW TO SET UP A LIMITED LIABILITY COMPANY

To gain the many benefits that an LLC can offer, you must first set up your LLC. Although the process of forming an LLC varies from state to state, the concepts and legal procedures are similar. The tax, business, and other planning is often based on federal law and general legal principles applicable to all states. Thus, the discussion in this chapter will provide many useful planning ideas, tax tips, and sample documents. However, an attorney in the state where the LLC will be formed and operated should always review your final documents and plans.

Most state statutes provide that LLCs are created when the Articles of Organization (also known as the Certificate of Formation in some states) are signed by one or more of the people organizing the LLC, and are filed with the appropriate state filing authority, often the secretary of state. In most states, the organizers do not have to be Members, or owners, of the LLC, but even so, they generally are. Sometimes, to expedite the signing and filing of the necessary certificate a secretary in your lawyer's office may sign.

STATE LAW GOVERNING SETTING UP YOUR LLC

Each state that permits the formation of LLCs has a group of laws (statutes) that are commonly called an "enabling statutes." This is a particular state's statutes under which individuals and/or entities may create an LLC (or other type of business entity; e.g., an enabling statute for a corporation). So long as the organizers properly follow the enabling statute they will create a valid LLC.

TECHNICAL REQUIREMENTS OF SETTING UP YOUR LLC

In most states, the enabling statutes address the issues discussed in the following sections.

TIP: Since the laws differ from state to state, you should at minimum obtain a copy of your state's LLC laws. Most public libraries will have books containing all state laws. Be certain to find out how the books are updated so that you can be sure you are looking at the most current law. Many statute books have what are called "pocket parts." On the inside of the back cover of each book in the set a slot is provided for inserting the most current update. You will often have to read the pertinent sections of the book and then check this pocket part to see whether any changes have been made to the law. Since many state LLC laws are so new, you may only find them in the pocket part; they were not enacted when the statute book was published, so that the entire LLC statute will appear in the later update. The contents to the LLC law section will probably have an entry similar to "formation" that will direct you quickly to the appropriate provisions. Many legal publishers print state specific forms that you can use. These may include instructions as well.

CAUTION: Many form books are available to provide guidance in setting up your own corporation. Undoubtedly, similar books for laypersons will be published in many states on how to set up your own LLC. These books are generally pitched as giving you all the forms and instructions you need. While such books can be helpful, the quality varies tremendously. Many, if not most, only reprint the laws you can find yourself in the library's copies of statute books (which may be more current considering publishing time requirements), and forms available for a few dollars from legal publishing companies in your state (or perhaps the state's office where the forms are filed). Be careful. While you're always best hiring a lawyer, if you try to go it alone don't rely on one of these "how-to" books without reading the current law and contacting the secretary of state (or other appropriate department) for forms and instructions.

Who May File the Articles of Organization

All state enabling statutes set forth the execution and filing requirements for an LLC's Articles of Organization. The Articles of Organization are filed with the appropriate state authority by the LLC's "organizer(s)." Some statutes require only one organizer to form the LLC, while others require at least two. In addition, in some states, the organizer(s) must be a Member, and in others there is no such requirement. Moreover, some states require that only "natural persons" may act as organizers, whereas others allow entities as well as natural persons to serve in this capacity.

The organizer(s) is the person who or which signs the Articles of Organization and files (also referred to as "delivers" in some states) that document with the appropriate state authority.

TIP: In most simple situations, you and your Members (if you have one or a few partners) can and even should sign the form. Apart from the legal requirements that you must meet, if you have only one or two partners, it's probably best from a "political" point of view if all of you sign all key legal documents. Not only does this avoid having one or more partners feel left out, but it assures that all of your names are in the public record as owners and that no partner can claim he or she did not know the contents of the certificate.

Filing and Other Fees

Each state has its own filing fees and other charges with respect to forming an LLC. Some states require annual license taxes, entry taxes, or franchise taxes. Filing fees usually range between $50 and $200. Currently, the largest minimum filing fee is $500, imposed by Illinois. Some states require LLCs to notify the public of its existence by publication in a newspaper of general circulation, which may add a substantial cost to the formation process.

EXAMPLE: In New York, there are strict requirements on publishing a notice of the LLC's existence. The cost can run from $500 to over $2,000.

CAUTION: The failure to publish, where required by your state, could prevent you from obtaining the benefit of limited liability, a key reason for using the LLC. Worse, if your state requires publication for proper formation of the LLC (i.e., it is an essential requirement of the LLC enabling statute), then you will not even have a properly formed LLC if you don't publish a notice.

When an LLC's Existence Begins

The exact time at which an LLC's existence begins varies from state to state. Depending on each particular state and the information in the Articles of Organization, your LLC may come into existence:

- Retroactively on the date the Articles of Organization were executed (signed by the organizers), as long as the Articles of Organization were submitted within a specified period after the date of execution.
- On the date of submission to the appropriate state authority.
- On the date of official approval.
- On some date within ninety (90) days (or later if your state's laws permit) after the date of the filing.

To have an effective date other than the filing date, the Articles of Organization for your LLC must state that its formation will be effective at that date. Some states, such as Colorado and Virginia, insist that the LLC can only legally begin with the issuance of a certificate by the state authority.

Before the appropriate state authority files the Articles of Organization, however, it will review that document to make sure it complies with the state statute. Generally, this review involves ensuring that the document includes the information required by the state statute. Additionally, the review will determine whether the name for the LLC is permitted, which is discussed later in this chapter.

CAUTION: If your company begins doing business before the state completes its review process and the state finds a defect in the documents and rejects the filing, your LLC's Members may be subject to personal liability as if they were doing business on behalf of an entity that was not yet formed. In such a case, the liability of the LLC's Members would be similar to the preincorporation transactions of general partners or corporate organizers. This means all of your personal assets (house, car, personal bank accounts, etc.) could be jeopardized if your LLC is sued before the formation situation is remedied.

If the state authority does not approve the filing of the Articles of Organization, the LLC will not be created. In such a case, the organizers may make the necessary technical adjustments to conform the Articles acceptably with the state statute. A minority of the states allow for an appeal process with respect to Articles of Organization that are not accepted for filing.

TIP: Many times, the LLC Articles of Organization are rejected over a minor technicality. Where you file the document yourself, ask the clerk for the state authority why it was rejected. The problem might be something you can fix and initial right then and there to finish the filing. Many attorneys send paralegals to the appropriate government office to personally file for this reason. Where the government office is not nearby, many attorneys use companies that, for a modest fee, file Articles of Organization (and many other certificates) with the various state authorities. While the use of this type of company may add a modest fee to your bill, it is often worthwhile since it can often assure a timely filing.

On the official formation of your LLC, the following four events occur or are deemed to occur:

1. The LLC becomes a separate legal entity.
2. The Members become protected from liabilities and obligations of the LLC.
3. A presumption arises that all conditions precedent to the existence of an LLC have been satisfied.
4. The Articles of Organization may constitute notice (in certain states) of all information required by statute to be set forth in the Articles.

TIP: In many states, you can file two certificates and ask the secretary of state (or other appropriate government agency) to stamp the second copy and return it to you for your files. This is an important step although it may add additional cost to the process. The stamped copy of the certificate you receive back will prove that the LLC was properly formed, will establish the date it was properly formed, and so on. You should keep this original document with important LLC records. You may need to send photocopies of the Articles of Organization, which has the stamp indicating when it was filed to the County Clerk (or other government property office), if you try to record a deed to real estate being transferred into your LLC. In addition, your bank may want a copy to complete a loan to the LLC.

Defective Formation and Its Consequences

A primary goal of creating an LLC is to have an entity that provides limited liability protections to its owners. This liability protection does not arise until the LLC is formed. Accordingly, if individuals begin doing business before formation takes place, those individuals risk being personally liable for the actions of the not-yet-formed LLC. As mentioned earlier, this is a possible scenario when businesspeople or investors believe they have created an LLC but a technical defect in the formation documents has prevented its creation.

If this situation occurs and individuals have done business on behalf of the not-yet-formed LLC, the following two arguments, which are taken from corporate law, can be made to protect the individuals from liability for actions committed before technical formation:

1. *De facto formation.* The personal liability protection would shield the individuals if the following three items are satisfied:
   a. An enabling statute permitting the creation of LLCs exists, which it does in almost all states.

b. A good faith effort has been made by the acting individuals to comply with the state's LLC statute.

c. The individuals have conducted themselves and their business as if the LLC had been formed. This de facto argument has been applied to corporations but not yet to LLCs. Its rationale, however, would seem to apply to LLCs as well. Although some state statutes seem to offer protection against this risk (if properly formed the liability protection is granted) the law is simply too new, and the risks too great, to rely on mere formation of the entity.

CAUTION: How you prove a good faith effort is a question of fact for a court to interpret. It is not worth the risk. You will generally be better off waiting for the proper formation of your LLC to be confirmed than to risk undertaking transactions before it is confirmed. You must follow all the formalities described in later chapters for properly operating your LLC.

---

2. *Estoppel.* The legal doctrine (concept) of estoppel, historically applied to corporations, may be argued in the LLC context. Estoppel would serve to bar creditors who have entered into contracts believing the LLC was formed and thus part of the bargain was that the liability of only the entity was available to the creditors. This doctrine would only apply to contract and not tort creditors.

EXAMPLE: This situation is typical of many LLC situations. Since LLCs are so new compared with other forms of business entities, the laws have simply not had the opportunity to develop to the extent that they have for partnerships and corporations. This is in fact an important drawback to using an LLC—what will the courts say? A "good faith" effort may depend on how a judge views your efforts to properly form the LLC, not how you view it. Therefore, you're always better off using caution to assure proper formation. Don't rely on a "good faith" attempt to form your LLC to get off the hook. You may not succeed.

LLC TERMINOLOGY

To understand and work with LLCs, you must understand new legal jargon. While the terms are similar to those used in discussing other entities such as partnerships or corporations, there are differences.

Members

What Are Members?

The owners of an LLC are called "Members." A Member is analogous to a shareholder in a corporation or a partner in a partnership. Most state statutes require at least two Members to participate in an LLC; there is no limit on the maximum number of the Members and no restrictions on the identity and types of Members. Thus, an LLC may have more than 35 Members, which is the current limit for an S corporation, although proposals are pending to ease many of the S corporation restrictions.

Some state statutes specifically define the term Member and some state statutes do not. Some states that specifically define the term Member provide that a Member is a person with a Membership interest; some states provide that a Member is a "person who has been admitted to Membership . . . and has not ceased to be a Member," and one state defines a Member as a "person reflected in the required records of an LLC as the owner of some governance rights of a Membership interest."

Who May Be a Member of an LLC?

Under all states authorizing LLCs, any individual or entity may be a Member of an LLC, so long as such individual or entity has the capacity to contract.

EXAMPLE: Someone who is incompetent (as a result of disease, age, mental incapacity, etc.) may not an acceptable person to be a Member of an LLC.

To become a Member of an LLC, a person or entity must be admitted to the LLC. An LLC's Membership may include many types of persons or entities not permitted to be owners of other entities. Nonresident aliens, partnerships and corporations, trusts, foreign LLCs (i.e., an LLC organized under the laws of another state or foreign country), custodians, nominees, or any other individuals or entities, generally may own Membership interests in an LLC. In addition, an LLC may have subsidiaries, thus serving as a holding company for different investments. This lack of restrictions on who can be a Member of an LLC may be a tremendous advantage to the LLC over the S corporation.

Rights and Obligations of Members

Generally, Members are not personally liable for an LLC's debts, liabilities, and other obligations, which is a similar outcome as limited partners of a limited partnership and shareholders of a corporation. Unless the Operating Agreement or Articles of Organization provide otherwise, all Members are of the same class and have equal rights, unlike a limited partnership, which has two classes of partners, limited and general.

CAUTION: This is an important drawback to the use of an LLC. For corporations, the shareholders, and for limited partnerships, the limited partners, are likely to be treated as having limited liability automatically. For an LLC, you may still have to "do things right" to qualify to be a Member.

Unless otherwise provided in an LLC's Operating Agreement, profits and losses of an LLC are usually allocated according to the value of capital contributed to the LLC and not yet returned (known as adjusted capital).

Other states allocate either (1) per capita; (2) according to capital contributions until return and then per capita; (3) book value of contributions; (4) agreed value of contributions; (5) the value of contributions; or (6) capital interests. Therefore, it is essential to address the method for allocation in the Operating Agreement (analogous to a shareholders' agreement for a corporation). Since for federal income tax purposes, an LLC is treated as a partnership (if properly structured), any special allocation (a disproportionate allocation) must have "substantial economic effect" to be valid. This means that the allocation must be realistic and affect the actual economic returns of the people involved (not just the tax benefits).

In most states, any Member of an LLC may, but is not obligated to, lend money to, borrow money from, act as a surety, guarantor, or endorser for, or guarantee or assume one or more specific obligations of, provide collateral for, and transact other business with the LLC, unless provided to the contrary in the Operating Agreement. Accordingly, the Operating Agreement of every LLC must address which of these rights a Member should, or should not, have.

Every Member, pursuant to most statutes, is given the right to demand and receive true and full information regarding the status of the business and financial condition of the LLC, a copy of the LLC's federal, state, and local tax returns, a current list of all Members and Managers, true and full information regarding the amount of Members' contributions, and a description of the agreed value of any property or services contributed by each Member. This information availability statute is a valuable protection, particularly for noncontrolling Members. This protective measure does not, however, mean that the typical accounting, disclosure, audit right, and related provisions included in the governing agreement for a business transaction can be ignored when drafting an Operating Agreement.

Classes and Groups of Members

Limited Liability Companies may have different classes or groups of members, with different rights, powers, and duties if provided for in the Articles of Organization and Operating Agreement. For example, certain groups or classes of Members may be given the right to take specified actions without the vote or approval of other Members. The Operating Agreement may grant certain Members the right to vote separately or as a group. For example, where a business comprises active participants and less active investors, the investors could comprise one class of Members and could be authorized by the Articles of Organization or Operating Agreement to make certain financial related decisions without requiring the consent of participants, who would comprise a separate class of Members. Similarly, the participant-Members class could be empowered to make all daily operating type decisions without requiring consultation with or the consent of the investor-Members class.

Where voting rights are provided, the Operating Agreement should provide provisions concerning a quorum of Members for voting, notice required prior to a vote, time a vote shall occur, proxies, and so on.

TIP: The importance of having proper legal documentation is vital.

When Is a Person Admitted as a Member?

Generally, an individual or an entity can become a Member of an LLC in one of the following two scenarios:

1. By the LLC issuing a Membership interest to the Member.
2. By assignment of an existing Member's interest and obtaining the necessary consent required under statute or the Operating Agreement from the nontransferring Members. If a Member is to obtain his or her Membership

interest by issuance directly from the LLC to such Member, the following issues come into play:

The Decision to Admit a Member

The default rule provided by the state statute or the Operating Agreement will provide a requisite consent that must be obtained before an additional Member may be admitted to an LLC. The Members who have the ability to participate in any such consent requirement will vary by each particular state statute and each LLC's Operating Agreement.

Contribution by Member. Generally, a new Member obtains his or her Membership interest from the LLC in exchange for such person or entity making a contribution to the LLC. The Members whose consent is required to admit any additional Members must be satisfied with the proposed contribution. Any such contributions must also be permitted by the particular state statute.

Recording Membership Status. Most state statutes require the LLC to make some type of recordation relating to the admission of an additional Member. In fact, most states require that the LLC maintain a record of all Members. The value of a Member's contribution to the LLC is particularly important under the default rules of most states' LLC statutes. According to these rules, the value of a Member's contribution (investment) will determine a Member's voting power, allocation of profits and losses, and rights to distributions from the LLC. You can change this only if the Articles of Organization or the Operating Agreement for your LLC state that the Member will have a different vote.

EXAMPLE: You contribute property worth $50,000 to your LLC. Your friend contributes $50,000 of cash. However, it is your knowledge and know-how, and the unique property you are contributing, which will make your new LLC profitable. You and your friend agree that you should have 60 percent of the vote and profits. Unless this is in the Articles of Organization or the Operating Agreement, it may not be valid.

When Does a Member Cease Being a Member?

In some states, where a Member either (1) makes an assignment for the benefit of creditors, (2) files a voluntary petition in bankruptcy, (3) is adjudicated bankrupt or insolvent, or (4) files a petition or answer seeking reorganization, his or her status as a Member of the LLC will terminate. Additionally, Members who transfer all the underlying economic rights to their interest in the company may terminate their status as Members.

Membership Interests

The ownership interest in an LLC is given a different name by the states that have enacted LLC statutes. In some states the ownership interest is referred to as a "Membership interest." In other states, it is merely referred to as an "interest," and in further states it may be referred to as a "limited liability company interest." In all cases, the ownership is the same—your interest in the LLC as a Member is analogous to the stock owned by a shareholder in a corporation.

Ownership of LLC Interests

Personal liability aside, Members of an LLC are similar to partners in a partnership. Members have "interests" or "Membership interests," not shares in the LLC. Some states expressly provide that a Member's interest in an LLC is personal property and other states do not address this issue. In the states that are silent in this regard, it is improbable that an interest in an LLC is anything but personal property.

TIP: The issue of whether your interest in an LLC is personal property or not can have important ramifications. If you live in New Jersey but own real estate in New York, your estate would be have to go through probate in New York (for the property located there) and may even owe New York estate taxes. If, however, you transfer your real estate in New York to a New Jersey LLC and if the LLC Member's interest is considered personal property under New York law, you would not be subject to probate or taxation on death as a result of owning the New York real estate.

This property interest may be held in many forms. The simplest and most common ownership form is a "sole owner." A second form of ownership is as "tenants-in-common," where the parties hold their interest together, but it is subject to division by each owner by several distinct titles. With the tenants-in-common property interest, the interest share of each tenant is distinct from that of other owners, and if a coowner dies, his or her interest does not pass to the surviving coowners. Until the interest is divided, no Member can claim a specific portion of the Membership interest. A "tenant in common" is allowed to transfer his or her interest in the Membership interest without affecting the interest rights of other coholders.

A third form of ownership that can be used for an LLC Membership interest is "joint tenancy with rights of survivorship." Typically used by husbands and wives (also known as a tenancy-by-the-entirety), the parties own an undivided interest in the LLC, which they acquired at the same time. In the case of the husband and wife, neither can transfer his or her interest without the consent of the other. Upon the death of a joint tenant, if a coowner dies, his or her interest passes to the surviving coowners. A joint tenancy is terminated by divorce, death, or voluntary separation.

As discussed earlier in this chapter, LLC statutes allow different classes of Membership interests to be created in an LLC. There may be Members who participate in management and non-Members who have only an economic interest in the LLC but have no right to participate in the LLC's management. Additional classes of Members may be created if not restricted by state law.

Contributions

Contributions (investments) may include cash, property, services rendered, or a promissory note or other obligation contributed to the LLC by a Member, in his or her capacity as a Member. For services to be treated as a contribution, however, they must be designated as a contribution in the LLC's Operating Agreement. In some instances, services may include furnishing guarantees of LLC debt, which may be valuable to a thinly capitalized LLC.

NOTE: In the "For Your Notebook" section following this chapter, several sample documents appear that you can use to invest assets other than cash in your LLC. Cash doesn't require any special documents. It is invested simply by writing a check out to the LLC and depositing it in the LLC bank account.

Distributions

LLC Members are generally not entitled to distributions (cash; analogous to dividends from a corporation) from the LLC, other than on the LLC's liquidation, unless provided otherwise in the Articles of Organization or in the Operating Agreement. Distributions to Members other than on the LLC's liquidation (otherwise known as "interim distributions") can be made on the basis of the following factors, which vary from state to state: (1) in the same manner as profits and losses are allocated, (2) in accordance with adjusted contributions of the members, (3) on a per capita basis, (4) on the book value of contributions, and (5) on the capital value. The methods set forth in the preceding sentence are various default rules which are contained in the statutes of the states which have enacted LLC legislation and these rules can generally be modified to a specific situation pursuant to the LLC's Operating Agreement.

EXAMPLE: Don't let your state's default LLC laws tell you when money can be distributed from your LLC. All the Members should come to some basic agreement. This may include some formula (e.g., a percentage of profits or sales) or a fixed amount for salary. You may also consider some type of point system for distributing profits above salaries (e.g., each Member active in the LLC is assigned points by agreement of the Members for generating business, hours worked, and so on and then profits are distributed based on the number of points each Member has). These arrangements can be revised in the future as circumstances change by simply amending your LLC's Operating Agreement.

An LLC can make distributions to its Members either in cash or in property. The tax implications to the Members relating to the distributions they receive may depend on the type of distribution. Distributions from an LLC to its Members are governed by the partnership tax law distribution rules, assuming your LLC is taxed as a partnership (which is what most should be).

When an LLC is taxed as a partnership, Members of the LLC generally may receive distributions of appreciated property without recognizing gain. As mentioned earlier, unless otherwise provided in the Articles of Organization or Operating Agreement, distributions do not have to be made to the Members prior to the LLC's dissolution. Once entitled to a distribution, a Member becomes a creditor of the LLC with respect to such distribution. This gives the Member the same rights as a creditor to sue for the money, put a lien on the LLC or its assets, or any other steps the law permits.

HOW TO CREATE AN LLC

Step 1.   Determine Whether an LLC Is the Appropriate Entity

The extensive discussion in the earlier chapters concerning the differences and similarities among general partnerships, limited partnerships, limited liability companies, C corporations, and S corporations should be considered first when determining the appropriate structure for your business entity. If the end result of your analysis of business entities is that the LLC is the preferable vehicle for the particular investment or business venture, then the basis for such decision should be documented in writing, and you should use the following procedures for implementing the LLC.

CAUTION: The decision to use an LLC can be quite complicated. Although this book makes every effort to give you guidance as to when and how to choose the right entity, it is impossible to anticipate the particular or unique situations of every investment, business, or estate. Even if you're trying to go it alone to keep your costs down, you should consider confirming your decision to use an LLC with an attorney and/or an accountant. If you've read and thought through the many points in this and preceding chapters, you will have accomplished your goal of minimizing professional fees because the professionals' clocks won't have to be ticking for basic issues and fact-finding you've done. But don't be "penny-wise and pound-foolish." Get professional confirmation of your decision.

Step 2. Draft and File the Articles of Organization/Certificate of Formation

Before moving forward with the formation of an LLC, it is advisable for the prospective owners to enter into a formation agreement. In this fashion, decisions regarding the choice of entity, the internal affairs, and the operation of the business will be spelled out and put in writing before the formation of the LLC. This formation agreement is also an excellent opportunity to record that all persons involved were properly advised on the formation of the entity, made their choice after a proper analysis, and understood the risks and potential problems, as well as any requirements. The content of the formation agreement may contain the business purpose and plan of the LLC, the job description of the management, and the identities and duties of the Members. See the sample formation agreement in the "For Your Notebook" section following this chapter.

To form an LLC, the Articles of Organization or Certificate of Formation (which is similar to a certificate of incorporation and a certificate of limited partnership) must be filed with the appropriate state agency, and the filing fee must be paid. To properly file any certificate, including the Articles of Organization, you must have it executed by one or more authorized persons (known as "organizers"), who generally do not have to be Members. Some states require at least two organizers to execute and file the Articles of Organization. Generally, unless the Operating Agreement provides to the contrary, any authorized person or agent may execute any certificate of the LLC, or the Operating Agreement itself.

TIP: It can be convenient to put a provision in the LLC's Operating Agreement stating that the Members designate and appoint the certain named individual as their attorney-in-fact (agent) to file the LLC's Articles of Organization and certain types of amendments to the certificate that are mere formalities and not changes in the substantive relationship of the Members. In many situations, however, the Operating Agreement is not signed until long after the LLC is formed and business begun (not the recommended approach) so that this provision is useful only for future amendments.

CAUTION: Carefully consider limiting the rights of any Members or persons to amend or file any certificate without obtaining some form of consent from the other Members.

General Rules Concerning Certificates

As described in this chapter, most states have minimal statutory requirements for forming an LLC. Usually, a brief certificate must be filed with the appropriate state agency. As discussed earlier in this chapter, the filing of the Articles of Organization is generally effective to create the LLC, but the effective date of the formation of the LLC may be a later date (or in some cases may be retroactive) as set forth in the Articles. In many cases, substantial compliance with the pertinent state enabling statute is sufficient to effect the formation of the LLC.

What Information to Include in the Articles of Organization

Every state's LLC statute sets forth a list of information that must be set forth in the Articles of Organization. Usually, the basic requirements are to state the name of the LLC, the name and address of the registered agent for service of process, the purpose of the LLC, the LLC's duration of existence, and the address of its principal office. The requirements in each state's statute, however, may differ from those in the Articles of Organization for other states. If the drafter of the Articles of Organization fails or intentionally omits information, the particular state statute will provide a set of default rules that would apply to the LLC with respect to the topic that was omitted. (For a detailed summary of each state's statutes regarding LLCs see Appendix A.)

The Name of the LLC. The requirements in setting forth the name of an LLC do not vary much from state to state. An LLC's name generally must include either the phrase "Limited Liability Company" or "LLC." Some states, however, require the phrase "Limited Company" or "LC." The name may, but is not required to, include the name of a Manager. The name must be distinguishable from the name of any other corporation, limited partnership, business trust or LLC reserved or registered with the state's records, unless that other party provides written consent to use an indistinguishable name. A name may be reserved in advance of formation.

TIP: Pick a name that has something in it that is not extremely common. For example, "Consultants International" is probably too simple and common to be accepted. If you can use "YOUR NAME Consultants International" you will be far more likely to have the certificate approved. You generally cannot use a word in your LLC's name that relates to a regulated industry (unless you have met the appropriate requirements). These could include "bank," "securities," and so on.

The Address for the Registered Office, and Registered Agent for Service of Process. Every state requires that the Articles of Organization set forth a registered agent for the LLC and a registered office. Each state, however, has different rules regarding this requirement. A registered agent and office ensures a name and address where service of process (notice) of a lawsuit or other important matter can be given. Generally, the registered office does not have to be a place of business of the LLC. In some states, the registered agent must sign a written consent to appointment that must be filed with the Articles.

The registered agent, with notice to the LLC, may change the registered office by filing a certificate with the appropriate state authority. In addition, where there is a change in the identity of the LLC's registered agent, a certificate must be filed with the appropriate state authority. Usually, the new registered agent, and not the replaced agent, is the party that files such a certificate. Moreover, many states provide a specific procedure for the resignation of a registered agent. Generally, resignation is accomplished by the registered agent sending a notice of resignation to the LLC. An affidavit of such service and a copy of the notice of resignation must then be filed with the appropriate state agency. In many states, the LLC has two years to appoint a new registered agent after its current registered agent resigns. If it fails to do so, the LLC's name may be transferred to an inactive list and the LLC may be subject to monetary penalties.

NOTE: Some lawyers routinely list themselves or their firms as registered agents. While your lawyer may be the first person any notice should be sent to, if you decide to change lawyers you will have to spend more legal fees to have your new lawyer change the name and address of the old lawyer's listing as registered agent. Lawyers have services provided by national organizations that specialize in filing certificates for all types of entities, monitoring notices issued to LLCs, corporations, and so on. You may wish to incur the annual fee they charge to list them as registered agent to assure that you will get every notice you should. The least expensive choice is to list yourself. However, if there are other Members in the LLC (and in most states you must since few states permit one-person LLCs), you may not want another Member to be the agent, and he or she may not want you to be the agent. Also, if you move to a new home, you will have to incur legal fees to amend the certificate to the new address.

Dissolution Date.   An LLC must specify, in its Articles of Organization, a specific date for the LLC's dissolution, if the dissolution date is to differ from the statutory termination period. Dissolution is when the business of the LLC will be wound up and the LLC terminated, and its assets liquidated. While the Members can, at that future date decide to continue the business of the LLC, a dissolution date must still be provided. The statutory, or default (i.e., in the absence of a statement to the contrary) termination period, is usually the earliest of:

- The occurrence of an event specified in the Operating Agreement.
- The voluntary written consent of the Members. Most states require unanimous consent of the Members in this regard, while other states only require majority consent.
- Expiration of the limited liability company's life (i.e., its specified period of duration either by the default rule set forth in your state's laws or at some other date set forth in the Articles of Organization). Many state laws provide that the LLC will end thirty years from the date of the formation of the LLC, unless this is changed in the Articles of Organization.
- The entry of a decree of judicial dissolution. This could occur, for example, where a Manager applies to the court where it is not reasonably practical to carry on the LLC's business in conformity with the Operating Agreement.

- The death, retirement, resignation, expulsion, bankruptcy, or dissolution of a Member or the occurrence of any other event that terminates the continued Membership of a Member in the LLC, unless the business of the LLC is continued either by the consent of all of the remaining Members, or pursuant to a right to continue the business of the LLC as stated in the Operating Agreement.

NOTE: A limited duration for the LLC is important for the LLC where you want the LLC taxed as a partnership.

Other Information That May Be Required in the Articles of Organization

- A provision providing that the LLC may carry on any lawful business or purposes permitted under state law. The purposes clause can be very broad since LLCs can be used for a wide variety of activities. It may be advantageous in some situations to provide a more restrictive definition of the activities of the LLC. This may be appropriate where a noncontrolling Member wishes to restrict the possible activities of the LLC.

- A statement that the LLC has at least two or more Members (in states that require this).

- Any other permitted matters that the Members wish to include. For example, Members holding noncontrolling interests may wish to include certain restrictions on the transfer of Membership interests or control by Members or Managers in the Articles to protect their interests.

- If required by the state, the provision in the Articles of a "principal" office where the LLC will conduct its business or location where its records will be kept.

Additional Information That May Be Required to Be Included in the Articles of Organization. In addition to the preceding requirements, the Articles of Organization may include the following information:

- The management structure of the LLC. In some states, it is required that the Articles provide whether the LLC will be managed by its Members or by Managers and the names and addresses of such individuals.

TIP: Be certain to address the management issue in detailed terms in the Operating Agreement since the Articles of Organization is only a sketchy and short document.

- Capital structure of the LLC. Some states require the disclosure of the description of contributions received by the LLC and a description of any promised future contributions.

- Every state's LLC statute enables the organizers to include any additional information in the Articles that is not inconsistent with law. An argument can be made, however, that there is no viable reason to include any additional information, other than the required information, in the Articles.

Amending Articles of Organization

The events that require the amendment of the Articles vary from state to state. Many states require amendments on the occurrence of any of the following:

- Any event that terminates the Membership of a Member.
- A change in the LLC name or purpose.

NOTE: In most cases, your Articles of Organization will simply state that your LLC can do anything permitted by law. This is so general that you will never have to amend the Articles if the LLC's business changes. However, this is not necessarily the best approach. If you put a more restrictive business purpose in, you will limit the scope of what the other Members or even the Managers can do. This can protect you by preventing them from expanding the scope of the business beyond what was agreed to. For example, you may state in the Articles of Organization that the purpose of the LLC is "to invest in residential rental properties of one to four family units, in XYZ county, only." Now everyone involved knows the limits.

- A change in Membership or management.
- A change in the registered agent or office.
- Discovery of an inaccuracy in the Articles.

In most states, a unanimous decision of the Members is required to amend the Articles of Organization. Other states, however, require merely the majority consent of the Members to amend the Articles. At least one state allows the Managers to amend the Articles by a majority vote. And yet other states require approval by both the Managers and the Members to amend the Articles. Still other states, are silent on the issue of the consent required to adopt an amendment. In those states, it may be proper to apply the unanimity standard to ensure that the amendment will be valid.

If one of the preceding events occur after which an amendment of the Articles is required, and the Articles are not so amended, there can be drastic results to the LLC. For example, under some statutes, the failure to amend when required may result in the involuntary dissolution of the LLC. In other states, the failure to amend may result only in damage claims by any individuals who are misled by false statements in the Articles.

The filing fee for such an amendment is usually minimal.

Step 3.   Negotiate and Draft the Operating Agreement

Operating Agreement

Although most states provide default provisions to govern the relationship between the Members of an LLC, once an LLC is formed, the Members should prepare and enter into a written "Operating Agreement." In some states, it is referred to as "regulations" or the "limited liability company agreement." The Operating Agreement is a contract that governs the operation of the LLC and the relationship of the Members and Managers (if the LLC has Managers) to each other and to the LLC. Although an Operating Agreement is not required in most states, it is certainly advisable to enter into one every time you form or invest in any LLC.

In most states, the Operating Agreement must be adopted by the initial Members. In other states, the Articles of Organization may permit the LLC's Managers to adopt the Operating Agreement. It is essentially analogous to what a partnership agreement is to a partnership.

NOTE: In most states, the Articles of Organization are merely a formality and will not disclose or discuss much of the agreed-on relationship among the Members/Managers and the LLC. Therefore, the Operating Agreement is the document that will most likely be relied on to memorialize such agreements.

Most LLC statutes require a unanimous consent of the Members to adopt the Operating Agreement. In states that do not expressly require unanimity, such a requirement may be implied by general contract principles. States vary in their requirements as to whether or not the Operating Agreement must be in writing. Some states do not require that the overall Operating Agreement be in writing, but merely that particular items which the Members agree to must be in writing. Moreover, if an Operating Agreement is to modify the default rules of any particular state's statute, then there must be a written version of that agreement. If you are doing business in a state that expressly permits oral Operating Agreements, it is still unwise not to have a written agreement. People and the relationships between people can change over time, and individuals may have different understandings and perceptions of oral agreements made several years in the past.

What happens if the Members decide to amend the Operating Agreement? Who can make the amendment? Generally, the default rule under most statutes is that the unanimous consent of the Members is required to amend the Operating Agreement. Under other statutes, the default rule specifies that a majority of the Members are required to amend. Moreover, other statutes allow the Managers to amend if such power is given in the Articles of Organization, and other statutes permit both the Managers and the Members to have control over amending the Operating Agreement if provided by the Articles of Organization.

If an LLC is structured so that it will be taxed as a partnership, because of Internal Revenue Code partnership tax considerations, the Operating Agreement must discuss the Members' understanding on the formula for distributions to the Members and the allocation of profits and losses. The agreement may also provide for other aspects of business transactions among the Members of the LLC. It should address the transfer of Membership interests to other Members and third parties, as well as the relative classes, rights, powers, and duties of each class or group of Members.

Voting rights of Members should be addressed in the Operating Agreement. The Operating Agreement may provide that certain actions by the LLC require a certain percentage of votes and other actions may be taken either without a vote or with a different percentage of votes required. It may provide for classes or groups of Members having the rights, powers, or duties of Managers. In some states (e.g., New Jersey), if the Operating Agreement has no provision vesting management in certain individuals, the management of an LLC will be vested in its Members with voting rights in proportion to each Member's respective share of the LLC's profits.

The LLC Operating Agreement may provide for a Manager (or group of Managers) who functions in a manner similar to a general partner in a limited partnership relating to managing the affairs of a partnership. Whether the management of the LLC operations will be vested in a Manager or in the Members should always be addressed in the Operating Agreement. If a Manager(s) is selected to manage the LLC, the details as to the rights and obligations of the Manager(s) and Members should be discussed. It may be practical to include penalties or other provisions in the event that a Manager or Member fails to comply with the terms of the Operating Agreement. Operating Agreements must be drafted carefully to avoid future management problems, abuse by majority owners, and potential operational deadlock.

Checklist for Drafting Terms of an Operating Agreement

- What decisions require the unanimous consent of the Members versus a majority or other percentage vote of the Members? Perhaps such situations as a sale of the entire business or major business assets, serving as a guarantor on debt, or settling major litigation claims, should require the unanimous consent of the Members. A unanimous consent or "major decisions" clause, as it is sometimes called, can be critical to protecting the interests of a non-controlling Member with respect to major decisions of the LLC.

- What decisions can be relegated to the Manager with respect to daily business operations that do not require Member approval? For example, should the Managers have unfettered discretion to make all but major decisions? In many instances setting such parameters can be useful to avoid potential problems.

- Carefully define in specific terms the nature and extent of the LLC's business. This is important so that extensions beyond the primary business purpose must be approved by the requisite percentage of Members. For a new business, this requirement can assure that all participants agree on the business approach being taken by the LLC. Often when this is reduced to writing, different views on where and what the business should be and the direction it is moving are brought out and addressed. This can be helpful to solve fundamental problems at a later date.

- What types of notice provisions should be given to Members and Managers for meetings and other matters that may arise under the agreement?

- Under what conditions, if any, may a Manager be permitted to resign?

- When and how may a Member resign or withdraw from the LLC?

- Should the Operating Agreement provide penalties or other specified consequences where a Member or Manager does not comply with its terms?

- Should the Manager be permitted to withhold and not disclose certain confidential data (trade secrets) to the Members; or alternatively, should the Operating Agreement specifically override this right?

- Should different groups of Members be provided for in the Operating Agreement? What relative rights and obligations and duties should the Members of each particular group have?

- Should precautionary language concerning each Member's purchase of interests in the LLC, such as purchase of an investment, without intent to resell, be included? Alternatively, is it considered certain enough based on an analysis of applicable law and the particular facts in the situation at hand that such language can be avoided?

- Should penalties be levied on a Manager who fails to perform as required under the Operating Agreement? Should the statutory default standard relating to liability of Managers be changed by the Operating Agreement so that a Manager can be held liable for acts or omissions at a lesser standard than "gross negligence" or "willful misconduct"?

- Since a Member and Manager are generally protected by a state's statute for relying in good faith on the LLC's records, who should be responsible for maintaining such records and what specific provisions, if any, should be included in the Operating Agreement concerning such records?

- Generally, Member contributions may be in cash, property or services, a promissory note, or the obligation to contribute other cash, property, or services. Should any such contributions be accepted, or should contributions be limited to cash? Where services are to be contributed, the Operating Agreement should specify the specific services to be rendered, a standard to approve the quality of the services rendered, the terms of the services, and an agreed value for the services.

- How should profits and losses be allocated among the Members? If incentives for different performances or contributions for specific assets are to be provided for, be certain that you meet the LLC requirement that services must be stated to be as contributions in the Operating Agreement if they are to be treated as such.

- How should compensation of the Members and Managers be determined? How can it be changed? Are perks permitted and how should they be determined? It is essential to set forth the items in detail in the Operating Agreement in a family business where certain children or family members are to receive salaries and be active in the business and other family members are not active in the business. If the formula for compensation of Members is not carefully structured, the family members in the business might not be fairly compensated for their work if nonparticipating family members control the Membership vote. On the other hand, if a specific formula is not imposed, those active in the business could potentially remove all profits from the business in the form of salaries, leaving nothing for the nonparticipating family members to receive as distributions of profits.

- How much vacation time should be allowed for each Member and how much notice should be given to the LLC and other Members before vacation dates? If several Members would like to take the same vacation time, perhaps a rotational basis should be provided for in the Operating Agreement.

- Who should be a Manager of the LLC? In the event of the permanent disability or death of a Manager, how should successors be selected (by remaining Managers or by the Members)? How should tie votes or deadlocks of Managers and/or Members be resolved?

- Several statutes provide that if a person is required to execute a Certificate of Amendment to the Articles of Organization on behalf of an LLC and fails or refuses to do so, any person who is adversely affected by such failure or refusal may petition the court to direct the execution of any such certificate. A similar provision is contained in some state statutes relating to a person who may be required to execute an Operating Agreement but refuses to do so. As a result, consideration should be given to include specific instructions in the formation agreement as to when a court can and cannot require a Member or Manager to execute a particular document.

- What should happen if a Member becomes disabled? Will disability income insurance be purchased by the LLC so that it may continue to pay salary to the disabled Member? Will the business self-insure (i.e., pay out of its own pocket) for a period of time (e.g., six months) to obtain lower premiums on its disability income insurance? After what length of a disability may a Member return to his or her former position with the LLC? One year, two years, or perhaps a longer time period? How long should benefits other than salary (e.g., health, pension) be continued during disability? What should happen to voting rights of a Member during disability? At what point, if any, should there be a mandatory buyout of a disabled Member's interest in the LLC? In the event of a buyout of a disabled Member's interest, who will be the purchasing party—the LLC or the nondisabled Members? Will the purchase price be funded with disability buyout insurance?

- What should happen if a Member dies? Will the legal representatives of the deceased Member's estate be obligated to sell the deceased Member's Membership interest? Who will be the party required to purchase such interest— the LLC or the surviving Members? Would the purchase price for such deceased Member's interest be funded with life insurance?

- If there is a buyout on a Member's death or permanent disability, how should such buyout be structured? Different types of buyout arrangements may be utilized for different circumstances. For example, if a buyout is provided for on the death or permanent disability of a Member, an appraisal of the LLC may be used to determine the purchase price (with the purchase price equal to the appraised value of the LLC divided by the interest in the LLC being purchased) so that the surviving and nondisabled Members cannot take advantage of the deceased or disabled Member's family by having an artificially low purchase price. In some cases, a stated or agreed-on value for the LLC, determined annually by the Members, can be used. It must be determined whether a formula method, an agreed-on value method, or an appraisal method is more appropriate to determine the purchase price. If a Member receives a third-party offer to purchase his or her Membership interest, should the LLC and/or other Members have a right of first refusal to purchase such Member's interest in the LLC? If so, on what terms? In some types of businesses, such as certain real estate ventures, it is important to give a Member the right to "put" or offer the entire property and business to a third party, which may be the only way to realize a fair value. Would a person purchase 1/10 of a real estate venture for exactly 1/10 of the appraised value of the company when the purchaser would have no control over distributions to the Members or Managers of the business?

- Should expenditures on the LLC's behalf in excess of a certain amount (i.e., $5,000) require more than one Member's or Manager's signature?

- If more capital is needed by the LLC, how should it be obtained? Should the Operating Agreement require mandatory loans by Members to the LLC on prearranged terms from existing Members? Should new Membership interests be offered to new Members after a right of first refusal for additional Membership interests is given to existing Members to contribute capital for additional Membership interests?

SUMMARY

Each state that allows for the formation of limited liability companies has its own specific formation requirements contained in statutes called "enabling statutes." An LLC is formed by the LLC's "organizers," who file Articles of Organization (also known as a "Certificate of Formation" in some states) with the appropriate state authority. In most states, the organizer does not have to be a Member of the LLC. A filing fee, which varies from state to state, must accompany the Articles of Organization when the organizer submits them to the appropriate state filing authority.

Generally, an LLC is officially formed on the date the Articles of Organization are filed or at some later date (usually not to exceed 90 days after the filing date) that may be set forth in the Articles.

The owners of an LLC are referred to as "Members." Most states require that an LLC must have at least two Members. There are no limitations relating to the maximum number of Members nor are there any restrictions as to who or what may be a Member of an LLC.

Generally, Members of an LLC are not personally liable for the debts and obligations of the LLC, which is a similar liability position as a shareholder in a corporation and a limited partner in a limited partnership. An LLC may have various groups and classes of Members. Such classes may vary with respect to voting rights and rights to allocations of profit and losses and management responsibilities, among other things.

An Operating Agreement governs the internal operations of an LLC. Once an LLC is formed, the Members should enter into an Operating Agreement with such agreement in writing so that there will be no uncertainty as to the agreement among the Members at a later date. The Operating Agreement should address the management structure of the LLC, set forth the contributions of each Member to the LLC, set forth the allocations of profits, losses, and so on, for the Members, provide for scenarios relating to the death or disability of a Member, and address the transfer of Membership interest to other Members and third parties.

A Member's interest in an LLC is personal property and thus can be owned by the Members in any manner in which personal property can be owned. As such, a Member can be a "sole owner," a "tenant-in-common" or "a joint tenant with rights of survivorship" with respect to his or her Membership interest.

For Your Notebook:

SAMPLE LLC FORMATION AGREEMENT

NOTE: This form is a sample of the type of document you and other Members about to form an LLC should consider signing. The goal is to avoid problems at a later date by assuring that everyone involved has been fully informed and understands the decisions made. In some situations, especially if you wish to control legal costs, you may skip this document and sign a comprehensive Operating Agreement that includes many of these items.

AGREEMENT dated as of _____ between and among LIST THE NAME AND AD-DRESS OF EACH PROSPECTIVE LLC MEMBER HERE (collectively the "Prospective Members"); and LLC NAME, an LLC in the process of formation (the "LLC") (collectively, the "Parties").

RECITALS

(a) The Prospective Members hereto have evaluated the benefits, risks, requirements of causing an LLC to be formed for the purpose of engaging in the trade or business of DESCRIBE BUSINESS (the "Business").

(b) The parties hereto wish to confirm their decision to form an LLC to operate the Business.

AND, THEREFORE, AGREE TO THE FOLLOWING TERMS AND CONDITIONS:

1. *Decision Regarding the Choice of Entity.*

The Prospective Members have evaluated individually, and with their individual legal, tax, accounting and business advisers, the benefits, costs, risks, requirements and other relevant considerations of using an LLC rather than other types of arrangements, for the purpose of organizing and conducting the Business. Each Prospective Member based on such evaluation concurs in the use of an LLC for the Business.

2. *Internal Affairs and Operation of the Business.*

The Prospective Members agree that the Business shall have its affairs and operations conducted in generally the following manner:

DESCRIBE KEY POINTS AGREED TO.

3. *Preliminary Agreement; Operating Agreement to Be Signed.*

The Prospective Members acknowledge that this LLC Formation Agreement is only a preliminary agreement and that the parties intend and shall execute a comprehensive Operating Agreement at some future date. The terms and provisions of this LLC Formation Agreement shall govern until such Operating Agreement is executed.

4. *Business Purpose and Business Plan of the LLC.*

In addition to the description above of the intended Business of the LLC, the Prospective Members acknowledge and agree that the

DESCRIBE ADDITIONAL BUSINESS DETAILS.

The Prospective Members further acknowledge that they have received, reviewed, and generally accepted the draft Business Plan and Projections attached to this LLC Formation Agreement.

5. *Description of the Management of the LLC.*

The Management of the LLC shall be conducted by

DESCRIBE IN GENERAL TERMS.

6. *Voting Rights of Members.*

The Membership Interests anticipated to be issued to LIST VOTING MEMBERS shall be voting Interests. The Membership Interests issued to LIST NONVOTING MEMBERS (if any) shall be nonvoting Interests.

7. *Limitation on Other Activities of Prospective Members.*

Except for MEMBER NAME, who shall serve as DESCRIBE DUTIES, nothing in this LLC Formation Agreement shall be deemed to restrict in any way the freedom of any Prospective Member to conduct any other business or activity whatsoever at any location other than the Business, so long as such business or activity does not directly compete with, or conflict with the Business of the LLC.

8. *Identities and Duties of the Prospective Members of the LLC.*

Member Name	Member Address	Tax ID Number	Intended Duties	Intended Contibution

9. *Independent Advice of Counsel.*

Each party hereto has been advised to seek the advice of independent legal, tax, business, and accounting counsel prior to executing this LLC Formation Agreement. Each party, by executing this LLC Formation Agreement, acknowledges that he has been advised to seek independent counsel and that the execution of this Agreement can affect their legal rights, that reasonable time to consult with independent counsel has been afforded, and that he or she has consulted with independent counsel, or has of his or her own volition decided not to do so.

10. *Arbitration.*

Any dispute under this LLC Formation Agreement shall, upon notice to the parties be submitted to binding arbitration, in LOCATION, in accordance with the rules of the American Arbitration Association.

IN WITNESS WHEREOF, the parties hereto have hereunto set their hands and seals the day and year first-above written.

_____
NAME 1, Prospective Member

_____
NAME 2, Prospective Member

_____
NAME 3, Prospective Member

For Your Notebook:

SAMPLE AMENDMENT TO LLC OPERATING AGREEMENT FOR PROPERTY CONTRIBUTIONS

LLC NAME
Action Taken by Unanimous Written
Consent of All Members
to Accept Property Contribution and
Issue Membership Interest of the LLC
and Amend the LLC NAME Operating Agreement

NOTE: The following form is a consent to be signed by all Members indicating their agreement to the contribution (investment) of noncash assets. This consent is in the form of an amendment to what is assumed to be an existing Operating Agreement. If property is invested at the outset, when the LLC is first formed, the nature of the property and the LLC Membership Interests received in exchange, should all be spelled out in the original Operating Agreement.

NOTE: You may not need all Members to sign. It depends on the terms of your Articles of Organization and Operating Agreement. The safest and preferable approach in all cases where there are a limited number of Members in your LLC is to have all Members sign off as agreeing on any contribution to capital of the LLC as well as any other significant transaction. This avoids the problems later of any Members claiming they didn't agree with a particular transaction, weren't advised of it, and so on.

The undersigned, being all of the Members of LLC NAME, hereby take the following action:
RESOLVED, Authorize the issuance of the following Membership Interests in the LLC to the Members listed below, at the price and for the consideration listed:

Member Name	Membership Interests	Contribution
Member 1 NAME		$15,000
Member 2 NAME		2 pickup trucks
Member 3 NAME		lathe and other equipment
Member 4 NAME		$4,000 and office equipment

NOTE: Attach detailed descriptions of all noncash assets to the consent, including vehicle registrations, sales receipts evidencing the Members' earlier purchase of the equipment, and so on. The descriptions attached should include, at minimum: (1) contributing Member's name; (2) description of property contributed; (3) agreed value of property contributed; (4) agreed Membership Interests issued for such property.

RESOLVED, that the LLC accept the transfer of the above assets under the Bill of Sale, and Assignment of Contract forms attached hereto.

NOTE: If the LLC is run by one or more Managers as opposed to by all Members, the language in this form would have to be changed. However, it is still ideal to have Members sign off. Where a Member is also a Manager, the signature lines at the end of this form should be revised to indicate that person is signing in both capacities.

RESOLVED, That the aforesaid offers of contributions to the capital of the LLC in exchange for Membership Interests in the LLC are agreed as being fair, adequate, and reasonable, and should be and are hereby accepted by the LLC and its Members and Manager.

RESOLVED, That the entire amount of the above payments be credited on the LLC's books and records in the manner designated by the LLC's accountant as contributions to the LLC's capital.

RESOLVED, that the Manager of the LLC are directed and authorized to take all necessary actions to implement the above resolutions.

RESOLVED, that this Unanimous Consent, signed by all Members, is hereby deemed an amendment to the LLC-NAME Operating Agreement, originally signed on MONTH, DAY, YEAR.

Dated: SIGN DATE

_____
MANAGER 1 NAME, Manager

_____
MEMBER 1 NAME, Member

_____
MEMBER 2 NAME, Member

_____
MEMBER 3 NAME, Member

_____
MEMBER 4 NAME, Member

For Your Notebook:

SAMPLE BILL OF SALE

NOTE: This form is used to transfer personal property (furniture, equipment, a car, but not real estate) to an LLC.

CAUTION: Where personal property is transferred, check with your accountant to see whether a sales or other local tax may be due. Also, check with your lawyer to see if any other documents also have to be prepared. For example, if you use a bill of sale to transfer ownership (title) to a car or truck to your LLC, you must also sign and transfer the vehicle's official registration issued by your state.

KNOW ALL MEN BY THESE PRESENTS, that MEMBER 1 NAME an individual who resides at MEMBER 1 ADDRESS (the "Transferor") for and in consideration of the sum of $1.00 and Membership Interests in the LLC, to LLC NAME, doing business at LLC's ADDRESS (the "Transferee"), has granted, transferred, and conveyed and by these presents does grant, transfer, and convey unto the said Transferee, and said Transferee's successors and assigns property as hereinafter described:
ALL THE RIGHT TITLE AND INTEREST in the following asset ("Asset"):

DESCRIBE ASSETS TRANSFERRED

including all Transferor's right, title and interests in the Asset.
Transferor hereby represents and warrants that he/she has good and marketable title to the ASSET NAME hereinabove, subject to no liens, mortgages, security interests, encumbrances, or charges of any nature.
This Bill of Sale has been executed to complete the transfer as a contribution to capital of LLC NAME, in accordance with the provisions of Section 721 of the Internal Revenue Code of 1986, as amended, and as contemplated herein. Nothing herein contained shall be deemed or construed to confer upon any person or entity other than Transferee any rights or remedies by reason of this instrument.
TO HAVE AND TO HOLD the same unto the said Transferee and the Transferee's successors and assigns forever; and the Transferor covenants and agrees to and with the said Transferee to warrant and defend the said described Asset against all and every person or persons whomsoever.
IN WITNESS WHEREOF, the Transferor has set his/her hand and seal to be hereto affixed this DAY day of MONTH, YEAR.

Sworn, Signed, Sealed, and Delivered

_____

MEMBER 1 NAME, Transferor

in the Presence of:

_____

WITNESS

For Your Notebook:

SAMPLE ASSIGNMENT OF CONTRACTS

EXAMPLE: Use this form to transfer existing contracts to your LLC. For example, you may have an equipment or property lease, a service contract for you to provide services for certain customers, and so on. In many cases, filling in and signing this general assignment of contracts form is only the start. Each contract right you assign has to be reviewed and special documents prepared where required. Say you operated a retail store as sole proprietorship. You wish to limit your liability exposure. You must review the lease for the requirements you must meet. You will almost always need the landlord's approval. Most likely, the landlord will insist that you sign a personal guarantee of the new LLC's performance under the lease (paying rent, keeping the premises clean, etc.). The landlord should insist on this because otherwise the transfer to an LLC with limited assets (the LLC will have less assets than you did personally (e.g., your house will remain in your name) will leave the landlord less protected in the event of a default or other problem under the lease. You will thus probably have to sign a personal guarantee, and either an assignment of lease (where you assign all your rights and interests in the lease to the LLC, or a sublet agreement (where you remain the main tenant and your LLC is a subtenant under you—this is less desirable from a liability perspective).

THIS AGREEMENT made as of the DAY day of MONTH, YEAR, between LLC NAME, doing business at LLC's ADDRESS ("Assignee"); and MEMBER 1 NAME, an individual who resides at MEMBER 1 ADDRESS ("Assignor").

NOTE: While you must at minimum attach a listing of the contracts, you should also attach a copy of each contract signed in its entirety.

WHEREAS, the Assignor wishes to assign all his right title and interest in those certain contracts more particularly set forth and described in Schedule "A" hereto (hereinafter called the "Contracts"); and Assignee wishes to accept the assignment of the Contracts.

NOW, THEREFORE, THIS AGREEMENT WITNESSETH that the parties hereto covenant and agree as follows:

1. In consideration of One Dollar ($1.00) and _____ Membership Interests in the LLC, Assignor hereby assigns, transfers, and sets over unto Assignee the said Contracts and all rights, titles and interests of Assignor therein and thereto, together with all rights, benefits, privileges, and advantages of Assignor to be derived therefrom, subject to the rights of certain third parties to approve, or consent to such assignments, as provided in the Contracts.

2. The Assignor covenants and agrees with the Assignee that Assignor shall at the request of the Assignee, do and perform all such acts and things, and execute and deliver all such consents, documents and other writings as may be required to give full force and effect to the assignment herein contemplated.

3. Assignee accepts the within assignment to it of the said Contracts and agrees with Assignor to assume, carry out, observe, perform, and fulfill said Contracts in accordance with their terms.

4. This Agreement shall, subject to the terms and conditions of the individual Contracts, enure to the benefit of and be binding upon the parties hereto and their successors and assigns.

5. This Assignment of Contract has been executed to complete the transfer as a contribution to capital of LLC-NAME, in accordance with the provisions of Section 721 of the Internal Revenue Code of 1986, as amended, and as contemplated herein.

IN WITNESS WHEREOF, the parties hereto have executed and delivered this Agreement as of the day and year first above written.

NOTE: Although the form is not set up to be notarized, where a transaction is between related parties (i.e., a Member and the LLC he or she owns an interest in) having a form notarized even if not required by law is a desirable step. It helps prove to the IRS (and others) that the documents were really signed when they indicate that they were. Also, if the LLC is controlled by its Members instead of a Manager, the signature line for the LLC should be revised below. Again, it is ideal to have all Members sign off if possible. If every Member signs the Assignment of Contract form and you follow the suggestion above to attach a copy of the entire contract involved, no Member can later claim that the contract assigned was a bad deal for the LLC.

WITNESSES:

ASSIGNEE:
LLC NAME, Assignee

_____

By: _____
       MANAGER NAME, Manager

ASSIGNOR:

_____

_____

MEMBER 1 NAME, Assignor

For Your Notebook:

SAMPLE CERTIFICATE OF FORMATION

NOTE: The following sample certificate is based on a hypothetical New Jersey LLC. Be sure to contact a lawyer in your state or obtain the appropriate forms as explained in the chapter.

Certificate of Formation
of
LLC NAME
Under Article 42:2B of the New Jersey Statutes

The undersigned, each over the age of majority, and in order to form an LLC pursuant to Article 42:2B of the New Jersey Statutes Annotated, under Section 11 of the New Jersey LLC Act, hereby certify as follows:

(a) The name of the LLC shall be:

LLC NAME

(b) The address of the initial registered office of the LLC shall be LLC ADDRESS, and the name of the registered agent of the LLC at that address is MANAGER NAME.

(c) The LLC has at least two or more Members.

(d) The LLC shall dissolve and terminate at the earliest of the following events:

(i) The occurrence of the termination events specified in the operating agreement of the LLC.

(ii) Written consent of all Members.

(iii) Thirty years from the date of the formation of the LLC.

(iv) The entry of a decree of judicial dissolution.

(v) The death, retirement, resignation, expulsion, bankruptcy, or dissolution of a Member or the occurrence of any other event which terminates the continued Membership of a Member in the LLC unless the business of the LLC is continued by the consent of all of the remaining Members within the time period, and in accordance with the requirements, provided in the Operating Agreement.

(e) The LLC may carry on and engage in the DESCRIBE BUSINESS, and all activities related or incident thereto.

(f) This Certificate of Formation shall be effective upon the initial filing and recording with the Secretary of State of the State of New Jersey.

(g) The undersigned persons executing this Certificate of Formation are properly authorized persons to do so as such term is defined under N.J.S.A. 42:2B-15.a.

IN WITNESS WHEREOF, We the undersigned sign our names this DAY of MONTH, YEAR and I affirm under the penalties of perjury that the statements in this Certificate are true.

_____   _____
MANAGER NAME   MEMBER 3 NAME

_____   _____
MEMBER 1 NAME   MEMBER 4 NAME

_____   _____
MEMBER 2 NAME   MEMBER 5 NAME

State of New Jersey   )

                           :ss.:

County of   )

On this DAY of MONTH, YEAR, before me personally came, MANAGER NAME to me known and known to me to be the individual described in and who executed the foregoing instrument, and such person duly acknowledged to me that he or she understood the meaning of the instrument and that he or she executed the same as his or her act and deed, and as a Member of the LLC named therein, and with full authority to act on behalf of such LLC, and that he or she is over the age of 18.

_____

Notary Public Signature

My commission expires: _____

State of New Jersey   )

                           :ss.:

County of   )

On this DAY of MONTH, YEAR, before me personally came, MEMBER 1 NAME to me known and known to me to be the individual described in and who executed the foregoing instrument, and such person duly acknowledged to me that he or she understood the meaning of the instrument and that he or she executed the same as his or her act and deed, and as a Member of the LLC named therein, and with full authority to act on behalf of such LLC, and that he or she is over the age of 18.

_____

Notary Public Signature

My commission expires: _____

State of New Jersey   )

                           :ss.:

County of   )

On this DAY of MONTH, YEAR, before me personally came, MEMBER 2 NAME to me known and known to me to be the individual described in and who executed the foregoing instrument, and such person duly acknowledged to me that he or she understood the meaning of the instrument and that he or she executed the same as his or her act and deed, and as a Member of the LLC named therein, and with full authority to act on behalf of such LLC, and that he or she is over the age of 18.

_____

Notary Public Signature

My commission expires: _____

State of New Jersey   )

                           :ss.:

County of   )

On this DAY of MONTH, YEAR, before me personally came, MEMBER 3 NAME to me known and known to me to be the individual described in and who executed the foregoing instrument, and such person duly acknowledged to me that he or she understood the meaning of the instrument and that he or she executed the same as his or her act and deed, and as a Member of the

LLC named therein, and with full authority to act on behalf of such LLC, and that he or she is over the age of 18.

_____
Notary Public Signature
My commission expires: _____

State of New Jersey   )
                             :ss.:
County of   )

On this DAY of MONTH, YEAR, before me personally came, MEMBER 4 NAME to me known and known to me to be the individual described in and who executed the foregoing instrument, and such person duly acknowledged to me that he or she understood the meaning of the instrument and that he or she executed the same as his or her act and deed, and as a Member of the LLC named therein, and with full authority to act on behalf of such LLC, and that he or she is over the age of 18.

_____
Notary Public Signature
My commission expires: _____

State of New Jersey   )
                             :ss.:
County of   )

On this DAY of MONTH, YEAR, before me personally came, MEMBER 5 NAME to me known and known to me to be the individual described in and who executed the foregoing instrument, and such person duly acknowledged to me that he or she understood the meaning of the instrument and that he or she executed the same as his or her act and deed, and as a Member of the LLC named therein, and with full authority to act on behalf of such LLC, and that he or she is over the age of 18.

_____
Notary Public Signature
My commission expires: _____

For Your Notebook:

SAMPLE ARTICLES OF ORGANIZATION

Articles of Organization
of
LLC NAME
Under and Pursuant to Section 203 of the
Limited Liability Company Law of the State of New York

The undersigned, being the organizer(s) of the Limited Liability Company does (do) hereby certify as follows:

(h)   The name of the Limited Liability Company is:

LLC NAME

(i)   The principal office of the Limited Liability Company shall be located in the County of COUNTY NAME.

(j)   The Limited Liability Company has a specific date of dissolution in addition to the events set forth in Section 701 of the LLC Law of the State of New York. Such date is which is the latest date upon which the Limited Liability Company is to dissolve.

The Limited Liability Company shall dissolve and terminate not later than the earliest of the following events:

(i)   The occurrence of the termination events specified in the operating agreement of the LLC.

(ii)   Written consent of all Members.

(iii)   Thirty years from the date of the formation of the Limited Liability Company.

(k)   The Secretary of State is designated as the agent of the Limited Liability Company upon whom process against the Limited Liability Company may be served, and the address to which the Secretary of State shall mail a copy of any process against the Limited Liability Company served upon him is AGENT ADDRESS.

The Limited Liability Company shall have a registered agent. The address of the initial registered office of the Limited Liability Company shall be AGENT ADDRESS, and the name of the registered agent of the Limited Liability Company at that address is AGENT NAME.

(l)   The Limited Liability Company shall be managed by one or more MANAGERS one or more members of a class or classes consisting of DESCRIBE.

(m)   All of specified class of members are to be liable in their capacity as members for all or specified debts, obligations, or liabilities of the Limited Liability Company as authorized pursuant to Section 609 of the Limited Liability Company Law of the State of New York.

(n)   The Members of the Limited Liability Company elect to include the following additional provisions in these Articles of Organization for the regulation of the internal affairs of the Limited Liability Company:

(i)   The Limited Liability Company may carry on and engage in
any lawful business of purposes permitted under state law.
DETAIL-SPECIFIC PURPOSE
OTHER PERMITTED MATTERS

(ii)   The following limitations on the authority of Members and/or Managers or a class of Members to bind the Limited Liability Company DESCRIBE

(iii)   [Describe any additional provisions permitted under Section 417].

IN WITNESS WHEREOF, I [We] the undersigned sign my (our) name(s) this DAY of MONTH, YEAR and affirm under the penalties of perjury that the statements in these Articles are true.

_____

NAME 1, Organizer

_____

NAME 2, Organizer

State of STATE NAME   )
                                         :ss.:
County of COUNTY NAME   )

On this DAY of MONTH, YEAR, before me personally came, NAME 1 to me known and known to me to be the individual described in and who executed the foregoing instrument, and such person duly acknowledged to me that he or she understood the meaning of the instrument and that he or she executed the same as his or her act and deed, and as a Member of the LLC named therein, and with full authority to act on behalf of such LLC, and that he or she is over the age of 18.

_____
Notary Public Signature
My commission expires: _____

State of STATE NAME   )
                                         :ss.:
County of COUNTY NAME   )

On this DAY of MONTH, YEAR, before me personally came, NAME 1 to me known and known to me to be the individual described in and who executed the foregoing instrument, and such person duly acknowledged to me that he or she understood the meaning of the instrument and that he or she executed the same as his or her act and deed, and as a Member of the LLC named therein, and with full authority to act on behalf of such LLC, and that he or she is over the age of 18.

_____
Notary Public Signature
My commission expires: _____

For Your Notebook:

SAMPLE OPERATING AGREEMENT
FOR
BIG-DEAL PROPERTIES LLC,
A MICHIGAN LIMITED LIABILITY COMPANY

NOTE: The following is a sample LLC Operating Agreement for a Michigan LLC formed by a small group of investors for the sole purpose of investing in a particular parcel of land. The LLC vehicle was used to limit their liability exposure from owning the land. Many of the provisions governing the management and operation are tailored to reflect this limited purpose. Because complex allocations of income and gain are not relevant to the particular deal, many more sophisticated tax-related provisions are not included in the agreement.

THIS OPERATING AGREEMENT is made and entered into as of DATE by and among BIG-DEAL Properties LLC, a Michigan Limited Liability Company (the "Company") and the persons executing this Operating Agreement as Members of the Company and all of those who shall hereafter be admitted as Members (individually, a "Member" and collectively, the "Members") whose names and signatures shall appear on "EXHIBIT A MEMBER LISTING; CAPITAL CONTRIBUTIONS," below, hereby agree as follows:

WITNESSETH:

NOTE: From a tax perspective, the investors in this LLC want to make it clear that they are merely holding land as an investment, which should qualify for capital gains treatment when sold. If the LLC developed, subdivided, or improved the land they purchased they could, depending on the facts and circumstances, be characterized as a dealer in real estate. If this occurred, the gain on sale could then be characterized as ordinary income, taxable at a much higher tax rate.

---

1. Whereas, the Members desire to enter into this operating agreement ("Operating Agreement" or "Agreement") for the purposes of governing the Company, to and for the purpose of investing in, purchasing, selling, granting, or taking an option on raw land solely for investment purposes and not as a trade or business ("Business"). The Company shall not conduct any other business unless related to the Business, unless approved by unanimous consent of all Members.

2. Whereas, the Members intend to operate the Business, appoint a person or persons to assume responsibility for certain management matters (the "Manager") and provide for the restriction on the transfers of ownership interests in the Company ("Interests").

NOW, THEREFORE, in consideration of the mutual premises below, and other good and valuable consideration, the receipt and sufficiency of which are hereby acknowledged, it is agreed as follows:

I. ORGANIZATION

1. *Formation.* The Company has been organized as a Michigan limited liability company under and pursuant to the Michigan LLC Act, being Act No. 23, Public Acts of 1993 (the "Act") by the filing of Articles of Organization ("Articles") with the Department of Commerce of the State of Michigan as required by the Act.

2. *Name.* The name of the Company shall be the "BIG-DEAL Properties LLC." The Company may also conduct its business under one or more assumed names.

3. *Purposes.* The purpose of the Company is to engage in any activity for which limited liability companies may be formed under the Act for purposes only of advancing the Business as defined above. The Company shall have all the powers necessary or convenient to effect any purpose for which it is formed, including all powers granted by the Act.

NOTE: The duration for the LLC should be consistent with the duration specified in the Articles of Organization.

---

4. *Duration.* The Company shall continue in existence for the period fixed in the Articles of Organization for the duration of the Company of thirty (30) years, or until the Company shall be sooner dissolved and its affairs wound up in accordance with the Act or this Operating Agreement.

NOTE: The following provision assures a continuation of a Registered Agent if the first named Agent resigns, without the need for an approval of the Manager or Members. This can be a useful precautionary step.

---

5. *Registered Office and Resident Agent.* The Registered Office and Resident Agent of the Company shall be as designated in the initial Articles or any amendment thereof, MANAGER-NAME, who resides at MANAGER'S-ADDRESS. The Registered Office and/or Resident Agent may be changed from time to time. Any such change shall be made in accordance with the Act. If the Resident Agent shall ever resign, the Company shall promptly appoint REPLACEMENT AGENT, who resides at REPLACEMENT-AGENT ADDRESS, as the successor. If he/she is unable or unwilling, then he/she shall designate a successor Manager by giving written notice to the Members.

6. *Intention for Company.* The Members have formed the Company as an limited liability company under and pursuant to the Act.

NOTE: The following statement makes clear that the intent of the Members is for the LLC to be taxed as a partnership. Even if the IRS permits a simple "check the box approach" for an LLC to designate how it wants to be taxed on its tax return, every Operating Agreement should clearly state the Members' intent concerning tax classification: partnership or corporation.

The Members specifically intend and agree that the Company shall not be, for legal purposes, a partnership (including, a limited partnership) or any other venture, but a shall be a limited liability company under and pursuant to the Act, desiring partnership tax treatment.

No Member or Manager shall be construed to be a partner in the Company or a partner of any other Member, Manager, or person; and the Articles, this Operating Agreement, and the relationships created thereby and arising therefrom shall not be construed to suggest otherwise.

II. BOOKS, RECORDS AND ACCOUNTING

1. *Books and Records.* The Company shall maintain complete and accurate books and records of the Company's business and affairs as required by the Act and such books and records shall be kept at the Company's Registered Office.

NOTE: There is no requirement to designate a specific accountant. In this transaction, several of the Members were comfortable with a particular accountant and felt that it would give stability to the venture, and help avoid disputes, to assure that a particular accountant was involved. This is simply an example of the many ways any agreement can be tailored to meet the specific needs you and your partners have for your LLC, the investment involved, and so on. The key point is, do not simply fill in the blanks on a form and assume you've obtained reasonable protection. Every document should be tailored to the specific situation. The more effort expended in the beginning on addressing and resolving likely issues in the Operating Agreement, the less likely it will be that significant, costly, and disruptive disputes will arise later.

---

2. *Fiscal Year; Accounting.* The Company's fiscal year shall be the calendar year. The particular accounting methods and principles to be followed by the Company shall be selected by the accountant for the Company ("Accountant") who is hereby designated as JOE ACCOUNTANT & Co., CPAs, Accounting Road, BIG CITY, Michigan, its successor or assigns. The Accountant may be changed by written Notice of the then serving Manager, consented to in writing by at least Two (2) Members.

NOTE: Since this particular deal involves only raw land, an annual accounting report is adequate. If you have a retail business, you may want to insist that you (and all Members) receive some type of monthly report. Tailor the provision to meet the reasonable needs and expectations you have for the business, without creating undue cost or administrative burdens.

---

3. *Reports.* The Managers shall provide reports concerning the financial condition and results of operation of the Company and the Capital Accounts of the Members to the Members in the time, manner, and form as the Manager determines. Such reports shall be provided at least annually as soon as practicable after the end of each calendar year and shall include a statement of each Member's share of profits and other items of income, gain, loss, deduction and credit.

4. *Member's Capital Accounts.* Separate Capital Accounts for each Member shall be maintained by the Company. Each Member's Capital Account shall reflect the Member's capital contributions and increases for the Member's share of any net income or gain of the Company. Each Member's Capital Account shall also reflect decreases for distributions made to the Member and the Member's share of any losses and deductions of the Company.

(a) *Definition of Capital Account*

A separate capital account shall be maintained for each Member or Assignee in accordance with the provisions below ("Capital Account").

(b) *Increases in Capital Account*

Each Member's Capital Account shall be increased by:

(i)   The amount of money contributed by the Member to the Company.

(ii)   The fair market value of property contributed by the Member to the Company (net of liabilities secured by such contributed property that the Company is considered to assume or take subject to under Code Section 752). If any property, other than cash, is contributed to or distributed by the Company, the adjustments to Capital Accounts required by Treasury Regulation Section 1.704-1(b)(2)(iv)(d), (e), (f) and (g) and Section 1.704-1(b)(4)(i) shall be made.

(iii)   The Member's share of the increase in the tax basis of Company property, if any, arising out of the recapture of any tax credit.

(iv)   Allocations to the Member of Profit.

(v)   Allocations to the Member of income or gain as provided under this Agreement, or otherwise by Regulation Section 1.704-1(b)(2)(iv).

(c) *Decreases in Capital Account*

Each Member's Capital Account shall be decreased by:

(i)   The amount of money distributed to the Member by the Company.

(ii)   The fair market value of property distributed to the Member by the Company (net of liabilities secured by such distributed property that such Member is considered to assume or take subject to under Code Section 752).

(iii)   Allocations to the Member of Losses.

(iv)   Allocations to the Member of deductions, expenses, Nonrecourse Deductions and Net Losses allocated to it pursuant to this Agreement, and the Member's share of Company expenditures which are neither deductible nor properly chargeable to Capital Accounts under Code Section 705(a)(2)(B) or are treated as such expenditures under Treasury Regulation Section 1.704-1(b)(2)(iv)(i). "Nonrecourse Deductions" shall have the meaning set forth in Treasury Regulation Section 1.704-2.

(v)   The Member's share of the decrease in the basis of the Company's property under Code Section 48(q) arising from the allowance of any tax credit.

(d) *Capital Account of Transferee*

In the event of a permitted sale or exchange of an Interest in the Company, the Capital Account of the transferor shall become the Capital Account of the transferee to the extent it relates to the transferred Interest in accordance with Regulation Section 1.704-1(b)(2)(iv).

(e) *Capital Accounts Shall Comply with Code Section 704(b).*

NOTE: A paragraph similar to the following should appear in every LLC Operating Agreement where the LLC is to be taxed as a partnership. The purpose is to assure that the business meets the tax rules for how capital accounts must be maintained. If they are not, the consequences can be dire. Where your deal has all Members receiving only distributions that are proportionate to their Membership Interests (e.g., a 10% Member receives 10% of all income, losses, gains, and distributions, and a 42% Member receives 42% of all items) problems are far less likely and a general provision as below could suffice (but have your tax adviser review the Operating Agreement to be sure). Where distributions are nonproportionate (e.g., you are a 25% Member but receive 45% of the profits from the sale of a particular parcel of property the LLC purchased, etc.) be certain to get competent tax advice and use a more sophisticated Operating Agreement.

CAUTION: Where Members of the LLC are family members (e.g., you give Membership Interests to your children as gifts to reduce your estate), additional tax provisions, called the family partnership rules under Section 704(e) of the Internal Revenue Code, should be discussed with your tax adviser. These rules are addressed in a later provision of this form.

The manner in which Capital Accounts are to be maintained pursuant to this Agreement is intended to comply with the requirements of Code Section 704(b) and the Regulations thereunder. It is the specific intent of the Members that all such further or different adjustments as may be required pursuant to Code Section 704, and any Regulations thereunder be made, so as to cause the allocations prescribed hereunder to be respected for tax purposes. Therefore, if in the opinion of the Accountant (or if the Accountant is unable or unwilling to act, the Manager), the manner in which Capital Accounts are to be maintained pursuant to this Agreement should be modified to comply with Code Section 704(b) and the Regulations thereunder, then notwithstanding anything to the contrary contained in this Agreement, or any other agreement between the Parties, the method in which Capital Accounts are maintained shall be so modified. However, any change in the manner of maintaining Capital Accounts shall not materially alter the economic agreement between or among the Members. Each Member hereby appoints the Manager the Tax Matters Member and agent for the purpose of making any amendment to this Agreement solely for purposes of complying with this provision.

III. CAPITAL CONTRIBUTIONS

NOTE: It's best for all investments to be made at the outset since it is simplest. If a Member will make a contribution at a later date, see the Amendment and related forms in the "For Your Notebook" section of this chapter.

1. *Initial Commitments and Contributions.* By the execution of this Operating Agreement, the initial Members hereby agree to make the capital contributions set forth in the attached Exhibit A. The interests of the respective Members in the total capital of the Company (their respective "Sharing Ratios," as adjusted from time to time to reflect changes in the Capital Accounts of the Members and the total capital in the Company) is also set forth in Exhibit A. Any additional Member (other than an assignee of a membership interest who has been admitted as a Member) shall make the capital contribution set forth in an Admission Agreement. No interest shall accrue on any capital contribution and no Member shall have any right to withdraw or to be repaid any capital contribution except as provided in this Operating Agreement.

2. *Additional Contributions.* In addition to the initial capital contributions, the Managers may determine from time to time that additional capital contributions are needed to enable the Company to conduct its business and affairs. Upon making such a determination, notice thereof shall be given to all Members in writing at least ten (10) business days prior to the date on which such

additional contributions are due. Such notice shall describe in reasonable detail, the purposes and uses of such additional capital, the amounts of additional capital required, and the date by which payment of the additional capital is required. Each Member shall be obligated to make such additional capital contribution to the extent of any unfulfilled commitment. Any Member who has fulfilled that Member's commitment, shall have the right, but not the obligation to make the additional capital contributions needed according to that Member's Sharing Ratio.

3. *Failure to Contribute.* If any Member fails to make a capital contribution when required, the Company may, in addition to the other rights and remedies the Company may have under the Act or applicable law, take such enforcement action (including, the commencement and prosecution of court proceedings) against such Member as the Managers consider appropriate. Moreover, the remaining Members may elect to contribute the amount of such required capital themselves according to their respective Sharing Ratios. In such an event, the remaining Members shall be entitled to treat such amounts as an extension of credit to such defaulting Member, payable upon demand, with interest accruing thereon at the federal midterm rate provided for under Code Section 1274(d), plus Two percent (2%) until paid, all of which shall be secured by such defaulting Member's interest in the Company, each Member who may hereafter default, hereby granting to each Member who may hereafter grant such an extension of credit, a security interest in such defaulting Member's interest in the Company.

IV. ALLOCATIONS AND DISTRIBUTIONS

1. *Allocations.* Except as may be required by the Code as amended or this Operating Agreement, net profits, net losses, and other items of income, gain, loss, deduction, and credit of the Company shall be allocated among the Members in accordance with their Sharing Ratios.

CAUTION: Distributions can be a real tough area to address. Some Members who need funds will want to have all available cash distributed. Others, who have a longer term interest in the business may prefer to "play it safe" and leave more funds in the business for an emergency, to fund future repairs and so on. Some mechanism must be included in every Operating Agreement establishing rules for how distributions should be made. If the LLC has two or three active Members, you may simply hash it out at year end. Where there are many passive Members not involved in management, the decision may be given to the Manager to make. In-between situations are tougher to call. But it is important to negotiate something workable to avoid fights later.

CAUTION: When the LLC is taxed as a partnership, every Member will have to report his or her share of income on his or her tax return regardless of the income distributed. Example: You're a 10 percent Member and the LLC earns $58,000 for the year. Because of anticipated repairs to the roof of the LLC's rental property, no distributions are made. You have what tax experts call "phantom income." You will have to report your share, or $5,800 (10% × $58,000) on your personal tax return and pay tax. Your tax cost could be $2,436 ($5,800 × 42% marginal federal and state tax rate). You're now out of pocket $2,436 and have received no distributions from the LLC. This is why the $5,800 is called "phantom income." You have to report it, but you didn't receive it. Be sure to discuss this issue with other Members. If you are a nonvoting Member or a voting, but noncontrolling, Member, you may want to negotiate a requirement that the Manager or other Members must distribute not less than say 40 percent of taxable income to the Members unless 75 percent or more of the Members agree otherwise.

---

2. *Distributions.* The Managers may make distributions to the Members from time to time. Distributions may be made only after the Managers determine in their reasonable judgment, that the Company has sufficient cash on hand which exceeds the current and the anticipated needs of the Company to fulfill its business purposes (including needs for operating expenses, debt service, acquisitions, reserves, and mandatory distributions, if any). All distributions shall be made

to the Members in accordance with their Sharing Ratios. Distributions shall be in cash or property or particularly in both, as determined by the Managers. No distribution shall be declared or made if, after giving it effect, the Company would not be able to pay its debts as they become due in the usual course of business or the Company's total assets would be less than the sum of its total liabilities plus, the amount that would be needed if the Company were to be dissolved at the time of the distribution, to satisfy the preferential rights of other Members upon dissolution that are superior to the rights of the Members receiving the distribution.

3. *Family Partnership Savings Provision.* Notwithstanding anything in this Operating Agreement to the contrary, should any provision of this Operating Agreement, or any act of the parties, result in a violation of the family partnership provisions of Code Section 704(e) or the regulations and cases thereunder, the Managers may amend this Agreement, or take any other actions reasonably necessary to prevent such violation, or to correct such violation.

V. DISPOSITION OF MEMBERSHIP INTERESTS

NOTE: The following provision is quite tough and may make it impossible for an unhappy Member to sell his or her interest. These provisions are a balancing act: you want any Member who is very unhappy, or who the other Members are unhappy with to be able leave. On the other hand, you don't want to make it so easy for any Member to dispose of his or her Membership Interest so that an outsider can get involved. Where the LLC is owned only by yourself and a limited number of close friends or business associates, you would not wish an outsider to be able to become a Member. Many approaches can be used to address this. A right of first refusal, for example, gives the LLC or other Members the right to purchase any Membership Interests any Member wishes to sell. Only if the LLC and other Members turn down the opportunity can the selling Member sell his or her interests to a third party. An advantage of this method is that an independent sale to a third party sets the price, not a battle of who has greater clout in the LLC. This method is not without problems however. A right of first refusal for a noncontrolling interest in an LLC is often difficult, if not impossible, to sell.

---

1. *General.* Every sale, assignment, transfer, exchange, mortgage, pledge, grant, hypothecation or other disposition of any Membership Interest shall be made only upon compliance with this Article. No Membership Interest shall be disposed of if the disposition would cause a termination of the Company under Section 708 of the Internal Revenue Code of 1986, as amended; without compliance with any and all state and federal securities laws and regulations; and unless the assignee of the Membership Interests provides the Company with the information and agreements that the Managers may require in connection with such disposition, including but not limited to an executed counterpart of this Agreement. No Member shall be entitled to assign, convey, sell, encumber, or in any way alienate all or any part of its Membership Interest in the Company and as a Member except with the prior written consent of a majority in interest of the non-transferring Members, which consent may be given or withheld, conditioned, or delayed (as allowed by this Agreement or the Act), as the non-transferring Members may determine in their sole discretion. Transfers in violation of this provision shall only be effective to the extent of an assignment of such interest with only the rights set forth in the following provision "Permitted Dispositions."

2. *Permitted Dispositions.* Subject to the provisions of this Article, a Member may assign such Member's Membership Interest in the Company in whole or in part. The assignment of a Membership Interest does not itself entitle the assignee to participate in the management and affairs of the Company or to become a Member. Such assignee is only entitled to receive, to the extent assigned, the distributions the assigning Member would otherwise be entitled to, and such assignee shall only become an assignee of a Membership Interest and not a substitute Member.

NOTE: An "assignee" of an LLC interest is entitled to only the income and distributions of that Membership Interest. He is not entitled to the other rights of being a Member unless he becomes a "substitute Member." Where unanimous consent is required, this can be an important control on who can become a Member and have the rights of a Member. Also, this restriction is an important issue in asset protection planning since it can prevent a creditor from obtaining full rights of your interest in an LLC to satisfy a lawsuit.

3. *Admission of Substitute Members.* An assignee of a Membership Interest shall be admitted as a substitute Member and shall be entitled to all the rights and powers of the assignor only if the other Members unanimously consent. If admitted, the substitute Member has, to the extent assigned, all of the rights and powers, and is subject to all of the restrictions and liabilities of a Member.

VI. MEETINGS OF MEMBERS

NOTE: Voting and control issues must be addressed in every Operating Agreement. In more complex business or investment transactions, you may have a series of different requirements as to what each Member can vote on, different percentages of Membership Interests required to pass various matters, and so forth. The key point is to identify what are the most important issues likely to affect a particular LLC, what the major concerns of the Members are, and what mechanisms can be used to protect the LLC and Members as a whole from those issues and concerns. For example, 80 percent plus vote may be required to sell an LLC's only rental property, while only a 51 percent vote of Membership Interests may be necessary to approve a lease to a tenant in one of the apartments in the LLC's building.

1. *Voting.* Except to the extent provided to the contrary in this Agreement, all Members shall be entitled to vote on any matter submitted to a vote of the Members. Notwithstanding the foregoing, the Members shall have the right to vote on all of the following: (a) the dissolution of the Company pursuant to the provisions of this Operating Agreement that permit a dissolution of the Company upon the unanimous consent of all Members; (b) the merger of the Company; (c) a transaction involving an actual or potential conflict of interest between a Manager and the Company; (d) an amendment to the Articles of Organization; or (e) the sale, exchange, lease or other transfer of all or substantially all of the assets of the Company other than in the ordinary course of business.

2. *Required Vote.* Unless a greater vote is required by the Act or the Articles of Organization, the affirmative vote or consent of a majority of the Sharing Ratios of all the Members entitled to vote or consent on such matter shall be required.

3. *Meetings.* An annual meeting of Members for the transaction of such business as may properly come before the Meeting, shall be held at such place, on such date and at such time as the Managers shall determine. Special meetings of Members for any proper purpose or purposes may be called at any time by the Managers or the holders of at least ten percent (10%) of the Sharing Ratios of all Members. The Company shall deliver or mail written notice stating the date, time, place, and purposes of any meeting to each Member entitled to vote at the meeting. Such notice shall be given not less than ten (10) and no more than Sixty (60) days before the date of the meeting. All meetings of Members shall be presided over by a Chairperson who shall be a Manager. A Member may participate and vote at such meeting via telephone conference call.

4. *Consent.* Any action required or permitted to be taken at an annual or special meeting of the Members may be taken without a meeting, without prior notice, and without a vote, if consents in writing, setting forth the action so taken, are signed by the Members having not less than the minimum number of votes that would be necessary to authorize or take such action at a meeting at which all Membership Interests entitled to vote on the action were present and voted. Every written consent shall bear the date and signature of each Member who signs the consent. Prompt notice of the taking of action without a meeting by less than unanimous written consent shall be given to all Members who have not consented in writing to such action.

VII. MANAGEMENT

1. *Management of Business.* The Company shall be managed by MANAGER 1, NAME ("Manager"), so long as she is able and willing to serve. If MANAGER 1, NAME shall ever resign, or be unable or unwilling to serve as Manager, then MANAGER 2, NAME, who resides at FANCY

STREET, BIG CITY, Michigan, shall serve as the successor. If MANAGER 2, NAME is unable or unwilling to so serve, then MANAGER 3, NAME, who resides at 123 Main Street, Anytown, Michigan, shall serve as Manager. If he is unable or unwilling, then he shall designate a successor Manager by giving written notice to the Members. The terms, duties, compensation, and benefits, if any, of the Managers shall be as follows: MANAGER shall receive compensation for serving as Manager as follows: DESCRIBE COMPENSATION. The duties of the Manager shall be those duties reasonably necessary to conduct the Business of the Company, and shall include, but not be limited to: DESCRIBE DUTIES.

2. *Removal of Manager.* Any Manager may be removed at any time, with or without cause, by the affirmative vote of seventy-five percent (75%) of the Membership Interests in the Company then entitled to vote.

3. *General Powers of Managers.* Except as may otherwise be provided in this Operating Agreement, the ordinary and usual decisions concerning the business and affairs of the Company shall be made by the Managers. The Managers have the power, on behalf of the Company, to do all things necessary or convenient to carry out the business and affairs of the Company, including, the power to: (a) purchase, lease, or otherwise acquire any real or personal property; (b) sell, convey, mortgage, grant a security interest in, pledge, lease, exchange, or otherwise dispose or encumber any real or personal property; (c) open one or more depository accounts and make deposits into and checks and withdrawals against such accounts; (d) borrow money, incur liabilities, and other obligations; (e) enter into any and all agreements and execute any and all contracts, documents, and instruments relating to the Business; (f) engage consultants and agents, define their respective duties and establish their compensation or remuneration; (g) obtain insurance covering the Business and affairs of the Company and its property; (h) commence, prosecute, or defend any proceeding in the Company's name; and (i) participate with others in partnerships, joint ventures, and other associations and strategic alliances only where same are directly in pursuit of the Business, as defined above.

As an express limitation on the nature of the Business and the powers granted the Managers herein, the Company is intended to hold real estate for investment purposes only, and no activities inconsistent with such limited purposes shall be undertaken.

4. *Limitations.* Notwithstanding the foregoing and any other provision contained in this Operating Agreement to the contrary, no act shall be taken, sum expended, decision made, obligation incurred or power exercised by any Manager on behalf of the Company except by the consent of seventy-five percent (75%) of all Membership Interests with respect to (a) any significant and material purchase, receipt, lease, exchange, or other acquisition of any real or personal property or business; (b) the sale of all or substantially all of the assets and property of the Company; (c) any mortgage, grant of security interest, pledge, or encumbrance upon all or substantially all of the assets and property of the Company; (d) any merger; (e) any amendment or restatement of the Articles or of this Operating Agreement; (f) any matter which could result in a change in the amount or character of the Company's capital; (g) any change in the character of the business and affairs of the Company; (h) the commission of any act which would make it impossible for the Company to carry on its ordinary business and affairs; or (i) any act that would contravene any provision of the Articles or of this Operating Agreement or the Act.

5. *Standard of Care; Liability.* Every Manger shall discharge his or her duties as a manager in good faith, with the care an ordinarily prudent person in a like position would exercise under similar circumstances, and in a manner he or she reasonably believes to be in the best interests of the Company. A Manager shall not be liable for any monetary damages to the Company for any breach of such duties except for receipt of a financial benefit to which the Manager is not entitled; voting for or assenting to a distribution to Members in violation of this Operating Agreement or the Act; or a knowing violation of the law.

VIII. EXCULPATION OF LIABILITY: INDEMNIFICATION

1. *Exculpation of Liability.* Unless otherwise provided by law or expressly assumed, a person who is a Member or Manager, or both, shall not be liable for the acts, debts or liabilities of the Company.

2. *Indemnification.* Except as otherwise provided in this Article, the Company shall indemnify any Manager and may indemnify any employee or agent of the Company who was or is a

party or is threatened to be made a party to a threatened, pending or completed action, suit or proceeding, whether civil, criminal, administrative, or investigative, and whether formal or informal, other than an action by or in the right of the Company, by reason of the fact that such person is or was a Manager, employee or agent of the Company against expenses, including attorney's fees, judgments, penalties, fines, and amounts paid in settlement actually and reasonably incurred by such person in connection with the action, suit or proceeding, if the person acted in good faith, with the care an ordinarily prudent person in a like position would exercise under similar circumstances, and in a manner that such person reasonably believed to be in the best interests of the Company and with respect to a criminal action or proceeding, if such person had no reasonable cause to believe such person's conduct was unlawful. To the extent that a Member, employee, or agent of the Company has been successful on the merits or otherwise in defense of an action, suit, or proceeding or in defense of any claim, issue, or other matter in the action, suit, or proceeding, such person shall be indemnified against actual and reasonable expenses, including attorney's fees, incurred by such person in connection with the action, suit, or proceeding and any action, suit, or proceeding brought to enforce the mandatory indemnification provided herein. Any indemnification permitted under this Article, unless ordered by a court, shall be made by the Company only as authorized in the specific case upon a determination that the indemnification is proper under the circumstances because the person to be indemnified has met the applicable standard of conduct and upon an evaluation of the reasonableness of expenses and amounts paid in settlement. This determination and evaluation shall be made by a majority vote of the Members who are not parties or threatened to be made parties to the action, suit, or proceeding. Notwithstanding the foregoing to the contrary, no indemnification shall be provided to any Manager, employee, or agent of the Company for or in connection with the receipt of a financial benefit to which such person is not entitled, voting for or assenting to a distribution to Members in violation of this Operating Agreement or the Act, or a knowing violation of law.

IX. OTHER ACTIVITIES

Any Member and the Managers may engage in other business ventures of every nature, including, without limitation by specification, the ownership of another business similar to that operated by the Company. Neither the Company nor any of the other Members shall have any right or interest in any such independent ventures or to the income and profits derived therefrom.

X. DISSOLUTION AND WINDING UP

1. *Dissolution.* The Company shall dissolve and its affairs shall be wound up on the first to occur of the following events: (a) at any time specified in the Articles or this Operating Agreement; (b) upon the happening of any event specified in the Articles or this Operating Agreement; (c) by the unanimous consent of all of the Members, (d) upon the death, withdrawal, expulsion, bankruptcy, or dissolution of a Member or the occurrence of any other event that terminates the continued membership of a Member in the Company unless within ninety (90) days after the disassociation of membership, a majority in interest of the remaining Members consent to continue the business of the Company and to the admission of one or more Members as necessary.

2. *Winding Up.* Upon dissolution, the Company shall cease carrying on its business and affairs and shall commence the winding up of the Company's business and affairs and complete the winding up as soon as practicable. Upon the winding up of the Company, the assets of the Company shall be distributed first to creditors to the extent permitted by law, in satisfaction of Company debts, liabilities, and obligations and then to Members and former Members first, in satisfaction of liabilities for distributions and then, in accordance with their Sharing Ratios. Such proceeds shall be paid to such Members within One Hundred Twenty (120) days after the date of winding up.

XI. MISCELLANEOUS PROVISIONS

1. *Terms.* Nouns and pronouns will be deemed to refer to the masculine, feminine, neuter, singular, and plural, as the identity of the person or persons, firm, or corporation may in the context require. The term "Code" shall refer to the Internal Revenue Code of 1986, as amended.

2. *Article Headings.* The Article headings and numbers contained in this Operating Agreement have been inserted only as a matter of convenience and for reference, and in no way shall

be construed to define, limit, or describe the scope or intent of any provision of this Operating Agreement.

3. *Counterparts.* This Operating Agreement may be executed in several counterparts, each of which will be deemed an original but all of which will constitute one and the same.

4. *Entire Agreement.* This Operating Agreement constitutes the entire agreement among the parties hereto and contains all of the agreements among said parties with respect to the subject matter hereof. This Operating Agreement supersedes any and all other agreements, either oral or written, between said parties with respect to the subject matter hereof.

5. *Severability.* The invalidity or unenforceability of any particular provision of this Operating Agreement shall not affect the other provisions hereof, and this Operating Agreement shall be construed in all respects as if such invalid or unenforceable provisions were omitted.

6. *Amendment.* This Operating Agreement may be amended or revoked at any time by a written agreement executed by all of the parties to this Operating Agreement, except where a lesser percentage of Membership Interests is permitted elsewhere in this Operating Agreement. No change or modification to this Operating Agreement shall be valid unless in writing and signed by all of the parties to this Operating Agreement.

7. *Notices.* Any notice permitted or required under this Operating Agreement shall be conveyed to the party at the address reflected in this Operating Agreement and will be deemed to have been given, when deposited in the United States mail, postage paid, or when delivered in person, or by a national overnight courier or by facsimile transmission (the receipt of which is confirmed).

8. *Binding Effect.* Subject to the provisions of this Operating Agreement relating to transferability, this Operating Agreement will be binding upon and shall inure to the benefit of the parties, and their respective distributees, heirs, successors and assigns.

9. *Governing Law.* This Operating Agreement is being executed and delivered in the State of Michigan and shall be governed by, construed, and enforced in accordance with the laws of the State of Michigan.

IN WITNESS WHEREOF, the parties hereto make and execute this Operating Agreement on the dates set below their names, to be effective on the date first above written.

WITNESSETH:

LLC NAME, LLC

By: _____
    MANAGER 1 NAME, Manager

MEMBERS:

_____
MEMBER 1 NAME, Member

_____
MEMBER 2 NAME, Member

John Doe Investment Trust

By: _____
    Thomas Trustworthy Trustee

_____
MEMBER 4 NAME, Member

For Your Notebook:

SAMPLE EXHIBIT A
MEMBER LISTING CAPITAL CONTRIBUTIONS

Members	Capital Contributed	Percentage Interest
MEMBER NAME 1	$10,000	50%
MEMBER NAME 2	$10,000	50%
Total	$20,000	100%

Date: _____ _____ , 1996

ACCEPTED AND AGREED:
LLC NAME, LLC

By: _____
       MANAGER 1 NAME, Manager

MEMBERS:

_____
MEMBER 1 NAME, Member

_____
MEMBER 2 NAME, Member

John Doe Investment Trust

By: _____
       Thomas Trustworthy Trustee

_____
MEMBER 4 NAME, Member

4 CONVERSION OF YOUR EXISTING BUSINESS TO A LIMITED LIABILITY COMPANY

Chapter 3 explained how to organize and set up your LLC. A twist on this standard approach may be necessary for many investors or business owners who already own the business or investment involved.

If you are an existing business owner or investor and have heard of the new form of doing business known as a "limited liability company" and believe that an LLC is the right entity for you, you should consider a conversion of your existing entity into an LLC. Before converting an existing entity into an LLC, however, make sure that a conversion from the existing entity into an LLC is permitted under state law and determine whether the conversion into an LLC will result in a taxable event that might outweigh the benefits achieved by the conversion.

Several other issues must be closely scrutinized before moving forward with an entity conversion into an LLC. For example, will the conversion trigger any "due on sale" clauses contained in any loan documents, or will the conversion cause a default on the entity's part in any contracts in which it is a party? In either of these two cases, there is the potential for the entity to incur severe conversion costs.

TIP: Identify and organize copies of all contracts to which the business or investment is a party. These should include mortgages, notes, and other loan documents, equipment and real property leases, license agreements, employment agreements, and so on. Have each document reviewed by your attorney to determine the consequences of conversion such as causing a loan to be accelerated or a lease to be violated. You should have your attorney obtain the necessary approval from the other side to each agreement affected. The cost of this process often can be more than legal fees. In many cases, a landlord or lender who is asked to approve a transfer may look on the request as an opportunity to extract some type of concession from you.

Generally, a conversion to an LLC will involve either a general partnership, a limited partnership, a corporation, or a sole proprietorship. Usually, the conversion from the partnership format or the sole proprietorship to an LLC can occur on a tax-free basis (with certain exceptions), but a conversion from a corporation to an LLC will involve a liquidation of the corporation (whether actual or constructive), which may result in severe tax consequences and expenses.

The opposite type of conversion may also be necessary in some instances. It may also be possible for a limited liability company to convert out of LLC status into a partnership. This may also be done on a tax-free basis in many situations.

When making the determination as to the desirability of an entity converting into an LLC, the business planner must keep in mind the following five factors:

1. The nature and purpose of the business.
2. The states where business will be conducted.
3. The business laws of each state in which business will be conducted.
4. Psychological factors to owners and employees.
5. The importance of having an IRS ruling which holds that an LLC formed under that particular state law may be classified as a partnership for federal tax purposes.

TO CONVERT OR NOT TO CONVERT

Generally, a conversion from an existing entity to an LLC must satisfy the following five issues:

1. There must be a state statute that allows for the creation of an LLC.
2. The conversion must not be disallowed under state law.
3. The particular business or investment must be permitted to be conducted in the LLC form.
4. The LLC generally must have two owners.
5. The consent of the company's creditors, lenders, lessors, and so on, generally must be obtained to avoid being in breach of any agreements.

CONVERSION OF A SOLE PROPRIETORSHIP INTO AN LLC

The conversion of a sole proprietorship into an LLC could happen by the sole proprietor contributing all of his or her business assets (subject to business liabilities) to an LLC and a second party (an individual or another entity) contributing other assets such as cash. Accordingly, the LLC would have two Members, which is required in most states. The contribution of the business assets and other assets is generally a tax-free transaction pursuant to Section 721 of the Code. However, if the amount of business liabilities that are transferred to the LLC exceed the basis (in rough terms, your investment increased and decreased by various adjustments) in the business assets of the sole proprietor, the sole proprietor might have to recognize gain equal to the difference. Moreover, if an interest in the LLC is issued to the new second Member in exchange for services to be rendered by the new incoming partner (Member), the new partner may have taxable consequences if the Membership interest is an interest in the LLC's capital and/or profits.

TIP: It may be feasible to gift some portion of the interest in the business to your spouse. There is no gift tax cost on the transfer to a spouse (where the spouse is a U.S. citizen).

Each specific situation where a sole proprietorship is potentially to be converted to an LLC must be carefully analyzed to determine whether the entire transaction will be tax-free or whether any parties will have to recognize gain on the transaction. It must also be determined whether the conversion will cause the sole proprietor to be in default of any contracts.

CONVERSION OF A PARTNERSHIP INTO AN LCC

Converting a General Partnership into a Limited Partnership

When analyzing a partnership conversion to an LLC, it is helpful to review the existing law relating to the conversion of a general partnership into a limited partnership. The conversion from a general partnership to a limited partnership is desirable for many reasons including, but not limited to the following:

- To provide limited liability protection to certain owners.
- To facilitate gift-giving transfers to children or other beneficiaries by making gifts of equity in the company without relinquishing any control.

For example, if a building, business, investment, or other asset is owned in a general partnership format, many of the benefits of a limited partnership can be obtained by converting the general partnership into a limited partnership. The primary reason for converting a general partnership into a limited partnership is to provide the family business owners with limited liability, although there must always be at least one general partner with unlimited liability. This raises a number of issues.

If the conversion of a partner's general partnership interests into limited partnership interests constitutes a "sale or exchange" of partnership interest (as defined under Section 708 of the Internal Revenue Code) the termination of the general partnership could have adverse tax consequences. The IRS has held that such a conversion will not be deemed a sale or exchange. Nevertheless, tax commentators have noted a number of troubling points about the logic of the IRS position, so that where significant sums are involved, caution must be exercised and perhaps a ruling should be obtained from the IRS.

NOTE: To obtain a ruling (also called private letter ruling), your tax adviser submits a formal request to the IRS for its opinion on how a particular transaction will be treated for federal tax purposes. The tax adviser must explain all the facts in the ruling request. If the IRS then rules favorably (that the conversion of your general partnership will not trigger adverse tax consequences), then you can proceed. These private letter rulings are only applicable to the taxpayer for which the ruling is given. Thus, be very careful in relying on a private letter ruling issued to another taxpayer. The IRS is simply not bound to maintain the same position for you. Drawbacks to obtaining a private ruling are the cost and time involved. It could cost $7,500 or more and could take many months to obtain one.

Another potential tax problem can arise in converting a general partnership interest into a limited partnership interest if the conversion reduces a partner's share of partnership liabilities. This means as a partner (or Member in the LLC) you are personally liable for less partnership debts than you were before the change. A reduction in a partner's share of liabilities will be treated as a deemed cash distribution to such partner; the IRS will treat a reduction in your responsibility for partnership debt as if you had received a distribution of cash from the partnership in the amount of debt for which you are no longer responsible. If the reduction in your share of the partnership debt exceeds your basis in your partnership interest, taxable gain can result. Similar problems can arise where there are changes in any partner's interest in the partnership capital or profits.

Before converting a partnership into an LLC, the partners should consider whether there will be any other adverse consequences as a result of the conversion. For example, when converting the partnership's tangible personal property, the conversion may result in a transfer tax or sales and use tax. In many states, statutory conversions will not trigger sales taxes. Another result of a conversion may be the imposition of transfer taxes on real property that is transferred from a partnership to an LLC.

TIP: Most taxpayers plan based on federal income tax, and to a lesser extent federal estate and other transfer taxes. Do not underestimate the potential costs of local transfer and recording fees. They can be surprisingly large.

Converting Your Partnership into an LLC

Until recently, partners of partnerships that wanted to convert their partnerships to LLCs faced uncertainty about the tax consequences of the conversion. The only revenue ruling issued by the IRS on this issue dealt with the conversion of a general partnership into a limited partnership but did not address limited liability companies. Private letter rulings issued by the Internal Revenue Service, however, indicated that conversions by partnerships to LLCs could be accomplished on a tax-free basis. The IRS has issued some rulings on this point. However, since these rulings are of recent vintage given the young age of most LLC laws, exercise caution before taking any steps. Have your tax adviser check the current status of the law before you take any action.

In one of the IRS rulings, the IRS discussed the conversion of a general partnership into a limited partnership. The identity of the partners in their percentage interest in the partnership remained the same in the limited partnership as it was in the general partnership. Some of the partners, however, became limited partners, and the other partners remained general partners in the new limited partnership. The business of the general partnership continued to be conducted by the limited partnership and the conversion was accomplished by filing a document with the appropriate state filing authority.

In that ruling, the IRS determined that the conversion of the general partnership into a limited partnership would not result in the recognition of gain or loss by any of the partners provided that no partner's share of partnership liabilities was reduced excessively. By this, the IRS meant that no partner's share of liabilities should be reduced by an amount that would cause a deemed cash distribution in excess of that partner's basis. If this occurred, as explained earlier, the partner would have to recognize taxable gain. Moreover, the IRS held that there would be no modification in the partner's basis in the partnership provided that there were no changes in the partners' share of partnership liabilities. The IRS has indicated that it will consider this when determining whether a conversion of a general partnership or a limited partnership into a limited liability company results in any gain or loss to the partners/Members.

There are several different ways to convert a partnership (whether general or limited) into an LLC. The conversion may be accomplished by one of the following methods.

By Specific Statutory Authority Permitting Conversion

Some states have a specific statute in their partnership statutes and/or LLC statutes permitting a general or limited partnership to convert (change) directly into an LLC. This conversion is generally accomplished by the partnership filing Articles of Conversion, or a similar document, with the appropriate state filing authority. These Articles typically contain a statement that the partnership is converting into an LLC, the names of each general and/or limited partner, and the effective date, if any, of the conversion. Once the Articles have been filed with he appropriate state filing authority, the conversion will become effective (or at some allowable later date set forth in the Articles) and the partnership's assets and liabilities will be transferred to the LLC. Generally, statutes that permit the direct conversion of a partnership into an LLC provide that the unanimous vote of the partners, including limited partners, is required before such a conversion can occur. A conversion accomplished in this manner should generally not result in the partners/Members recognizing income or loss. As with all tax rules, however, this conclusion is subject to certain exceptions. One example is where there is a shift in liabilities among partners/Members which causes a partner/Member to recognize gain for income tax purposes.

Liquidation of Partnership Followed by Contribution of Assets to an LLC

Another method to convert a partnership into an LLC is for the partnership to liquidate and distribute its assets (and liabilities) to its partners in complete liquidation of the partnership followed by a contribution of the assets and liabilities to a newly formed LLC. Generally, this would not result in any gain or loss recognition to the partners. Gain may be recognized, however, if there is cash distributed to a partner, or a deemed distribution of cash to a partner (as a result of a reduction in his or her share of partnership liabilities) which exceeds the partner's basis (investment) in the partnership. There could also be gain recognition to a partner if he or she had contributed appreciated property to the partnership within the five-year period prior to the partnership's liquidation and received in the liquidation a distribution of property having a fair market value exceeding that partner's basis in his or her partnership interest.

As mentioned earlier, this conversion method should not ordinarily result in taxable gain or loss to the partners/Members. From a practical standpoint, however, a liquidation followed by a contribution involves two transfers of assets and liabilities—one transfer on liquidation of the partnership to the partners and another on the contribution by the Members to the LLC. The additional second transfer could result in additional costs of the conversion as other methods may require only one transfer. For example, if real property is involved, several deeds may be needed to effectuate this conversion, and many states impose a realty transfer fee on each transfer (deed).

Contribution by Partners of Their Partnership Interests to an
LLC in Exchange for LLC Interests

Other than the states that allow for a statutory conversion and except for a merger of a partnership with and into an LLC (discussed later in this chapter), this conversion method may be the simplest way to convert a partnership into an LLC. Under this conversion method, the partners of the existing partnership would form an LLC. In exchange for their Membership interests in the LLC, each partner would contribute his or her partnership interest to the LLC. The partnership would then have only one partner, which would be the LLC, and thus would be dissolved, wound up, and terminated, because a partnership must always have at least two partners.

In this case, the LLC would be a continuation of the partnership because the business of the partnership would continue after the conversion. Moreover, even though the partners contribute their partnership interests to the LLC, the partnership is deemed to continue (in the form of the LLC) after the conversion.

Again, this conversion method should generally result in a tax-free conversion.

CAUTION: To the extent that there is a shift among the partners/Members of their respective shares of partnership liabilities, a taxable gain may have to be recognized by the partners/Members.

Contribution by Partnership of Its Assets and Liabilities to an LLC

Under this conversion method, a partnership would transfer its assets and liabilities to an LLC, would receive LLC Membership interests, and would then distribute those same Membership interests to the partners in liquidation of the partnership. A technical problem of this conversion method is that initially the partnership would appear to be the only Member of the LLC and would thereafter transfer Membership interests to the partners. This may be avoided by having the existing partners of the partnership form the LLC along with the partnership followed by a liquidation of the partnership of its Membership interests. In this fashion, there would always be at least two Members of the LLC.

It is important to keep in mind that for the LLC to be taxed as a partnership for federal tax purposes, it generally must lack free transferability of interest. Therefore, the transfer of the Membership interests in liquidation of the partnership to the partners must be structured to avoid causing the LLC to have the corporate characteristic of free transferability of interests, which may be difficult to do in this scenario if the converting partnership distributes Membership interests on its liquidation.

Conclusion Concerning a Partnership Conversion

Partnerships, both limited and general, can convert to LLCs tax-free based on positions taken by the IRS. For tax purposes, a conversion would generally be treated as a nontaxable event, meaning that the Members would not recognize any gain or loss on the transaction. There may, however, be certain instances where gain or loss would be recognized, such as a reduction in a partner's share of liabilities that exceeds his or her adjusted basis in his or her partnership interest.

It does not matter how the conversion from a partnership into an LLC is achieved under state law. Thus, any method that is usable should suffice according to IRS rules.

The IRS has also provided that the converting partnership would not be deemed to terminate on the conversion and the resulting LLC may continue to use the federal taxpayer identification number originally issued to the partnership.

POTENTIAL GAIN RECOGNITION WHEN CONVERTING A PARTNERSHIP TO AN LLC

As stated earlier, the conversion of a partnership into an LLC will generally not be a taxable event. On the conversion of a partnership into an LLC, however, gain may be recognized if there is a reduction of a partner's share of liabilities in excess of such partner's basis in his or her partnership interest.

Generally, under the Internal Revenue Code, if a partner's share of partnership liabilities is decreased, such decrease is treated as a deemed distribution of money from the partnership to the partner. If a partner's share of partnership liabilities is increased, such increase is treated as a deemed contribution of money by the partner to the partnership.

Moreover, the deemed distribution of money to a partner will decrease the partner's basis in the partnership, but not below zero. A deemed contribution of money from the partner to the partnership would cause the partner's basis in the partnership to increase. These basis adjustments are important because a distribution (or deemed distribution) of money to a partner from the partnership will not cause the partner to recognize gain unless the distribution amount exceeds the partner's basis (investment) in the partnership. Therefore, the reduction of a partner's share in partnership liabilities as a result of a conversion into an LLC would constitute a deemed distribution of money to the partner and would cause the partner to recognize gain to the extent that the amount of such distribution exceeds the partner's basis in the partnership.

The analysis of a reduction or increase in a partner's share of partnership liabilities may depend on whether or not a liability is a recourse liability or a nonrecourse liability. A liability is a "recourse" liability to the extent that any individual partner bears the economic risk of loss for that liability. A liability is a "nonrecourse" liability to the extent that no individual partner bears the economic risk of loss for that liability. A discussion relating to the different effects that nonrecourse versus recourse liabilities have on shifts of partnership liability among partners is beyond the scope of this book.

ADDITIONAL ISSUES IN CONVERTING A PARTNERSHIP INTO AN LLC

In conversion to an LLC, it is important to avoid forcing a partnership that uses the cash receipts and disbursements method of accounting to convert its method of accounting to the accrual method. Such a change could force the partnership/LLC to accelerate the recognition of income, which could be a very unfavorable outcome.

This situation is especially prevalent when converting a professional practice (such as a law or accounting firm) from a partnership to an LLC. Several IRS letter rulings have held that the conversion of a professional practice partnership to

Some state LLC statutes explicitly permit LLC mergers with other entities and/or LLCs, while other states do not expressively provide guidance relating to mergers. LLCs in states that do not provide for mergers must look to partnership law regarding mergers. The special merger rules of the tax laws, relating to partnerships, should apply to the mergers of LLCs and partnerships. The tax laws provide that the merger of two or more partnerships will not trigger termination of the partnership if (1) the Members own an interest in the partnership of 50 percent of the capital and profits of the resulting partnership (in this case, the LLC); and (2) no portion of any business, financial operation, or venture of the partnership continues to be carried on by any of its partners in the partnership.

If a conversion of a partnership into an LLC is accomplished by a merger of the partnership with and into an LLC, the conversion will occur through operation of law, rather than through the coupling of distributions and contributions, as was the case for the nonstatutory conversion methods discussed earlier. The details of a merger vary by state. Some states only allow mergers of partnerships with domestic LLCs, while other states allow mergers with foreign LLCs as well.

The main advantage of converting your partnership to an LLC using merger statutes is that existing partnerships may be converted without exchanging assets. This can avoid sales, transfer, and use taxes because the transfer of assets to the LLC (conveyances) occurs by operation of law, and nothing else happens. State laws must still be reviewed to determine if transfer taxes apply even by a conversion through merger or conversion statutes. Another advantage is that a conversion through these statutes assures that the conversion is legally valid.

EXAMPLE: General Partnership (GP) is formed under the laws of State Y and owns two parcels of real property. GP wishes to convert to an LLC to provide its owners with limited liability protection. GP's state does not have a statute that expressly provides for the conversion of a general partnership into an LLC. GP does not want to do a nonstatutory conversion because it does not want to pay the realty transfer taxes that would result from transferring the parcels of real property to the LLC. State Y does have a statute expressly authorizing the merger of general partnerships and LLCs. Therefore, the partners of GP form an LLC and cause GP to merge with and into the LLC with the LLC being the surviving entity. By operation of law, all assets and liabilities of GP become owned and assumed by LLC and no deed transferring the real property to LLC is required. Therefore, no realty transfer tax should be triggered by this transaction.

SUMMARY

If a company that is already in existence believes that it would be advantageous to operate as a limited liability company, it should consider converting its existing entity into an LLC. Before moving forward with the conversion of an existing entity into an LLC, it is important to determine whether it is permitted under state law and whether the conversion will result in any tax costs or other expenses that might outweigh the benefits of operating in the LLC format.

General partnerships, limited partnerships, corporations, or sole proprietorship may all entertain the possibility of converting into LLCs. The conversion of a corporation into an LLC, however, will generally be a taxable event and the liquidation of the corporation may have adverse tax consequences. By contrast, generally the conversion of a partnership or sole proprietorship into an LLC can be accomplished on a tax-free basis. There are certain exceptions to this general rule. With the conversion of a partnership into an LLC, a partner whose share in liabilities is reduced pursuant to the conversion may recognize gain if the amount of the liability reduction exceeds that partner's basis in the partnership.

There are several methods to effectuate a conversion of an existing entity into a limited liability company. Nonstatutory methods to convert require the distribution and contribution of assets between companies and their owners; statutory methods require merely the filing of a document to effectuate the conversion. In addition, the conversion may also be accomplished by merging the existing entity with and into an LLC and having the LLC be the surviving entity of the merger. Not all states, however, have statutes that expressly permit a merger.

Regardless of how the conversion from a partnership to an LLC takes place, the IRS has ruled that the conversion will generally be a tax-free transaction. Again, however, gain may be recognized here to the extent of a liability shift and in other certain instances.

The LLC is an excellent form of transacting business and thus existing businesses may desire to convert into an LLC. Each conversion, however, must be thought out to determine whether the benefits of the conversion outweigh the costs or vice versa.

5 OPERATING AND MAINTAINING A LIMITED LIABILITY COMPANY

In prior chapters, you've made the decision that an LLC is the right choice for your business or investment situation. Then you've formed your LLC (or converted your existing entity into an LLC) and put in place the most important legal document, the Operating Agreement. Finally, you've transferred cash and other assets to the LLC so it can begin operations. Now you must operate your LLC.

Like any other form of business entity (i.e., corporations and partnerships), LLCs must be professionally and efficiently managed and operated to be productive, generate profits, provide liability protection, and achieve your other goals. Much of the success of an LLC depends on the individuals who manage the LLC and their rights and obligations in that management capacity. Retaining qualified legal, tax, accounting, business, and other advisers, and methodically implementing their advice is also essential. An important factor in ensuring smooth operations, maintaining limited liability, and professionally running your LLC is having in place the necessary legal documents. This chapter will provide an overview of many of these important points. The "For Your Notebook" section following this chapter includes several sample forms that may be helpful in operating your LLC.

CAUTION: Every business is unique, and every business transaction has its own nuances, so that every LLC will have need for different legal documents. The sample documents in the "For Your Notebook" section are some of the more commonly used types of documents. This should not be taken to mean that these are the only documents your LLC will need, or that the format of those documents is appropriate for the circumstances your LLC faces. The first step in making that determination is clearly defining the goals and objectives of your LLC, and precisely how those goals should be achieved. This will give your advisers the framework they need to help you implement the appropriate documents.

MANAGING AN LLC

Who Can Manage?

Members Generally Manage the LLC

In all but one state (Colorado), the default statutory rule is that management of an LLC is vested in the Members. No state LLC statutes, however, require that the Members themselves manage the LLC. In a few states, moreover, the default rule is that the LLC is to be managed by Managers. Depending on which state the

LLC is formed in, in order to change the default rule of Member management to Manager management, the Articles of Organization or the Operating Agreement must provide that management of the LLC is to be vested in Managers. If management is to be vested in Managers rather than Members, it may be advisable to set forth the management structure in the Articles of Organization rather than the Operating Agreement because the Articles of Organization is a public document that third parties can simply find in the public records. If the management structure is set forth in the Operating Agreement, which third parties may not have easy access to, this may complicate relations with third parties who may be relying on the LLC being managed by its Members instead of Managers, when, in fact, the opposite is true. Unless the Operating Agreement provides to the contrary, decision making and control in most states will be vested in the Members. Relating to voting standards in a Member-managed LLC, some states follow the one vote per Member approach (with a majority vote required for most actions) and other states allocate voting power in proportion to contributions made by the Members and not returned or in proportion to Members' profit shares. Under most LLC statutes, when a majority vote is called for, a majority of all voting Members is meant, not only the Members present at any specific meeting. In most states, the usual default rule is unanimous consent for the following issues: (1) admission of new Members, (2) continuation of the LLC's business after a Member dissociates, (3) amending the Articles of Organization, and (4) amending the Operating Agreement.

In every LLC, the Operating Agreement should specifically address the decision-making criteria for the Members. For example, the Operating Agreement should address the voting criteria for any particular decision, which persons or Members should have management control, what types of issues should be within the purview of a Manager, and which should require the input or approval of some portion of the Members.

Manager(s) May Be Designated to Manage the LLC

Instead of having the LLC managed by its Members, the Members can designate one or more persons to serve as Manager(s) of the LLC.

In some states, the default rule is actually that management of the LLC is to be by Managers rather than by Members. There are no requirements relating to the number of Managers that a Manager-run LLC must have. Some states require that a Manager must be a natural person, whereas other states do not have such a requirement. In fact, some states expressly state that the Manager does not have to be a natural person. This is a distinct difference from the law of corporations where a member of the Board of Directors cannot be an organization.

No LLC state statutes require that Managers be Members. Some states expressly permit nonmember Managers, and other states are silent on this issue. Moreover, it is not necessary for a Manager of an LLC to be a resident of the state in which the LLC is formed.

An LLC's Manager can be of the same class or group, or there can be different classes or groups of Managers. Being able to create different classes of Managers enables the LLC to designate authority with respect to different types of actions among different Managers.

TIP: Don't make the management structure more complex than the economics and the needs of the deal warrant. If you have a single residential rental property with four units in the LLC, tiers of managers for different structures are not only unnecessary but are unworkable. Even if the property is quite valuable, the situation should not be complex enough to justify a complex management structure. If, however, the four units are large commercial units in a multimillion-dollar warehouse, a more complex structure may be warranted. Not only does the economic value of this latter example justify a somewhat more complex arrangement, but the decisions are likely to be more complex. But in all situations, no matter how complex or large in dollar terms, always go with the simplest approach that works. Don't complicate any deal unless the complication serves an important purpose that can't be served in a less complex manner.

In some states, the Articles of Organization must provide the names of the initial Managers, while in other states there is no similar requirement. The general default rule for selection of Managers is that the majority vote of the Members is required to elect Managers. This majority vote requirement can be modified by either the Articles of Organization or the Operating Agreement. With respect to the length of a term for which a Manager can serve, the Operating Agreement should set forth specific guidelines. Most state LLC statutes provide default rules in this context, but the default rules may not necessarily represent exactly what the Members want to occur.

Some state statutes provide default rules for the removal of Managers (with or without cause, and others do not provide such rules). If an LLC is organized in a state whose LLC statute does not contain any rules relating to the removal of a Manager, such rules should be enumerated in the Articles of Organization or it may be virtually impossible to remove a Manager who is also a Member. This is because in such a situation there may be a requirement of unanimous consent of the Members to remove a Manager.

The resignation of a Manager, whether a Member or a non-Member, will not cause a termination of the LLC. Instead, each particular state's statute must be examined to determine the rules relating to the filling of a managerial vacancy. An LLC's Operating Agreement should contain specific rules relating to the filling of managerial vacancies. The failure to have such provisions in an Operating Agreement could cause a deadlock among the remaining Managers.

Transactions between the Manager and the LLC

Generally, a Manager may lend money to, borrow money from, act as a surety, guarantor, or endorser for, or guarantee or assume one or more specific obligations of, provide collateral for, and transact other business with the LLC, unless provided to the contrary in the Articles of Organization, Operating Agreement, or state statute.

TIP: In most deals, you will not want the Manager doing any of these things unless it is on an arm's length basis (terms no different than an uninvolved and unrelated person would obtain) and approved by a larger percentage of the Members.

Rights of the Manager

Managers are generally given the right to demand and receive (1) true and full information regarding the status of the business and financial condition of the

LLC, (2) a copy of the LLC's federal, state, and local tax returns, (3) a current list of all Members and Managers, and (4) true and full information regarding the amount of the LLC's cash, and a description of the agreed value of any property or services contributed by each member, so long as such disclosures reasonably relate to the person's position as Manager.

The Manager may even be given the right to keep confidential from the Members information that he or she reasonably believes to be trade secrets or other information the disclosure of which the Manager in good faith believes is not in the LLC's best interest. While this provision may be helpful in many instances, it may not be appropriate if the Members are all actively involved in the business of the LLC. Therefore, in negotiating and drafting an LLC Operating Agreement, consideration should be given to nullifying this right of the Manager, which may be the statutory default rule.

The Manager may be given the right to resign as Manager if events occur as specified in the Operating Agreement. The Operating Agreement may provide that the Manager does not have the right to resign. Such a clause will not prevent the Manager from resigning but it will provide the LLC with a cause of action for damages from a Manager's resignation.

Obligation and Liability of a Manager

An Operating Agreement can include penalty provisions that apply to a Manager who does not perform the duties required by statute, the Articles of Organization, and the Operating Agreement. Some statutes also provide that a Member may bring a derivative action against a Manager (or Members). This is a lawsuit for harm that the Manager (or Members) have done to the LLC or the LLC's business or assets.

NOTE: While these types of rights and protection may sound appealing, keep in mind that if the Operating Agreement or Articles of Organization are too unfair or too restrictive, no one will be willing to serve as Manager (or if you have an original Manager, it may be quite difficult to find a replacement).

Voting Rights

The Operating Agreement may provide for different classes or groups of Members and/or Managers, with different rights, powers, and duties. For example, certain groups or classes of Members may take specified actions without the vote or approval of other Members. The Operating Agreement may grant certain Members the right to vote separately or as a group. For example, where a business comprises active participants and less active investors, the investor-Members could compose a group that is authorized to make certain financial decisions without the consent of the active Members. Similarly, the active Members could be empowered to make all daily operating decisions without consultation with the investor-Members group.

Where certain specified voting rights are provided, the Operating Agreement may also include provisions concerning the notice required prior to any vote of the Members, such as the time and place that a vote shall occur.

TIP: Don't forget the principle discussed earlier. The acronym KISS means "Keep It Simple Stupid." The simpler and less complex an arrangement, the better. Only include a more complex arrangement if it really serves a specific and important purposes.

EXAMPLE: Multiple rules for different types of voting issues can sometimes be a useful method of resolving disputes such as where a larger percentage vote is required to sell the LLC's key asset than to take a more routine step.

Other Managerial Rights

Unless provided otherwise in the Articles or Operating Agreement, management may appoint committees and people to serve on them. Each committee may exercise the authority given to it by the management. Management does not need to have meetings unless required by a particular state's LLC act, the Articles, or Operating Agreement. Most states do not require the Managers or Members to have meetings.

Consent of Members

Where an LLC is managed by its Members, they must provide some form of consent, whether majority, unanimous, or otherwise, for the company to take action. In most states, there is no requirement that the Members engage in formal meetings to take managerial actions. Some states' statutes require the written approval of the Members to certain action. For the same reasons an Operating Agreement should be in writing, a meeting of the minds of the managing Members relating to management decisions should also be in writing. Having a written document would provide a record of the agreement of the Members to alleviate any potential confusion in the future. Putting agreements of the Members in writing is obviously more important for decisions that have a potentially greater impact on the LLC. Some states do in fact require formal meetings of the Members. This requirement may be modified through the Articles of Organization and the Operating Agreement.

TIP: In most cases, no matter what your state's laws require, it is best to have any major decision approved, in writing, by all Members and Managers in any LLC with a relatively small number of Members. The form illustrated in Chapter 3 as a Unanimous Consent of All Managers and Members can be adapted to have almost any type of action approved. Simply modify the form as needed to address the actions involved, attach complete copies of all relevant documents concerning the actions, and have everyone sign.

Decisions of the Managers

If an LLC is managed by more than one Manager, it is imperative to understand the state default rule relating to the necessary vote of the Managers to take managerial action. Unless there is a provision in the Operating Agreement to the contrary, Managers will act with a majority vote. Moreover, in a Manager-run entity, unless the Operating Agreement provides otherwise, a Member who is not a Manager does not have the right on his or her own to bind the LLC to any contracts or other decisions of the LLC with a third party.

Contractual Relationship

Although state statutes and court decisions may set standards relating to the duties of the managing individuals of an LLC, whether Member Managers or non-Member Managers, the Operating Agreement may be utilized to expand or limit the duties and obligations of such Managers, as the Operating Agreement creates a contractual relationship. Therefore, the Operating Agreement must pay careful consideration to these most important issues and lay out the important points of the Manager's relationship with the LLC and Members clearly and concisely. This is important to address in the beginning so that both the Manager and the Members will have similar expectations concerning the duties to be performed.

TIP: Although many people don't like long legal documents, including long Operating Agreements, or they dismiss them as a lawyer's ploy to make more money, writing out in detail how the LLC is to operate and how decisions are to be made can help the Managers and Members focus on matters they may not have thought about. Working through these items to find a reasonable resolution of different opinions in the beginning when everyone gets along and wants the deal to work can be very productive. Thus, it is the process of completing the Operating Agreement, not just the final paperwork, that is important. For this process to be productive, however, all the people involved, including the attorneys, must realize that everyone is working toward the common good and toward the benefit of all. One-upmanship and antagonism are not necessary or appropriate.

OPERATING AN LLC

LLC Periodic Reporting and Record-Keeping

It is essential for any management authority to record information about their entity to protect their respective interests and prevent ambiguity over past actions. Under the Revised Uniform Limited Partnership Act ("RULPA"), limited partnerships must maintain records at the partnership's principal place of business and the partners must have access to them. Partners must also have the right to a formal accounting of partnership affairs at specific times. A corporation must also keep certain records and information at a principal place of business. Such records include minutes from shareholder and directors' meetings, a list of shareholders, and the number and class of shares held by each.

LLCs may also be subject to certain record-keeping requirements depending on each state's statute. Some states require LLCs to maintain books and provide an accounting to Members, while other states have more informal information requirements. Most states require an informational annual report to be filed with the secretary of state. Some statutes are patterned after RULPA in that they require the LLC to keep at its registered office or principal place of business:

- A current list of Members.
- A copy of the filed Articles of Organization and any amendments thereto.
- Copies of tax returns and financial statements for the preceding three years.
- A list of events of dissolution and other specific information depending on each state.

It is also advisable that an LLC maintain minutes from meetings of its Members and/or Managers, written documentation of actions taken without meetings, and a record of its Members and their respective contributions. Failure to keep such records may create a problem when a crisis arises and may result in punishment for the company. Use the form in the "For Your Notebook" section of Chapter 3.

Tax Filing Requirements

Like a partnership, an LLC must file annual tax returns, (IRS Form 1065 and Forms K-1) and comply with any federal and state reporting or filing requirements that any partnership would normally have to comply with.

CAUTION: Even if you want to do your own tax return, where there are several Members in the LLC, it can be advantageous to have the tax return prepared by a professional accountant. Not only will this assure that these important matters are handled correctly, but an accountant can often be an excellent source of ongoing business advice and can serve as a mediator or go-between if issues arise. For the accountant to be effective in either capacity, a history with you, the LLC, and the business of the LLC can be extremely important. It is much harder for an accountant to assist you to resolve problems when he or she is called in after problems have occurred and where he or she has limited or no prior experience with the business. Where an accountant is engaged throughout, many problems can be prevented, and when they do occur, the accountant will have the knowledge of the business, and the trust of the Members, to best address them.

Ancillary Legal Documents

Where an LLC is treated as a partnership for federal tax purposes, and as a distinct legal entity (i.e., independent from its owners), any legal documentation that would ordinarily be required of any business entity would be required for an LLC. This could include, but not be limited to, employment agreements, buy/sell agreements, license and other agreements, and so forth. Periodically, the Articles of Organization and the Operating Agreement should be reviewed to assure that they have remained current and relevant in light of any changes in the ownership or nature of the business or investment involvements of the LLC. The Articles of Organization and the Operating Agreement were discussed in Chapter 3, and sample documents presented. The "For Your Notebook" section following this chapter includes other commonly used forms that may be useful for you during the operational stage of your LLC.

Additional Documents That May Be Filed on the LLC's Behalf

Certificate of Amendments/Correction

The filing of the Articles of Organization causes the creation of an LLC. The Articles must be amended when the information contained in the Articles is no longer correct. The information required to be contained in a Certificate of Amendment may vary from state to state, but in most states, it must include:

- The name of the LLC.
- The amendment that is being made to the Articles of Organization.

The amendment can be made to be effective on filing the document, or on a later date not more than a specified number of days (e.g., 90 days) following the date of filing, which is similar to the effective date rules relating to the creation of the LLC.

In addition, in most states a Certificate of Correction may be filed to correct any errors in the Articles of Organization or any amendments thereto.

Certificate of Ownership

Generally, no evidence of ownership is necessary for Members of an LLC. A Certificate of Ownership, however, may be filed with the appropriate state authority if restrictions on interests or classes of Members are desired. Most states permit this certificate to be filed for an LLC, and some states refer to this certificate as a "certificate of membership."

This certificate must contain:

- The name of the LLC, and the state of organization.
- Percentage of ownership in the LLC that the certificate represents.
- Name of the individual or entity to whom or which the certificate is issued.
- Any transfer restrictions imposed on such interest.
- Specific acts of termination of the ownership interests.

When used, the certificate of ownership must be signed by people authorized by the LLC. Restrictions of the certificate are to be placed conspicuously on the front or back of the certificate. Examples of restrictions are the enforcement of buy-sell agreements, preservation of exemptions under federal and state securities laws, and prohibition on the transfer of interests to designated parties.

Certificate of Foreign LLC Registration

Before an LLC may conduct business in a state other than the state in which it was formed, it must register with the appropriate state authority by filing an application. Many state statues provide comprehensive provisions governing the operation of a foreign LLC. If an LLC transacts business in a foreign state without registering, it could be subject to penalties and/or fines.

EXAMPLE: ABC Limited Liability Company is formed in state X. ABC wants to do business in state Z. Prior to engaging in business in state Z, ABC should file an application to do business in state Z.

Certificate of Alternate/Fictitious Name

Usually an alternate/fictitious name (a name other than the name under which an LLC is formed) may be registered and used by an LLC. This is accomplished by filing a document known in some states as a "Certificate of Registration of an Alternate Name" with the appropriate state authority setting forth the following information:

- The name, jurisdiction, and date of establishment of the LLC.
- The alternate name to be used by the LLC.
- A brief statement of the character or nature of the particular activities to be conducted using the alternate name.
- A statement that the LLC intends to use the alternate name in that state.
- A statement that the LLC has not previously used the alternate name. If the LLC has used the alternate name previously, the certificate usually must state when it commenced using the name. A fee for the period in which the alternate name was improperly used may be required.

In some states, the Certificate of Alternate Name is effective for a period of five years and may be renewed at any time within 90 days prior to the expiration of the five-year period. The LLC may be subject to penalties when false information is filed in this Certificate.

Certificate of Name Reservation

A person may reserve the exclusive use of a name for an LLC by filing a Certificate of Name Reservation. Such a certificate may be filed by any person intending to organize an LLC, and an existing LLC seeking to change its name. This is accomplished by filing with the appropriate state authority an application specifying the name to be reserved, as well as the name and address of the person applying for the reservation. The amount of time a name may be reserved and the amount of renewals vary from state to state. The right to use a particular name can be transferred to another person by filing a certificate of transfer. Obviously, only available names may be reserved.

Certificate of Merger or Consolidation

If an LLC is to merge or consolidate with another entity, a Certificate of Merger or Consolidation should be filed. Generally, the Certificate is filed by the surviving entity of the transaction and must provide:

- The name and jurisdiction of formation or organization of each LLC or other business entity.
- A statement that an agreement of merger or consolidation has been approved and executed by each LLC or other business entity that is to merge or consolidate.

- The name of the surviving entity.
- The future effective date or time certain of the merger or consolidation (if none is specified, it is effective on filing).
- A statement that the agreement of merger or consolidation is on file at a place of business of the surviving or resulting LLC or other business entity, and the address.
- A statement that a copy of the agreement will be furnished on request.
- If the surviving entity is not an LLC in the state of filing, a statement that the surviving entity can be served with process in the state of filing, and the address where it shall be served.

Certificate of Restatement

An LLC may file a certificate restating all previously filed certificates (Articles of Organization and amendments thereto) into a single certificate. Such a certificate restates and integrates previously filed certificates but does not act to amend the existing certificates on file. If it restates and amends (which in practice is likely to be the most common), the certificate should be labeled "Amended and Restated Articles of Organization."

Certificate of Cancellation

A Certificate of Cancellation may be filed to cancel the Articles of Organization on the dissolution and completion of the winding up of an LLC. The Certificate of Cancellation may also be filed where there are no longer at least two Members of an LLC in states where there is a two-Member minimum.

SUMMARY

It is essential to the success of an LLC that it be managed efficiently, professionally, and legally. In the vast majority of states, the default rule is that an LLC is managed by its Members. It is possible, however, for Managers to be appointed to manage the LLC. Managers must be provided with the information necessary for them to efficiently run the business. Moreover, a Manager is obligated to comply with the terms of the LLC's Articles of Organization and its Operating Agreement.

Whether managed by the Members or Managers, the LLC, in its Articles of Organization and/or the Operating Agreement, may provide for different voting requirements among the Members and/or Managers. Therefore, certain groups of Members and/or Managers may have more power with respect to certain managerial actions. If an LLC is to be managed by certain designated Managers, the Operating Agreement must contain provisions relating to the rights and obligations of the Managers as well as restrictions on transactions that may be entered into by the LLC with the Manager or any entity controlled by the Manager.

It is essential for the individuals who manage the LLC to maintain proper and accurate records of the LLC's business. In addition, the LLC must file the necessary tax documentation and other required legal documents.

For Your Notebook:

SAMPLE AMENDMENT TO AUTHORIZE LLC LEASING PROPERTY

CAUTION: The documents presented in this section are merely samples of common documents. Be sure the documents you use not only are appropriate for any given situation but are properly tailored to meet your needs. These samples will help you reduce legal and other professional fees by helping you think through the information you will need to convey to your attorney, financial adviser, and so forth. It is best, however, to retain a professional and not merely adapt a standard form.

LLC NAME
Action Taken by Unanimous Written
Consent to All Managers and Members
to Authorize LLC Leasing Property

The undersigned, being all of the Managers and Members of the LLC, hereby take the following action:

RESOLVED, The LLC adopts and becomes a party to a lease substantially in the form of attached hereto to enable the LLC to obtain the use of certain real property necessary and useful to the operation of the LLC's business.

RESOLVED, The Managers of the LLC are directed and authorized to execute such lease, obtain any insurance necessary or appropriate to protect the LLC's interest in such leased property, and take any additional actions necessary or desirable to facilitate the LLC's using such property.

RESOLVED, The Managers of the LLC are directed and authorized to take all necessary actions to implement the above resolutions.

Executed: SIGN DATE

_____

MEMBER 1 NAME, Member and Manager

_____

MEMBER 2 NAME, Member

_____

MEMBER 3 NAME, Member and Manager

_____

MANAGER 1 NAME, Manager

[Attach Lease to This Page]

For Your Notebook:

SAMPLE AMENDMENT TO AUTHORIZE CONSULTING AGREEMENT

NOTE: Use the following documents where the LLC wishes to retain a key person under a consulting agreement. Be sure to discuss with your accountant whether the person your LLC is hiring is really a consultant or whether the person should more properly be classified as an employee for tax purposes. This is a very important decision since the tax consequences of a mistake can be quite costly. There are also legal implications to classifying a person as an employee or consultant (independent contractor).

LLC NAME
Action Taken by Unanimous Written Consent
of All
Managers and Members
to Authorize Consulting Agreement

The undersigned, being all of the Managers and Members of the LLC, hereby take the following actions:

RESOLVED, The LLC retains CONSULTANT NAME as a consultant to the LLC on the terms and conditions set forth in the Consulting Agreement attached.

RESOLVED, The LLC enters into a Consulting Agreement substantially in the form attached.

RESOLVED, The Managers of the LLC are hereby authorized to take any and all actions to effect the above.

Dated: SIGN DATE

_____

MEMBER 1 NAME, Member and Manager

_____

MEMBER 2 NAME, Member

_____

MEMBER 4 NAME, Member and Manager

_____

MANAGER 1 NAME, Manager

[Attach a Signed Consulting Agreement to This Page]

For Your Notebook:

SAMPLE CONSULTING AGREEMENT

AGREEMENT dated DAY of MONTH, YEAR, between CONSULTANT NAME, an individual who resides at CONSULTANT ADDRESS (the "Consultant"), and LLC NAME, a New Jersey LLC doing business at LLC ADDRESS, (the "LLC").

WHEREAS, the LLC operates a DESCRIBE BUSINESS business (the "Business").

WHEREAS, the LLC wishes to retain the Consultant as an independent contractor, and the Consultant wishes to be retained in such capacity and perform certain services for the LLC, to promote the interests of the Business.

THEREFORE, the parties hereto agree as follows:

A. CONSULTING

1. LLC hereby retains Consultant and Consultant hereby accepts such engagement, for the term and under the conditions and requirements specified herein, as a consultant to the LLC, with such duties and responsibilities as may reasonably be assigned to pursuant to this Agreement. The Consultant's compensation shall be that specified below.

2. Consultant's principal duties shall include DESCRIBE DUTIES. However, Consultant shall have no authority to accept, reject or modify any contract entered into by the LLC's Members or Managers, or to negotiate the sale of any significant portion of the Business without the express written consent of the LLC.

3. Consultant shall receive an annual salary to be determined in the reasonable discretion of the Managers, which shall be based on going market rates for each of the various services consultant performs (including but not limited to leasing, managing, etc.), payable (the "Compensation"). Consultant shall bill LLC for all ordinary and necessary business expenses and the LLC shall pay such amounts.

4. The Consultant shall devote Consultant's best efforts, at the times and places Consultant reasonably deems appropriate to Consultant's duties hereunder. However, it is expressly agreed that Consultant may serve as a consultant, manager, investor, or employee to other persons, without limitation.

5. The principal place of business of the Consultant shall be at such places as Consultant, in Consultant's reasonable discretion, may choose from time to time. Consultant shall provide the LLC not less than Twenty (20) days advance Notice of any change in the principal place of business.

6. The Consultant shall be responsible to DETAIL ADDITIONAL ITEMS.

B. STATUS

The Consultant shall be treated in all respects as an independent contractor and the LLC shall not withhold any taxes on account of services rendered to it by Consultant. Consultant represents to LLC that Consultant regularly holds itself out as a consultant to others, maintains an office, has business cards other than for the services provided to LLC, and assumes all risk of Consultant's classification as an independent contractor and not an employee.

C. TERM OF RETAINER

The term for which Consultant shall be retained hereunder shall commence on the date hereof and shall terminate upon the earlier of: (i) the cessation of the Business of the LLC; (ii) the death, or substantial disability of Consultant; or (iii) the last day of the 24th month following the date of this Agreement, unless this Agreement is not canceled by the parties in which event it shall be renewed for One (1) additional year pursuant to this Agreement.

D. EXTENSION AND TERMINATION

1. If Consultant shall be terminated by LLC, Consultant shall be entitled to any amounts due and owing as compensation under their Agreement to the extent earned, as defined herein, on a pro rata basis, plus reimbursement for costs.

2. This Agreement can be terminated by either party on One Hundred Twenty (120) days written notice provided in accordance with the terms hereof.

3. If neither party hereto terminates this Agreement as provided herein, then the term of this Agreement shall be renewed for the following calendar month subject to all the terms and conditions hereof. However, notwithstanding anything herein to the contrary, this Agreement shall terminate on December 31, 2010.

E. DISABILITY OR DEATH

The Consultant shall be deemed substantially disabled if (i) the Consultant and the LLC agree that the Consultant is substantially disabled; or (ii) for a period of Sixty (60) consecutive days, the Consultant is unable, as a result of any physical, mental, or emotional illness, ailment, or accident to effectively discharge Consultant's duties hereunder. If the Consultant shall be substantially disabled as defined herein, the LLC may then immediately upon Notice to the Consultant terminate this Agreement and the LLC's obligation to pay the Consultant the Compensation hereunder.

F. EXPENSES

LLC shall be responsible for any and all expenses that Consultant reasonably incurs in performing the duties assigned hereunder. The Consultant shall be responsible to provide reasonable corroboration to the LLC of any such expenses.

G. NOTICES

All notices and other communications hereunder shall be in writing and shall be deemed given if delivered personally or mailed, by either registered mail or certified mail return receipt requested, to the parties hereto at the addresses listed herein, or at such other address for a party as shall be specified by notice given pursuant hereto ("Notice").

H. WAIVER

The failure of Consultant or LLC to seek redress for violation of, or to insist upon the strict performance of any covenant or condition of this Agreement shall not prevent a subsequent act which would have originally constituted a violation from having all the force and effect of an original violation.

I. MISCELLANEOUS

This Agreement constitutes the entire agreement between the parties hereto, supersedes all existing agreements between them and cannot be changed or terminated except by a written agreement signed by the parties and may not be assigned by either party. This Agreement shall be construed in accordance with the substantive law of STATE NAME.

LLC NAME

By _____
    MANAGER NAME, Manager

CONSULTANT

_____

CONSULTANT NAME

For Your Notebook:

SAMPLE AMENDMENT TO AUTHORIZE A LOAN

NOTE: In many businesses, especially start-up businesses, cash flow may be inadequate at different times. A common way this is dealt with is for investors to loan the business money. The following consent and note are samples of documents that can be used where one Member loans the LLC money. Be certain that the terms are reasonably arm's-length (what a noninvolved person would charge for interest, provide for maturity date, and accept as collateral). Also, be sure that the loan itself, and the terms, are not prohibited by the Operating Agreement. To avoid problems, it's best that all Members and Managers consent to this type of transaction. Also, be sure interest payments are made on a timely basis as required by the note.

LLC NAME
Action Taken by Unanimous Written Consent
of the
Managers and Members
to Authorize Loans to the LLC from a Member

The undersigned, being all of the Managers and Members of the LLC, hereby agree as follows:
RESOLVED, The LLC shall borrow from Member 1 NAME, [DESCRIBE THE LOAN'S PURPOSE] on the terms and conditions set forth in the Promissory Note attached.
RESOLVED, The LLC enter into a loan, and accept and receive the funds, substantially in accordance with the form Note attached.
RESOLVED, The Managers of the LLC are hereby authorized to take any and all actions to effect the above.

Dated: SIGN DATE

_____

MEMBER 1 NAME, Member and Manager

_____

MEMBER 2 NAME, Member

_____

MEMBER 3 NAME, Member and Manager

_____

MANAGER 1 NAME, Manager

For Your Notebook:

SAMPLE PROMISSORY NOTE

$000,000.00   **CITY, STATE**

DATE: SIGN DATE

FOR VALUE RECEIVED, the Undersigned promises to pay to the order of Member 1 NAME, or the holder hereof ("the Payee") at MEMBER ADDRESS or at such other place as the Payee may designate in writing to the Undersigned, the principal sum of LOAN AMOUNT Thousand Dollars ($00,000.00) in lawful money of the United States of America.

This Note shall be repaid in full upon the maturity hereof, on MATURITY DATE. Repayment shall include all then unpaid principal and any accrued but unpaid interest on this Note.

Interest shall accrue on this Note at the rate of RATE percent (%) per annum. Interest shall be due and payable within Thirty (30) days of each anniversary date of this Note.

The Undersigned shall, at any time, have the right to prepay, without penalty or premium, all or any portion of the loan evidenced by this Note.

The Payee shall not exercise any right or remedy provided for in this Note because of any default of the Undersigned to pay the sums due hereunder, until after the expiration of a Five (5) days' grace period from the Undersigned's receipt of any demand for payment.

If the Payee shall institute any action to enforce collection of this Note, there shall become due and payable from the Undersigned, in addition to the unpaid principal and interest, all costs and expenses of such action (including reasonable attorneys' fees) and the Payee shall be entitled to judgment for all such additional amounts.

The Undersigned irrevocably consents to the sole and exclusive jurisdiction of the Courts of the State of STATE NAME and of any Federal court located in STATE NAME in connection with any action or proceeding arising out of, or related to, this Note. In any such proceeding, the undersigned waives personal service of any summons, complaint, or other process and agrees that service thereof shall be deemed made when mailed by registered or certified mail, return receipt requested to the undersigned. Within Twenty (20) days after such service, the undersigned shall appear or answer the summons, complaint, or other process. If the undersigned shall fail to appear or answer within that Twenty (20) day period, the Undersigned shall be deemed in default and judgment may be entered by the Payee against the Undersigned for the amount demanded in the summons, complaint, or other process.

No delay or failure on the part of the Payee on this Note to exercise any power or right given hereunder shall operate as a waiver thereof, and no right or remedy of the Payee shall be deemed abridged or modified by any course of conduct.

The Undersigned waives presentment, demand for payment, notice of dishonor and all other notices or demands in connection with the delivery, acceptance, performance, default, or endorsement of this Note.

This Note shall be governed by and construed in accordance with the State of STATE NAME applicable to agreements made and to be performed in STATE NAME.

This Note cannot be changed orally.

UNDERSIGNED:

LLC NAME
LLC ADDRESS

By: _____
    MANAGER NAME, Manager

For Your Notebook:

SAMPLE EQUIPMENT LEASE

NOTE: The following is a simplified equipment lease that can be used for the LLC to lease equipment from or to another person. If the LLC intends to lease expensive equipment from a major corporation, such as a car or copy machine, the larger lessor will insist on the lease being on its form. In such instance, the LLC doesn't need to use the equipment lease following, but it can use one of the consent forms in this chapter or in Chapter 3 as a model for the Managers and Members to approve the lease.

AGREEMENT made this DAY day of MONTH, YEAR, between LESSOR NAME, doing business at LESSOR ADDRESS, (the "Lessor"), and LESSEE NAME, doing business at LESSEE ADDRESS, (the "Lessee").

1. *Lease agreement.* The Lessor hereby leases to the Lessee the machinery described in Schedule A attached hereto (the "Equipment"), upon the terms and conditions set forth in this agreement.

2. *Term of agreement.* The term of this agreement shall commence as of the date hereof and ends on the last day of the MONTH following the date of this Lease ("Termination").

3. *Rental payments.* The Lessee shall pay, as rental for the use of the Equipment, $ _____ per month commencing the first day of the first full month beginning after the date this lease is executed and ending on the Termination, for an aggregate rental of $ _____ . Said rent is payable without notice on the first day of each month, at the Lessor's address set forth above.

4. *Title to equipment.* Title to the equipment shall remain in the Lessor. The Equipment shall at all times be and remain personal property, however it may be affixed to realty.

5. *Removal, inspection, and return of equipment.* The Equipment shall not be removed from the premises of the Lessee to which originally delivered without the prior written consent of the Lessor. The Lessor shall have the right, upon reasonable prior notice to the Lessee and during the Lessee's regular business hours, to inspect the Equipment at the premises of the Lessee or wherever the Equipment may be located. Upon the termination of the lease with respect to the Equipment, the Equipment shall be returned, at the Lessee's expense, to any place reasonably designated by the Lessor.

6. *Maintenance and repair.* The Lessee shall pay all transportation and installation costs with respect to the Equipment. The Lessee shall be responsible for maintaining the Equipment in good mechanical condition and running order at all times during this Agreement, but the Lessor shall be responsible for the costs thereof. In consideration for the Lessor discharging Lessee's maintenance obligation hereunder and as full payment for Lessee's services, or the services of Lessee's employees or agents operating under Lessee's instructions and supervision, for maintaining and repairing the Equipment, Lessor shall pay the Lessee $ _____ per annum. Such amount shall be payable in equal quarterly installments on the last day of each calendar quarter commencing March 31. All additions, attachments, accessories, and repairs at any time made to or placed upon the Equipment shall become part of the Equipment and shall be the property of the Lessor. The Lessor shall deliver to the Lessee a copy of any warranty agreement it may receive from the manufacturer of the Equipment, and the Lessee shall comply with all the conditions of such warranty required to be performed by the Lessor. To the extent that such compliance required performance of normal maintenance and repairs, such compliance shall be at the expense of the Lessor to the extent provided for in this paragraph.

7. *Risk of loss and insurance.* All risk of loss or damage to the Equipment shall be borne by the Lessor. The Lessor shall, at his own expense, keep the equipment insured, at the full value thereof, against fire with extended coverage, and shall likewise insure the Equipment adequately against such other risks and in such amounts as the Lessor may reasonably deem necessary, and with insurance companies qualified to do business in the State of California or such other state in

which the Equipment may, with Lessor's consent, be located. Notwithstanding the foregoing, the lessee shall be responsible for procuring the insurance and naming the Lessor as an insured as the Lessor's interests may appear, and advancing the insurance premium. The Lessor shall reimburse the Lessee for the cost for insurance promptly upon receipt of the policies or evidence of insurance obtained by the Lessee and the insurance bills.

8. *Extraordinary damage to equipment.* Notwithstanding any extraordinary damage to the Equipment, the monthly rental for the Equipment shall continue to be paid by the Lessee. The Lessee shall have the responsibility for the repair of any damaged equipment, at the Lessor's expense only as described in this lease under paragraph 6 above, and the Lessee shall repair such equipment promptly after the damage. In every such instance, the Lessor shall assign to the Lessee any and all rights the Lessor may have under insurance policies carried by the Lessor with respect to such damage, as well as any rights the Lessor may have to be reimbursed for such damage pursuant to insurance coverage carried by others, as reimbursement to the Lessee for any sum or sums expended by the Lessee in connection with the extraordinary repair of such equipment.

9. *Taxes, etc.* The Lessee shall pay all use taxes, excise taxes, personal property taxes, assessments, ad valorem taxes, stamp and documentary taxes, and all other governmental charges, fees, fines, or penalties whatsoever, whether payable by the Lessor or the Lessee or others, on or relating to the use of the Equipment or the registration, rental, shipment, transportation, delivery, or operation thereof, and shall file all returns required therefor and furnish copies thereof to the Lessor. Upon demand, the Lessee shall reimburse the Lessor for any such taxes, assessments, charges, fines, or penalties which the Lessor may be compelled to pay in connection with the Equipment. The Lessor will corporate with the Lessee and furnish the Lessee with any information available to the Lessor in connection with the Lessee's obligations under this paragraph. The Lessor has paid the applicable sales tax on the purchase of the Equipment.

10. *Indemnity.* The Lessee shall indemnify and hold harmless the Lessor from and against all losses, damages, injuries, claims, demands, and expenses (including legal expenses) of whatever nature, arising out of the use, condition (including, but not limited to, latent and other defects and whether or not discoverable by him), or operation of the Equipment, regardless of where, how, or by whom operated. The Lessee shall assume the cost and responsibility for defending any legal proceedings brought with respect to any losses, damages, injuries, claims, demands, and expenses, and shall pay all settlements or judgments entered in any such legal proceedings. The indemnities and assumptions of liabilities and obligations herein provided for shall continue in full force and effect notwithstanding the termination of this Agreement.

11. *Assignment and sublease.* The Lessee may not sublet or assign the Equipment, without the Lessor's consent, which both parties agree Lessor may withhold without regard to reasonableness. If the Lessee assigns or sublets the Equipment without the Lessor's consent, such assignment or sublet shall be deemed to be a default under this agreement entitling the Lessor to immediately repossess the Equipment at the Lessee's expense.

12. *Lessee's default.* The following events shall constitute defaults on the part of the Lessee hereunder: the failure of the Lessee to pay any installment of rental within 30 days after the date on which the rent shall become due and breach or failure by the Lessee to observe or perform any of its other obligations hereunder and the continuance of such default for 30 days after notice in writing to the Lessee of the existence of such default; the insolvency or bankruptcy of the Lessee; the consent of the Lessee to the appointment of a trustee or receiver for the Lessee or for a substantial part of its property; the institution by or against the lessee of bankruptcy, reorganization, arrangement, or insolvency proceedings; or the Lessee's assignment or subletting of the Equipment without Lessor's consent. Upon the occurrence of any such default, the Lessor may, at its option and without notice to or demand on the Lessee, declare this agreement in default and thereupon all Equipment and all rights of the Lessee therein shall be surrendered to the Lessor. The Lessor may, by the Lessor's agents, take possession of the Equipment wherever found, with or without process of law, and for this purpose may enter upon any premises of the Lessee without liability for suit, action, or other proceeding by the Lessee and remove the same. The Lessor may hold, use, sell, lease, or otherwise dispose of the Equipment or keep any of it idle if the Lessor so chooses, without affecting the obligations of the lessee as provided in this paragraph. If the Lessee fails to deliver the equipment as provided in this paragraph, or converts or

destroys the equipment, the Lessor may hold the Lessee liable for a sum equal to the fair market value of the equipment, which the Lessee shall forthwith pay the Lessor. With respect to Equipment returned to the Lessor or reposed by the Lessor, the Lessor shall be entitled to any amounts realized by the Lessor through the sale, lease, or other disposition thereof.

13. *Purchase option.* The Lessee shall have the right to purchase the Equipment for its fair market value, as determined by appraisal, at the termination of this lease.

14. *Invalid provision.* Any provision of this agreement prohibited by law shall be ineffective to the extent of such prohibition without invalidating the rest of this agreement.

15. *Complete agreement.* This agreement and the Schedules executed by the parties contain the entire understanding of the parties, and such understanding may not be modified or terminated except in writing signed by the parties and by proper sublessee or assignee.

16. *Governing law.* This agreement shall be governed by the laws of the State of STATE NAME.

IN WITNESS WHEREOF, the Lessor and the Lessee have caused these presents to be duly executed.

Lessor:

By: _____

Lessee:

By: _____

6 SECURITIES LAWS AND LIMITED LIABILITY COMPANIES

At some point in the life cycle of your LLC, securities laws may become an important issue. Securities laws could be an issue when, as in Chapter 3, you organize and form your LLC. If you have a number of passive investors (do not participate in management) at that time, you may have to deal with both state and federal securities laws. On an optimistic note, after you have operated your LLC for a period of time, you may be sufficiently successful that you wish to bring in new investors. Depending on the numbers involved, and other factors, state and/or federal securities laws could be essential to address.

The application of federal and state securities laws to LLCs is still developing. On the federal level, lawyers and businesspeople will have to look to the courts for guidance as the federal statutes, enacted in the 1930s, are necessarily not dispositive. State legislatures, on the other hand, have been active in addressing the issue of LLC Membership interests.

LLCs AND SECURITIES LAW CONSIDERATIONS

The securities laws are enacted by each of the states as well as the federal government. One of the goals of the laws is to minimize security frauds and schemes that harm investors. This goal is achieved, in part, by requiring anyone issuing securities to file reports that must disclose a substantial amount of information in a specified format. Complying with these disclosures, especially when the security may be sold in several states, each with its own reporting requirements, can be quite expensive.

Corporations and limited partnerships have been common entities for structuring investment transactions. Where a number of passive investors have purchased stock in a corporation or partnership interests in a limited partnership, the stock and partnership interests have been classified as securities and the entities had to meet the security disclosure and other requirements. Since the LLC is a newer type of entity, some persons sponsoring investment transactions have argued that the Membership interest in an LLC is not a security and the expensive reporting and other requirements could be avoided.

Many regulators believe that some LLCs are being formed to offer and sell securities without registration under federal and state securities laws. Several states, as well as the Securities and Exchange Commission (SEC), have filed lawsuits against some LLCs to set an example and close down these investment-sales operations. Regulators say that most LLCs are formed to take legitimate advantage of the tax benefits and liability protection that LLCs offer. However, there are LLCs that are abusing the business entity by claiming exemption from securities laws but offering investment interests akin to those traditionally considered to be securities.

The term "security" is defined in the federal securities laws and in the Uniform Securities Act to include an investment contract. The term "investment contract" is not defined in any of the federal or state statutes but rather has been defined by the Supreme Court (*SEC v. Howey*, 328 U.S. 293, 298–299 (1946)) as a "contract, transaction or scheme whereby a person invests his money in a common enterprise and is led to expect profits solely from the efforts of the promoter or third party."

Under the tests set forth in the *Howey* court case, four necessary components for determining the existence of an investment contract are (1) an investment of money, (2) in a common enterprise, (3) having expectation of profits, and (4) whose profits are expected solely from the efforts of others.

LLCs should be concerned with the "investment contract" issue. LLCs encourage Members to retain management responsibilities and thus avoid having the corporate characteristic of centralized management. Investment contracts can occur in an LLC context unless all the Members control the major decision making, have the power to remove or employ management, and participate in voting on important business matters.

PARTNERSHIPS AND SECURITIES LAWS

LLCs resemble general partnerships in two significant aspects. First, each is to be managed by its partners or Members. Second, the management structure of both entities is extremely flexible. Consequently, in determining whether an LLC Membership interest is a security under the federal securities laws, reference to the federal case law analysis of the status of general partnership interests is useful. Under the *Howey* test, general partnership interests are usually not considered to be securities. Partners in a general partnership have the ability to participate in the management's decision-making. This ability removes the "solely from the efforts of others" component from the investment contract test in analyzing general partnership interests. Unlike general partnerships (*Williamson v. Tucker*, 645 F.2d 404 (5th Cir. 1981), cert. denied, 454 US 897 (1981)), in limited partnerships the limited partners are generally precluded, under the partnership agreement, from participating in the management of the partnership. This is why most limited partnership interests have been held to be securities.

Because an investment takes the form of a general partnership, however, does not inevitably mean that partnership interests are not securities. Courts have held that general partnership interests may be securities when the partnership agreement in fact distributed power as would a limited partnership and the partners are inexperienced or not knowledgeable in business affairs generally. The tests boil down to whether the partnership agreement leaves the partners in ultimate control, and whether they have the practical ability (are not disabled by their own inexperience, large numbers, or the manager's unique experience) to exercise that control.

Because of the similarity of LLCs and general partnerships, it can be expected that federal courts will look to the general partnership cases in determining the nature of LLC interests. The key to the determination will probably be the allocation of managerial rights. If the LLC is actually managed by the Members who collectively make all important decisions and may act on behalf of the LLC in dealing with third parties, it is likely that the LLC interests would not be considered securities. If a Manager is engaged to run the day-to-day operations of the LLC, the LLC interests are still likely not to be securities if the Members retain ultimate control (i.e., can vote to oust the Manager, or have a say in important business decisions). If, however, ultimate responsibility for managing is ceded to the Manager, with some or all of the Members having no real role in business matters (i.e., are treated as if they were limited partners), then the LLC interests are likely to be considered securities. Both the Articles of Organization and Operating Agreement are critical to the determination of whether an LLC interest is a security. Care should be taken to make it clear that the Members retain the power to make important business decisions and, if a Manager is retained, the power to periodically vote in removal or transaction of the Manager's contract.

As a final note in this analysis, the number of LLC Members may be dispositive of the issue. Interests in an LLC with hundreds of Members, for example, are assuredly to be considered securities because such large numbers of people cannot realistically expect to be actually involved in the exercise of management power.

EXEMPTION FROM REGISTRATION UNDER FEDERAL SECURITIES LAWS

Under the Securities Act of 1933 (the Securities Act), the offer and sale of securities must be made pursuant to the registration and prospectus delivery requirements of Section 5 of the Securities Act, or pursuant to an available exemption therefrom. In addition, many state securities laws (blue sky laws) require either registration or the availability of an exemption from registration. Failure to register when required may result in civil and criminal penalties. There are a number of exemptions from the registration requirements of Section 5 of the Securities Act. Some of the exemptions include:

- *The Intrastate Exemption.* This exemption is for securities offered and sold only to people residing in a single state and where the issuer is also a resident of and doing business in that state.
- *Regulation D Offerings.* Regulation D is a safe harbor promulgated by the Securities and Exchange Commission (SEC) pursuant to Sections 3 and 4 of the Securities Act. Regulation D consists of general rules (Rules 501 through 503, 507, and 508) and three separate offering exemptions (Rules 504, 505, and 506). Compliance with all the general rules and the provisions of the specific offering exemption rule ensures the availability of an exemption from the registration requirements of the Securities Act.

Limited offerings under $1 million (Rule 504). Under this exemption, non-reporting companies (companies that do not have a class of securities registered under the Securities Exchange Act) may sell up to $1 million of securities in any 12-month period. There are no specific disclosure requirements, and the offering may be sold through general advertising and solicitation.

Limited offerings under $5 million (Rule 505). For this exemption to apply, providing that the offer is not made by general soliciting or general advertising, issuers may offer securities totaling less than $5 million in any 12-month period to not more than 35 purchasers and any number of "accredited investors" (generally wealthy individuals or certain types of financial institutions). However, the issuer must provide certain specified disclosure materials if any sales are made to nonaccredited investors.

Private placement (Rule 506). Issuers may offer and sell any dollar amount of securities to up to 35 purchasers and any number of accredited investors provided that no general solicitation or general advertising is used. Once again, the issuer has to provide certain disclosure materials if any sales are made to any nonaccredited investors. In addition, the issuer must make a determination that each nonaccredited investor has such knowledge and experience in financial and business matters that he or she is capable of evaluating the merits and risks of the prospective investment.

- *The Accredited Investor Exemption.* This exemption is similar to Rule 506.

- *Regulation A.* Regulation A permits issuers to freely sell tradable securities to investors without complying with the registration requirements of the Securities Act. Regulation A's disclosure requirements are simpler than a registration under the Securities Act and permit forms of advertising and solicitation are not permitted in other nonregistered offerings. Issuers may provide unaudited financial statements if audited statements are not available. The dollar limit for a Regulation A offering is $5 million. An issuer relying on Regulation A may "test the waters" for potential investor interest prior to incurring the costs of preparing a Regulation A offering statement. Thus, an issuer may publish or deliver to prospective purchasers a written document or make scripted radio or television broadcasts.

Any securities issued in reliance on an exemption from the registration requirements of the Securities Act (except pursuant to Rule 504 or Regulation A) will be restricted securities and, as such, may not be offered or resold without registration under the Securities Act or an available exemption from registration therefrom.

Assuming LLC interests are securities and that an exemption from registration is available at the federal level, the antifraud provisions of the federal securities laws (most significantly Section 10 of the 1934 Act and Rule 10b-5 promulgated thereunder) are applicable to the offer, sale, and purchase of these investments.

STATE SECURITIES LAWS

In addition to complying with the federal securities laws, the offer and sale of securities must also be made in accordance with the securities laws (blue sky laws) of the various states. Various exemptions from state registration are available, including the Uniform Limited Offering Exemption (ULOE), which has been adopted in one form or another by most of the states. The ULOE tracks Rules 505 and 506, described previously and, with certain variations, provides for a state exemption for offerings that meet the requirements of either of these two rules. The ULOE has not, however, been extended to cover Rule 504 offerings.

The states have also addressed the question of whether LLC interests are securities. In doing so, they have applied the *Howey* investment contract analysis and the *Williamson* general partnership interest analysis. The analysis has been addressed in state statutes, administrative regulations and rulings, no-action letters, and policy statements.

The securities statutes of several states have been amended to include LLC interests within the definition of a "security." In certain instances, these statutes provide exceptions to the definition when, generally, all the LLC Members are actively engaged in the LLC's management. A number of state statutes also provide that the term security includes an LLC interest "unless the contract requires otherwise." Other states that have not included LLC interests within the statutory definition of a security, have arguably done so by implication by providing for the exemption from registration of LLC interests under certain circumstances (the implication being that registration may be required in other circumstances).

The securities acts of many states include LLCs within the statuary definition of "person" or "entity," thereby subjecting LLCs to registration requirements for brokers and/or dealers if they wish to offer and sell LLC interests within the state.

The state administrative orders and no-action letters issued have focused primarily on the numbers of investors, their participation in management, the experience of the investors, and whether the purchases were made for investment purposes. Further, a number of states with no official position have unofficially indicated that they would apply the *Howey* and *Williamson* tests on a case-by-case basis.

SUMMARY

In addition to reviewing the tax ramifications and other considerations of conducting business in the LLC format, the possible security law implications must be considered. Where your LLC is offering to sell LLC Membership interests to more than a few passive investors, always consult with a securities attorney before taking any steps to market the Membership interests to be certain that you have properly addressed any applicable state or federal security laws.

CAUTION: The consequences of failing to file the required documents and adhere to other security law requirements are severe. The position advocated by some that LLC Membership interests are not securities simply cannot be relied on. The conclusion will depend on all the facts in a particular situation. If there is any issue whatsoever, err on the side of caution and have securities counsel review the matter.

---

7 DISSOLUTION, WINDING UP, AND TERMINATION OF A LIMITED LIABILITY COMPANY

The chapters in this book have followed a natural sequence in the progression of your LLC. First you must make the decision to form an LLC. Next, you form and then operate the LLC. At some point, the business purpose of the LLC may cease, or some other event may trigger the end of the your LLC. This chapter addresses this next stage in the progression.

The final phase of the "operation" of an LLC is its ultimate demise, which is generally a three-stage process: (1) dissolution, (2) winding up, and (3) termination, in that order. Each of these three steps will be discussed in this chapter.

A dissolution is the first step in formally ending the legal existence of your LLC. It is followed by winding up and finally the formal termination.

Each state's LLC statute provides specific rules relating to the dissolution and ultimate legal termination of an LLC as a legal entity. The following discussion provides an overview of the concepts common to many states' laws.

WHAT CAUSES DISSOLUTION?

The first step in ending the legal existence of an LLC is a dissolution of the entity. The events that may cause a dissolution of an LLC may vary from state to state, but generally any of the following six events may trigger a dissolution:

1. The expiration of a fixed duration set forth in the Articles of Organization (in the sample in Chapter 3 a 30-year period was used).
2. By written agreement among the Members (the people involved decide it's time to move on and agree so in writing).
3. By dissociation of the Members (i.e., the death, retirement, resignation, bankruptcy, or expulsion of any Member).
4. The occurrence of a specific event set forth in the Articles of Organization or Operating Agreement (see the sample Operating Agreement in Chapter 3).
5. By judicial action (e.g., a court determines that a particular LLC should be dissolved, perhaps to pay certain assets to creditors).
6. A professional services LLC is no longer licensed to render professional services (e.g., one or more of the physicians in a LLC, where an LLC is permitted for professional practices, has his or her license revoked).

If dissolution is to occur because of the dissociation of a Member, dissolution can be avoided if all the remaining Members, other than the Member whose acts resulted in the dissociation, provide consent to continue the business after the dissociation event. Most state default statutes provide that the consent must be unanimous; however, the Operating Agreement could provide for a requisite level of consent that may be less than unanimous. The possibility of a Member's dissociation from the LLC poses the most likely potential cause of an LLC dissolution. As stated in the preceding sentence, if the Members give the requisite consent to continue the business after the dissociation of a Member, the LLC will not in fact dissolve.

CAUTION: Some legal advisers have suggested that the Members enter into advance agreements to continue the business upon the dissociation of a Member. Such an agreement, however, may prove fatal to the partnership tax classification of an LLC because it might cause the LLC to possess the corporate characteristic of continuity of life. Therefore, extreme caution should be exercised.

PROCESS OF WINDING UP

An LLC winds up by satisfying its obligations and liabilities to creditors and making distributions to its Members. To provide the funds necessary to satisfy creditors, the LLC's assets may have to be sold. In some states, a Member owning more than 50 percent of the interests in profits of an LLC may wind down the LLC's affairs.

Filing Requirements

In many states, on an LLC's dissolution the law requires that a notice of intent to dissolve, articles of dissolution, or notice of dissolution must be filed first, and then the Certificate of Cancellation or Articles of Termination can be filed. For example, the Arizona, Wyoming, Florida, Louisiana, Maryland, Minnesota, Nevada, Oklahoma, and Utah statutes require an initial filing, then a second filing on the conclusion of the winding-up process. On the other hand, some states only require a filing relating to the final winding up of the LLC. Some of these forms are discussed in Chapter 5.

Distribution of Assets

Generally, on the winding up of an LLC, its assets are to be distributed in the following order of priority:

1. To creditors.
2. To Members in satisfaction of liabilities for distributions (for example if a Member loaned money to an LLC using the loan documents illustrated in Chapter 5, this loan would be repaid before all the Members were entitled to make claims for a return of their capital accounts).
3. To Members to return their capital contributions (this includes their initial investments in the LLC, as discussed in Chapter 3).

4. To Members based on their percentage interests in the LLC. In most simple LLC arrangements, this will be the same percentage by which profits and distributions had been shared in all years. In more complex arrangements, special allocations and complex adjustments may have to be made to determine how proceeds are to be distributed at this stage.

The winding up of an LLC is completed when all debts, liabilities, and obligations of the LLC have been paid and/or discharged, or adequate provisions have been made for such obligations, and all remaining property and assets of the LLC have been distributed to its Members.

PRACTICE TIP: Each state's LLC statute must be examined to determine whether an LLC in the process of dissolution and winding up must notify its creditors of such situation. If a creditor to whom notice is given does not respond within a certain time period to the LLC, depending on each particular state's statute, the LLC may be able to disregard the creditor's claim. With respect to unknown creditors, the LLC may be able to effectuate the same outcome by publishing a notice of its dissolution in a local newspaper. While there is a cost to publishing the various notices, the comfort of being able to cut off creditor claims, or at least to have a defense that you have reasonably endeavored to notify claimants, can be well worth the cost.

SUMMARY

After all the business of the LLC has been accomplished or at some sooner time as may be required, the LLC may be legally terminated. Each state's statute provides certain default rules under which an LLC may dissolve, wind up, and terminate unless otherwise provided in the Operating Agreement. There are various state filing requirements relating to the termination of an LLC and the distribution of assets at such time.

Part Three

USING LIMITED LIABILITY COMPANIES FOR SPECIFIC BUSINESSES AND FOR FINANCIAL GOALS

8 USING LIMITED LIABILITY COMPANIES FOR REAL ESTATE INVESTMENTS

An LLC may carry on any lawful business, purpose, or activity. However, an LLC offers an especially beneficial structure for owning real estate investments. Too many investors have structured real estate ownership in their individual names, or in the general partnership format. While these approaches have the benefit of simplicity from both a tax and legal perspective, there is no limitation on the personal liability of the owners. While many lenders may require personal guarantees of the principals regardless of the ownership structure, the use of an entity that provides limited liability to its owners for other potential claims, such as certain environmental, personal injury claims, and ordinary trade creditors, should always be considered.

NOTE: The reaction of some real estate owners is, "That's why I carry insurance." Insurance, however, is not foolproof. Premium payments can be missed causing policies to lapse. Insurance can cancel coverage or refuse to renew coverage. Every policy has exclusions. You may fail to adhere to conditions in a policy. Using an LLC should not be a reason to lessen insurance coverage. However, having insurance coverage should not be a reason to overlook the importance of the limited liability that an LLC can provide.

For many real estate transactions, a limited partnership with a corporate general partner has been the standard organizational format. The limited partnership structure provided the tax benefits of partnership flow-through taxation (the partners, not the partnership, pay tax). The limited partners have limited liability. However, at least one general partner must have unlimited liability. For this general partner to avoid unlimited liability, an S corporation had to be formed to serve as general partner, with the individual owning the S corporation stock. The cost of forming and operating both the corporate general partner used in the typical arrangement, as well as the partnership itself, however, is very expensive for smaller transactions. Furthermore, the corporate general partner should have a net worth equal to 10 percent of the total capital contributions of the limited partnership. Since the general partner is liable for all partnership liabilities, this exposes more assets to fund these liabilities. Thus, the sole proprietor, tenancy in common, joint tenancy, or general partnership was frequently used.

CAUTION: The ownership of real estate as a sole proprietor, tenant in common, joint tenancy, or general partnership is potentially very dangerous from a liability prospective. In one situation that exemplifies the danger involved, two brothers owned a residential rental apartment complex. One day, they received an urgent phone call to come back to the complex. When they arrived, fire trucks were at the scene and all the tenants had been evacuated. Ultimately, a determination was made by the fire department that gas was coming up from the ground and spreading throughout the building. The brothers have now been subject to a class action lawsuit by the tenants and all their assets have now become vulnerable to a potential judgment against them.

CAUTION: Another problem with the use of the sole proprietorship is that if the real estate is in a state other than where you reside, your heirs will have to incur the costs and time delays of probate in that state as well. Using a partnership, corporation, or LLC to own the property may obviate the need for ancillary probate.

The LLC can provide a cost-effective and simple approach for ownership in these smaller investments. While the LLC can clearly offer potential benefits to the larger real estate venture, smaller investments, such as a few friends or family members purchasing a rental property, can benefit most.

DISADVANTAGES OF USING S CORPORATIONS FOR REAL ESTATE INVESTMENTS

For real estate investments, using an S corporation as the ownership vehicle is rarely appropriate. This is because the entity level debt of an S corporation cannot be included in the tax basis of its shareholders even if the debt is personally guaranteed by the shareholders; and special allocations, common to many real estate ventures, cannot be structured within the scope of the S corporation one-class-of-stock requirement.

EXAMPLE: Assume an S corporation is owned by shareholders X and Y with X and Y making no capital contributions to the corporation. The corporation acquires the building and real estate for $1 million. The corporation obtains the funds necessary to buy the building and real estate by borrowing $1 million, which is personally guaranteed by X and Y. Assume further that there is a $25,000 net loss in the first year of business, primarily from depreciation deductions. Neither X nor Y is entitled to utilize any of the loss on their individual tax returns; they have no basis because the liability cannot be included in their tax basis and therefore their tax basis is zero.

Alternatively, if this entity is structured as an LLC, X and Y will get full benefit for the $1 million of debt even if neither of them personally guarantees the debt. Therefore, each of them will be able to take a deduction on their tax return for $12,500 subject to the passive loss rules.

Furthermore, some states, until very recently, have not recognized S corporations for state tax purposes and some that do, still impose a corporate level tax.

Therefore, the profits of the S corporation in such states may be subject to that state's corporate income tax.

GENERAL PARTNERSHIP VERSUS LIMITED PARTNERSHIP VERSUS LLC TO OWN REAL ESTATE INVESTMENTS

As a result of the problems attendant to utilizing an S corporation to own real estate, many owners elected either to use a general partnership or a limited partnership. With a general partnership, the partners expose themselves to unlimited liability. Utilizing either a limited partnership with a corporate general partner or an LLC would be more prudent for limiting this liability.

When comparing the use of a limited partnership with a limited liability company, both entities can limit the liability of its owners. In a limited partnership, however, the general partner will still have unlimited liability. This problem can be alleviated by setting up a corporation as a general partner. However, since the general partnership should ideally have a net worth equal to at least 10 percent of the total capital contributions to the limited partnership, those assets would be exposed to the liabilities of the partnership. The capital funding requirement can be completely eliminated by utilizing a LLC.

Moreover, the LLC, which avoids the need for two entities (the corporation as a general partner and the limited partnership), requires less cost to start up and fewer annual tax returns and complications.

Although the LLC can be used to protect the Members from outside creditors, the LLC's Operating Agreement can still be used to require additional capital from Members for reasons common in real estate investments. These include construction overruns, debt service deficiencies, and working capital needs resulting from expiration of leases such as broker's commissions and tenant fit-up costs. The LLC Operating Agreement can provide that capital will be called for such needs and can further provide various remedies for failure to contribute, such as dilution of percentage of total Membership interests in the LLC for non-contributing Members. Nonetheless, the agreement can also provide that no Member is personally liable to the LLC, its Members, or any third party for failure to so contribute.

Thus, for real estate investors in particular, the choice often was between a limited or general partnership. The LLC offers an excellent option for ownership of real estate.

THE LLC COMPARED WITH LIMITED PARTNERSHIP SYNDICATION

Real estate syndications (almost invariably structured as limited partnerships) were the rage prior to the Tax Reform Act of 1986, which attacked the tax shelter industry and severely wounded the real estate industry in the process. As a result of the abusive tax-oriented real estate syndications of the 1980s, many wealthy investors seeking to diversify their portfolios into passive real estate investments view anything called a real estate syndication (or real estate limited partnership) as a four-letter word. The LLC offers an important advantage over the limited partnership because its name is not tainted by the negative experience so many associate with real estate syndications, even if the advantage is primarily a psychological edge.

REAL ESTATE INVESTMENTS TRUSTS AND LLCs

A real estate investment trust (REIT) is a trust or corporation organized to hold real estate assets. It is typically owned by a large number of shareholders. Although a REIT may be classified as a corporation, it can qualify—if it meets the many strict REIT tax requirements—to avoid tax on most of its income, which it then passes through to its shareholders. The requirements are complex. The LLC may offer a possible alternative to the use of a REIT in some instances. An LLC can have a significant number of investors, own real estate, and provide many of the benefits of the REIT for real estate investing. Most importantly for real estate investors, this can all be accomplished with far less complexity and administrative cost.

TAX CONSIDERATIONS

For real estate investments, especially if depreciation and other deductions generate a tax loss, the passive loss limitations rules are an important tax-planning consideration. The passive loss rules generally limit a real estate investor's ability to deduct losses from real estate and other passive investments to the income from passive investments. In some cases it can therefore be advantageous to have a loss from a real estate rental treated instead as active.

The LLC provides an opportunity for real estate owners to characterize income and losses derived from the entity as potentially active income losses. In a limited partnership, a limited partner's allocable share of income and losses derived from the partnership will generally be treated as passive. Depending on the activity of a Member, his or her participation may be deemed active and hence the income and losses flowing from the LLC may be active.

Real estate transactions have historically relied more heavily on special allocations of income, gain, and loss from an investment than has any other type of business or investment transaction. The LLC offers more flexibility than any type of corporate entity to allocate tax benefits.

In a limited partnership (heretofore the entity of choice for real estate investments), mortgage debt for which the lender had recourse to the general partner could not be allocated to the limited partners, thus adversely affecting the limited partners' ability to claim deductions. An LLC is not subject to this restriction. All investors obtain limited liability (the goal sought by limited partners under the traditional real estate limited partnership), and they can also have recourse liabilities allocated to them. This contrasts favorably to the limited partnership where limited partners were only allocated nonrecourse liabilities.

OTHER REAL ESTATE ISSUES

When drafting an Operating Agreement for a real estate transaction, specify in detail the person or persons necessary to authorize a particular action. Who can approve a new mortgage, or sign a deed? One Manager, all Managers, a majority of Members, two-thirds of the Members, and so on. The greater the detail as to key operating actions, the easier it will be for the LLC itself to engage in significant transactions such as the purchase, financing, or sale of real estate.

Where you wish to convert an existing property owned by you outright, or in a general partnership, into an LLC, be certain to investigate the necessity of obtaining new casualty insurance as well as the effect on the validity of your title insurance policy.

SUMMARY

Utilizing an LLC for real estate investments has a substantial benefit over utilizing a corporation or partnership for such purposes. Anyone involved in real estate activities, whether a local vacation home rental property or a substantial commercial project, should give consideration to the use of an LLC.

9   PROFESSIONAL PRACTICES AND LIMITED LIABILITY COMPANIES

TIP: Before any professional invests any time completing the analysis of which entity to use, investigate which entities persons in your licensed profession need or can use in your particular state. For example, some states do not permit attorneys to practice as LLCs.

LIABILITY OF PROFESSIONALS

A very common form of ownership of a professional practice (e.g., accounting and law firms) has been the partnership, which creates the problem of vicarious liability of one partner for the acts of another partner. This means that each partner in a professional partnership is personally liable for all the debts of the partnership in addition to being potentially liable for the negligent or wrongful acts of his or her partners. This is the classic "weak link" scenario: One partner becomes the weak link by failing to perform at the appropriate professional level maintained by the rest of the firm. Every partner in the firm can be personally liable (to the extent of losing his or her home) for the acts of the single inept partner.

Because of the unlimited liability of each of the partners in the partnerships, many professionals have opted to utilize a professional corporation or professional association as the business structure for their practice. Generally, the professional corporation or professional association provides limited liability to each of the shareholders. There is an important exception to this limited liability. Under this exception, a shareholder remains personally liable for any acts of malpractice that he or she may commit as well as anyone under his or her supervision. The other shareholders remain insulated from such liabilities.

As for a limited liability company, the liability protection will generally be the same as that afforded a professional corporation or a professional association. Therefore, an LLC Member will only be liable for his or her personal malpractice and those under his or her supervision. The Member will not be liable for the malpractice committed by other Members nor for contractual liabilities of the LLC.

TAX CONSIDERATIONS OF THE LLC AND THE PROFESSIONAL CORPORATION

Professional corporations are classified as personal service corporations, which require significant monitoring at year end to avoid double taxation. This generally requires the payment of bonuses to shareholders resulting in cash flow problems and is difficult to monitor.

If an S corporation is utilized, concerns such as ownership restrictions and botched S elections. Furthermore, an S corporation requires proportionate distributions of income to its shareholders, which may not be appropriate for your professional corporation or a professional LLC.

Utilization of a professional service LLC will generally be preferable for accountants, lawyers, and other licensed professionals if and when the LLC format for these professionals is available. Such an entity provides greater flexibility as to requirements for Membership and distributions of income. It also permits clear avoidance of double taxation both during operation and on liquidation.

PROFESSIONAL SERVICE LLC

Licensed professionals who wish to practice within the type of limited liability structure offered by the LLC can organize themselves as professional service LLCs.

Where a professional firm (e.g., of accountants or lawyers) operates in several states, however, the limited liability partnership (LLP) can offer an important advantage of facilitating interstate operations while maintaining the limited liability characteristic of a professional corporation.

CAUTION: While initially the LLP may sound like the equivalent of a professional corporation (or professional association) providing limited liability, this may not be true. Although some state statutes grant the LLC similar liability protection afforded to the professional corporation, many LLP statutes do not. Instead, they do not provide any limitation on liability with respect to leases, bank loans, and so on.

LIMITED LIABILITY PARTNERSHIP

Another entity that may be used by professionals is the limited liability partnership. The LLP is a partnership that provides limited liability to its partners for liability arising from the malpractice of other partners. Similar to an LLC and a professional corporation, it does not protect the malpracticing partner from liabilities arising from his or her own malpractice and from those under his or her supervision. Furthermore, it generally does not provide protection to a partner for business and tort liabilities of the LLP. Therefore, each partner remains jointly and severally liable for all commercial debts such as leases, sexual harassment claims, and accounts payable of the LLP. Many professional service entities have opted to use an LLP rather than an LLC because LLCs in certain states such as Texas and Florida are subject to corporate level taxes.

In some states, such as Michigan, professional LLCs are permitted and have become prevalent. In other states, there is still less clarity as to whether or not LLCs may be used by professionals. Furthermore, the use of LLCs will generally need to be authorized by the appropriate licensing authorities.

The accounting profession has been quick to recognize the importance and advantages of LLCs. In January 1992, the American Institute of Certified Public Accountants amended its Rule 505 to allow accountants to utilize LLCs where available under state law.

EXAMPLE: Assume there are three partners in a general partnership, M, N, and O, who practice accounting. N commits malpractice giving rise to a $3 million judgment. Each of M, N, and O are liable for the entire $3 million liability.

If the entity were a professional corporation, an LLC, or an LLP, then the entity and only N would be liable for the $3 million liability. M and O would have no personal liability.

By using an LLP, a professional may escape liability for malpractice where he or she wasn't involved. Instead, the Member who supervised the person committing the malpractice would be held accountable. This situation can create a practical dilemma. Why should any Member wish to be the managing partner (Member) of a firm, or the head of a department that addresses risky legal issues? Members requested to serve in these capacities may only do so where they have a commitment from other firm members to make a contribution in the event of a lawsuit. Thus, an agreement for all Members to contribute may be inevitable. When evaluating the use of a LLP, you must take care in analyzing and drafting the provisions to include in the LLP Agreement. If the Agreement requires a partner to contribute where the LLP's assets are exhausted, the limited liability benefits of the LLP could be compromised. This risk can be addressed by stating that no third parties are to be beneficiaries of the provision requiring contribution. Further, the contribution provision could be made inapplicable in the case of fraud, wilful misconduct, and other acts where contribution by other partners is inappropriate. The reality, however, is that where a claimant is aware that the LLP Agreement includes a contribution provision, claims may be made for greater amounts, and the prospect of settling is lessened.

EVALUATING THE CHOICE OF ENTITY TO PROVIDE PROFESSIONAL SERVICES

When evaluating the choice for the organizational form of your professional service entity, various factors must be considered. Some of the factors include:

- Desired degree of protection from personal liability.
- Availability of the entities under state law.
- Securities law aspects.
- Costs and burdens of converting an existing entity to a new entity.
- Limitations on the transferability of ownership interests in a particular entity.
- Impact of an entity type on firm culture.

Protection from Personal Liability

All professional service providers are afraid of their firm's liability exposure. Many types of potential liability may arise from the membership in a professional practice. The preferred form of organization depends on the types of liabilities that may arise of concern to the owners.

In most states, the professional corporation and LLC provide protection for owners of professional practices from malpractice liability of another owner if there is no agreement among the owners to share in the liability. However, malpractice liability is not the only liability feared by professional practices. Another major source of personal liability for professionals is contract liability. Contract liabilities may include long-term office leases, equipment leases, accounts payable, and staff salaries. There is also significant concerns involving tort liabilities. Sexual harassment is a major form of this liability.

Availability of the Entities under State Law

In choosing a business format the owners must determine whether or not an LLC can be used to conduct business in that in the particular jurisdiction. A further necessary step is to determine whether or not the profession is permitted by its particular licensing authority to utilize an LLC in that particular jurisdiction.

Securities Law Aspects

In certain instances, interests in a professional firm may either constitute securities or be exempt from status as a security. Characterization of ownership interests as securities may affect a firm's ability to use the cash method of accounting, which could cause a firm to recognize income sooner than it otherwise would have been required. (For a more detailed discussion on securities law and LLCs, see Chapter 6.)

Costs and Burdens of Converting an Existing Entity to a New Entity

A careful determination needs to be made as to the cost of changing a partnership to a limited liability company. Generally, this transition is not subject to income tax (see Chapter 4). In some jurisdictions, this will require a formal assignment of the partnership assets to the LLC. Other states permit a merger of the partnership into an LLC, which is a much more streamlined transition.

The transition from a professional corporation to an LLC is a potentially costly conversion. If the professional corporation is a regular corporation, the transfer results in a liquidation of the professional corporation that could give rise to double taxation. If the professional corporation is an S corporation, it will still be a liquidation and will give rise to at least one level of taxation (under certain circumstances it will result in double taxation).

Limitations on the Transferability of Ownership Interests

LLCs typically prohibit the free transferability of LLC interests to help ensure that they are taxed as a partnership for federal tax purposes. Licensed professions, such as the accounting and legal professions, in general, preclude free transferability of ownership interests. While other professions may allow for free transferability, most members generally would want to maintain the control over the identities of their coowners.

Impact on Firm Culture

Conversion of a professional practice to an LLC can raise sensitive issues and cause a reexamination of the practice's business relationships. Some owners may not want to have centralized management such as in a Manager-managed LLC because they prefer the general partnership advantage of each partner having significant voting rights. However, avoidance of centralization of management is not critical for the LLC to be taxed as a partnership. Cultural aspects must be considered based on each firm's unique relationship with and among its owners and its history.

A major concept with which the owners of a professional practice must wrestle is whether or not the owner should be liable for the malpractice of another owner. In a partnership, all the partners remain liable for the malpracticing partners' liability. If an LLC (or an LLP and a professional corporation) is utilized, then the remaining Members are not liable for the liability arising from this malpractice. The owners must decide what the ultimate objectives are under this scenario.

LLCs AND LLPs AND PROFESSIONAL MALPRACTICE INSURANCE

Your use of an LLC or LLP should not in any manner encourage you to reduce your malpractice coverage. The LLC structure is not infallible so insurance coverage is essential. The professional firm itself likely has significant assets to be protected. Likewise, do not let the existence of malpractice insurance lull you into believing that you don't need an entity such as an LLC or LLP to limit liability.

NOTE: Some state LLC statutes permit the Members to select other Members who agree to be liable on specific debts, but not others.

Liabilities of Owners and Particular Entities

Type of Liability	General Partnership	Professional Corporation or Association	LLC	LLP
Liability for one's own malpractice	Yes	Yes	Yes	Yes
Liability for malpractice of others	Yes	No	No	No
Liability for the malpractice of others under one's supervision	Yes	Yes	Yes	Yes
General commercial and tort liability	Yes	No	No	Yes

SUMMARY

Professional practices (e.g., accounting and law firms) have been typically formed in the partnership format. Professional corporations have been used as an alternate form for transacting professional practice businesses. Certain states, but not all, allow for the practice of professionals in the LLC format. Before forming a professional practice in the LLC format, however, check with the appropriate state agency that regulates the professional practice to determine whether the agency has given permission for professionals in such state to practice as an LLC. In most states, an LLC must have two members so if you are a solo professional practitioner in one of those states you may not be able to utilize an LLC.

Even if the professional practitioner does form as an LLC, he or she will not be protected for personal liability for his or her professional malpractice or the malpractice of individuals under his or her direct supervision. Some courts have, for example, found partners vicariously liable for acts of others even where the others were not within their direct supervision.

Thus, for professionals, the LLP or LLC—depending on the laws applicable in your state—can be excellent vehicles to help minimize, although by no means eliminate, the risk of professional malpractice.

10 USING LIMITED LIABILITY COMPANIES FOR HIGH-TECHNOLOGY ENTERPRISES, FOREIGN INVESTORS, AND MULTISTATE OPERATIONS

HIGH-TECHNOLOGY ENTERPRISES

The LLC should be carefully considered when evaluating entities to use to form and to operate a high-technology enterprise. New hi-tech companies are typically associated with a high risk for their investors. Limiting one's personal liability where hi-tech investments are involved is very attractive, if not imperative, when facing significant investment risks.

Highly risky investments often use special allocations to compensate the various investors for the different types of risk each takes. Some investors who contribute more capital may want to be entitled to preferred distributions from the company, which would not be permitted in an S corporation, but is in an LLC.

The ability of an investor to limit his or her personal liability is essential. A high-risk venture may be highly leveraged with borrowed funds. To the extent the investors are not required to furnish personal guarantees for any such borrowed funds, they would want to be protected from personal liability due to the inability of the LLC to repay those loans.

Certain investors in many start-up ventures involving high technology and high risk may wish to have more control and input than a limited partner would have if the entity were structured as a limited partnership. If a limited partner is given too much control, he or she risks losing the personal liability shield that is so important to the investor. By contrast, with an LLC, an investor can participate in the entity's management and control without having to worry about risking personal liability. Thus, the combination of limited liability, participation in management, and flexible allocations, makes an LLC an ideal structure for new risky enterprises such as high-technology companies.

FOREIGN INVESTORS AND LLCs

LLCs resemble entities that have long been used in other countries, as was discussed in Chapter 1. This fact should make LLCs familiar to many foreign investors who may be less familiar with other entities used in the United States, such as limited partnerships. Accordingly, an LLC may be an ideal vehicle for international investors because of its pass-through tax treatment and limited liability protection to its owners.

For foreign investors, an LLC may be the ideal vehicle to structure investment and business transactions because the restrictions pertaining to who can be a shareholder in an S corporation prohibit nonresident aliens as shareholders. That restriction does not apply to LLCs.

EXAMPLE: Ten individuals want to organize a business venture in which each of the individuals will be actively involved. One of the individuals, J, is a Japanese citizen and is not a resident of the United States. All the entrepreneurs consider limited liability and pass-through taxation to be essential. The entrepreneurs can achieve all their goals only with an LLC. The business could not be formed as an S corporation because J is a nonresident alien and a corporation is ineligible to be an S corporation if it has a nonresident alien shareholder. The entrepreneurs could not achieve both their goal of maintaining joint control over the business and their goal of limited liability by forming a limited partnership, since limited partners may not participate in management without risking loss of limited liability. There would be unlimited liability if they were a general partnership. There would not be pass-through taxation if the entity was a C corporation. An LLC is perfect.

An LLC that is treated as a partnership for federal tax purposes should also be subject to the same rules relating to partnership withholding requirements relating to foreign partners. Accordingly, an LLC will be required to pay a withholding tax with respect to each foreign Member's distributive share of the LLC's income that is "effectively connected" with a trade or business in the United States. The amount of the withholding tax with respect to a foreign Member currently would be 35 percent (the highest corporate tax rate) in the case of a foreign corporate Member and 39.6 percent (the highest individual tax rate) in the case of a foreign noncorporate Member, multiplied by the LLC's effectively connected income allocable to each Member.

An LLC will also be required to pay a withholding tax with respect to each foreign Member's distributive share of the LLC's income that is not "effectively connected" with a trade or business in the United States. A flat 30 percent tax is levied on the gross amount of noneffectively connected "fixed or determinable annual or periodical gains, profits, and income," such as rents, dividends, and interest.

The preceding tax rates are subject to modification by specific tax treaties between the United States and foreign countries.

SUMMARY: FOREIGN INVESTORS AND LLCs

An LLC is an ideal vehicle for nonresident aliens to conduct business in the United States and maintain their limited liability. Accordingly, such entity would receive the pass-through tax treatment of partnerships with the limited liability protection typically associated with corporations. In addition, if an LLC is structured so that it will be taxed as a partnership, it is likely that the IRS would treat the LLC like a partnership in that the entity would be required to withhold taxes attributable to the distributive share of a foreign Member in the LLC.

MULTISTATE OPERATIONS

A key issue to address in determining whether a limited liability company is the right entity for you is an analysis of the states in which your LLC will operate its business. An LLC is known as a "domestic" LLC in the state in which it was organized and an LLC is known as a "foreign" LLC in a state other than the state of organization.

Since there has not yet been an enactment of a Uniform Limited Liability Company Act, each state has its own specific rules relating to LLCs. These specific rules vary from state to state. Therefore, the statutes of these specific states in which the LLC will operate must be carefully reviewed to determine in advance how a particular state will treat an LLC. It is obviously much better to know this information in advance, rather than being surprised at a later time. Accordingly, where a multistate operation is important to the company's business, it is important to determine what filing requirements, if any, are required of your LLC in a foreign jurisdiction (a state other than the state of organization).

STATES WITH NO LLC STATUTES

At the time this book was printed, there were two states that do not recognize LLCs (Hawaii and Vermont). Be sure, however, to verify the status of those states if you plan on setting up an LLC in either of them. Thus, it is possible that an LLC formed in a state that allows for the formation of LLCs may transact business in a state with no LLC statute. There is also the possibility that a state that does not recognize LLCs may impose personal liability on an LLC's owners under an analogy to general partnership law, where each partner is personally liable for the partnership's debts and obligations. To best protect themselves, it is important that Members who sign a document on the LLC's behalf (e.g., a contract or guarantee) sign only as an agent of the LLC and not in their individual capacity. Moreover, the LLC should take the requisite steps to register as a foreign entity in such state.

REGISTRATION OF FOREIGN LLCs

State Statutes Expressly Permitting Registration of Foreign LLCs

Not all states expressly provide in their statutes for the registration of foreign LLCs, even though such state may authorize the formation of LLCs. Generally, registration of a foreign LLC is a matter of filling out and filing some type of registration form with the appropriate state filing authority of the foreign jurisdiction. The information usually contained in such a registration form would be the name of the LLC, the jurisdiction of its organization, the name and address of a registered agent in the foreign jurisdiction, and under some states, the business purpose of the LLC. It is the approval of such registration by the appropriate state filing authority, not merely the filing of a document, that authorizes the foreign LLC to transact business in the foreign jurisdiction.

Some states require a foreign LLC, as well as domestic LLCs to file annual reports with the appropriate state filing authority and pay an annual filing fee.

Registration in Foreign Jurisdictions That Do Not Have Specific Registration Requirements for Limited Liabilities

What is required of an LLC to operate its business in a foreign jurisdiction that does not have a statute expressly dealing with the registration of foreign LLCs? In those states, it may be wise to proceed with any statutory filing procedures for foreign partnerships. If the state does not accept the registration of foreign partnerships (either general or limited), then proceeding with the foreign registration requirements for corporations may be appropriate. However, if an LLC follows the procedure of registration of a foreign corporation, it is important that the LLC does not in fact register as a corporation or else it may risk losing the partnership tax benefits of an LLC.

THE FAILURE TO REGISTER IN A FOREIGN JURISDICTION

Generally, if an LLC is required to register in a foreign jurisdiction and fails to do so, it will be precluded from bringing a lawsuit in the courts of that state. The failure to file a registration, however, should not alone invalidate any contract that the LLC had entered into in the foreign jurisdiction. Nor will the failure to file a registration impede the LLC's ability to defend itself in a lawsuit.

EXAMPLE: Assume a foreign LLC does business in another state and fails to get authorized to do business in that state. If the foreign LLC and its Members are sued in that foreign jurisdiction, the LLC would be able to defend itself in the lawsuit, and the individual Members would still benefit from limited liability. The LLC, however, may be limited in its ability to bring a counterclaim.

MULTISTATE TAX ISSUES

A complication to conducting business in the LLC format in several states is that not every state treats an LLC the same for state tax purposes. In most states, LLCs are treated for state tax purposes in the same manner in which they are treated for federal tax purposes. These are known as conformity statutes. In some states, however, an LLC that may be classified as a partnership for federal tax purposes will still be taxed as a corporation for state tax purposes.

This differing tax treatment by several states may cause administrative and accounting difficulties to the LLC. Therefore, before an LLC decides to conduct business in a foreign jurisdiction, it should make a determination that the LLC format will not cause any adverse tax consequences for state tax purposes that might outweigh the benefits of using an LLC.

EXAMPLE: An LLC formed in Florida, Texas, or Pennsylvania, or a foreign LLC doing business in any such state that is subject to that state's income tax, will be taxed as a corporation, rather than as a pass-through entity (i.e., partnership tax treatment), for state tax purposes.

SUMMARY: MULTISTATE OPERATIONS

Currently, 48 states and the District of Columbia recognize limited liability companies. Each state that recognizes LLCs, however, has its own distinct state statute and these statutes vary from state to state. Therefore, when forming an entity that will conduct business in several states, it is important to review and understand the LLC statutes in each state where business will be conducted.

If an LLC will be transacting business in a foreign jurisdiction, it is important to examine whether such foreign jurisdiction requires the registration of the LLC. If registration of a foreign LLC is required, then the LLC should comply with the filing requirements. If the LLC does not comply with the filing requirements, it may be subject to penalties and will not be able to initiate a lawsuit in the foreign jurisdiction.

Not every state, however, has a statute pertaining to the registration of a foreign LLC. In those states, the LLC should nevertheless move forward and comply with the filing requirements of a foreign partnership if there are such requirements.

11 DIVORCE AND LIMITED LIABILITY COMPANIES

LLCs are becoming a more and more popular form for organizing business and investment activities. The tax and legal advantages this hybrid of a partnership and corporation offers may make it the vehicle of choice for new transactions. As such, if you are getting divorced, you and your advisers must understand some of the nuances of LLCs that may affect how you will negotiate various financial and legal aspects of your divorce settlement. LLCs are important to understand in determining a spouse's earnings for alimony and child support calculations; for valuing a spouse's assets for determining equitable distribution; and in valuing a spouse's assets for negotiating a prenuptial agreement. Similarly, the terminology of LLCs is essential to understand when making discovery requests (a formal request by your lawyer for financial information from your spouse to help you and your financial advisers determine an appropriate settlement) and depositions (formal questioning of your spouse in front of a court reporter concerning various aspects of the marriage and financial matters) in the context of divorce litigation.

UNIQUE FEATURES OF LLCs

LLCs differ in many important ways from the more traditional business forms. These differences can have important implications on the matrimonial process. The following bulleted paragraphs highlight a few of these important differences.

- *Tax Valuation.* Whether an LLC is taxed as a partnership or as a corporation could be vitally important to the determination of the net of tax value of a spouse's interest in the entity. Earnings could also be affected. An LLC taxed as a corporation could be inclined to distribute all profits as salaries to avoid a corporate level tax, thus inflating the real "salary."

EXAMPLE: Abe owns 100 percent of the stock of B Corporation. This asset was acquired during the marriage and is subject to equitable distribution. Abe has drawn an annual salary of $300,000 for the three years preceding the divorce action and the corporation shows no profit on which a corporate level tax will be paid. Abe pays ordinary income tax on the $300,000; he loans to the corporation $50,000 of after-tax money to cover capital repayment in corporate debt. Will the court or the adversary representing Abe's spouse in the divorce action recognize this corporate need or seek to demonstrate that the loan by Abe to B Corporation is purely voluntary, not a beneficial tax device, and the full salary of $300,000 is available for alimony and child support. Since child support in many jurisdictions is controlled by "Guidelines" wherein the calculation is determined by fixed percentage of income as reported on the federal tax return, can or will the court adjust the information on the tax return?

An LLC taxed as a partnership could deflate or ignore salary payments since distributions can be made with no entity level tax, but the pass-through of an LLC's profits appears to be synonymous with earnings of an S corporation. This difference in tax treatment may cloud the determination of alimony and child support (i.e., what is the true cash flow available for these purposes).

EXAMPLE: Wife is currently in the midst of a divorce and owns 99 percent of an LLC that is taxed as a partnership. She has chosen for the past three years to draw $50,000 as salary and show a profit of $200,000 since she contemplates she may want to sell the business when the divorce ends. In calculating her share of child support as mandated by child support "Guidelines," is the $50,000 reported as salary the controlling number, or is the $200,000 profit also to be included? Husband works for AT&T. He earns $250,000. Is child support based on equal earnings or ⅙–⅚ shares. This was a long marriage. Does the husband pay alimony to the wife because of the disparate earnings?

- *Termination Date.* Many cases addressing the implication of a hypothetical tax have found the event triggering the tax too uncertain to justify an imputation of tax liability. Many LLC statutes require that the LLC be terminated no later than a specified number of years after formation. Will this date certain change the view of the courts as to the imputation of a tax? Even where no tax is imputed, will this statutory cutoff date provide a termination date for calculating future values of a business? If the statutory cutoff date is only five years away, can an appraiser assume the business will be reformed? Since the valuer for matrimonial purposes generally considers the five years preceding the filing of the complaint, what impact does the five-year termination have on the valuation?

- *Voting Rights.* An LLC may have different classes and groups of Membership interests, each with different voting and distribution rights. Where these different classes and groups are present, the valuation process will become quite complex. What is a voting right worth? Were voting rights avoided solely to argue for a reduced value in the matrimonial action? It may be necessary to make projections of distributions under different scenarios to value the potentially complex variations in distribution rights. While this might appear similar to the issues faced in valuing different classes of stock in a C corporation, it can be more complex since special allocations used in sophisticated investment LLC transactions can also be present.

- *Spouse as Manager.* Where a spouse is the LLC's Manager, the compensation as Manager, as well as the possible right to control compensation and distributions, must be addressed. Some states even permit the Operating Agreement to include penalties to charge a Manager for certain improper acts. Should these penalties reduce the value of the Manager's interests?

SUMMARY

As LLCs continue to become a more common vehicle for investments and businesses, those undergoing divorce, and their advisers, will be required to address a broad range of new issues and concerns in discovery, trial, and valuation matters and in determining child support and alimony.

In the context of matrimonial law, understanding the in's and out's of LLCs will be helpful in determining the value of a Membership interest. This knowledge will assure equitable distribution between divorcing spouses and will establish the wages of a particular spouse (who may or may not be an LLC's Manager) for purposes of determining child support and alimony.

12 FAMILY BUSINESSES AND LIMITED LIABILITY COMPANIES

When a business is family owned and operated, transferability of interests in the ownership of the business and estate planning for the firm's owners are important. LLCs, S corporations, and limited partnerships may all be good choices for certain family businesses. S corporations provide easy transferability of ownership interests through stock and the option of "deductible" estate planning through stock bonuses to family employees. By paying compensation to the family members, the corporation receives a deduction for the payment and the parent does not have to pay a gift tax since the money transferred is a wage and not a gift. Obviously, the amount paid for compensation must be within reason compared with what unrelated people would be paid or the IRS could challenge the transaction and recharacterize a portion of the salary as a dividend distribution to the parent followed by a gift to the child.

Only certain trusts, however, can be a shareholder in an S corporation, which significantly limits estate planning opportunities. This serious issue is often overlooked in many estate plans until a problem arises. LLCs can be owned by all types of estate planing vehicles (i.e., any trusts).

NOTE: As this book is being written, Congress is considering several changes that may affect the preceding discussion. For many years, Congress has considered plans to liberalize the laws concerning S corporations to make them simpler, more flexible, and to minimize some of the traps that lurk in the tax jargon. Also, there have been a number of proposals to minimize the estate tax on family-held businesses. One of these proposals would provide for what is effectively an estate tax deduction for some portion of the value of a qualifying family business owned at death.

Before making any final decision concerning the planning for your family's business, be certain to discuss these issues with a tax adviser to determine the current state of the law and how it may affect your planning.

CHARACTERISTICS OF A FAMILY LLC

The LLC has significant estate planning advantages over the family S corporation, which had been the entity of choice for the family business until the LLC laws became so widespread. The LLC is beneficial to the family business owner because it provides the tax benefits of a limited partnership (only one level of taxation and tremendous flexibility in allocating income to the various owners) and can prevent the transfer of voting rights to individuals outside the family (e.g., through restrictions in the Operating Agreement). Senior members of family businesses desire to maintain control of their business within the family. Because LLCs allow for different classes of Members and Managers, ownership interests can be transferred to younger family members, while older family members can retain management control.

When this approach is used to structure a family business, the tax issue discussed in Chapter 18 as to the proper classification of the LLC as a partnership or corporation can be an issue. The family LLC may be deemed to possess the corporate characteristic of centralized management. However, free transferability of interests usually is not a characteristic of family business entities due to agreements restricting the owners from transferring their interests. The third characteristic of corporate forms, which is limited liability, is also generally a characteristic of family LLCs. Family LLCs do not possess continuity of life because the entity can be terminated with events such as the death or bankruptcy of one of its Members, unless there is unanimous consent (or some other consent of the Members that is permitted under state law and has been approved by the IRS) to continue the LLC.

The LLC provides limited liability to family members who ultimately become Members in the LLC.

Compared with an S corporation, an LLC will permit distributions to some senior Members and not to other junior Members (e.g., children and grandchildren).

EXAMPLE: Assume that Pa and Ma are each 50 percent members of an LLC that is run by Managers. Pa and Ma could gift Membership interests in the LLC and have such gifted interests placed in trust for the benefit of their children. The trust would be a nonvoting Member and would not be a Manager in the LLC. Ma and Pa would continue to control the LLC as Managers of the LLC. In addition, Ma and Pa would be able to take a distribution of their share of the profits of the LLC and not be required to make corresponding distributions to the trusts for their children. If the company was an S corporation, there would have to be pro rata distributions of income to Ma and Pa as well as to the trust.

THE FAMILY PARTNERSHIP TAX RULES: INTERNAL REVENUE CODE SECTION 704(e)

When forming a family LLC, it is important to be familiar with the family partnership rules found in Section 704(e) of the Internal Revenue Code. Although an Operating Agreement will generally discuss the allocation of profits and losses among Members, special income allocation rules are provided when a donee owns a capital interest in a partnership, or an LLC taxed as a partnership, where that capital is a material income-producing factor. (See the sample Operating Agreement and the annotations in the "For Your Notebook" section of Chapter 3.) In that case, if the donee is a member of the donor's family, the IRS will reallocate the income of the LLC unless the Operating Agreement provides for both of the following:

1. *Reasonable Compensation for the Services of the Donor/Member.* Reasonable compensation is generally measured by what an unrelated person would earn for the same services. If a parent and coowner of the LLC works 65 hours a week as a skilled manager in a family manufacturing business, but only draws

a $100-a-week salary, the IRS will challenge the arrangement. The low salary would effectively result in the transfer of more earnings to the children who received gifts of Membership interests in the LLC from the parent. This would occur because the parent's low salary reduces the LLC's deductions, hence increasing the profits to be distributed to all Members. There is some range in which a salary may or may not be deemed fair so some degree of flexibility is possible.

TIP: If you become involved in this type of planning, the old tax-planning maxim should be your guiding light: "Cows get fat, pigs get slaughtered." You might be able to take a salary that is somewhat less than you believe you should earn, but you should not be so unreasonable as to expose the entire LLC arrangement to IRS attack.

TIP: If you believe that any family member's salary could be challenged, take steps to document and support it. Save copies of industry or trade organization salary and compensation services, use a time clock, or maintain time records to prove the actual hours worked, and so on.

In a family business, the opposite type of planning can also involve paying the child/employee an excessive salary to transfer wealth. This situation is subject to the same reasonable compensation limitations as the preceding scenario with the parent who takes an unreasonably low salary.

2. *Donee's Allocation of Income.* The donee does not receive an allocation of income attributable to the gifted capital in an amount proportionately greater than the portion of the donor's share that is attributable to his or her capital.

EXAMPLE: Parent gives Child 10 percent of the Membership interests in an LLC. Profits, after reasonable salaries for the year, are $50,000. Child must receive a $5,000 distribution and Parent $45,000. If Parent gives Child no distribution, the IRS may disallow the transaction claiming that Parent never really gave a gift of the Membership interest to Child.

If this rule is not followed and accounted for in the LLC's Operating Agreement, the IRS will reallocate the income of the LLC to make reasonable allowances for services provided by the donor. The purpose behind Section 704(e) of the Code is to prevent an assignment of income from noncapital items, such as salary, to family members.

THREE DISCOUNTS ON VALUING LLC MEMBERSHIP INTERESTS FOR GIFT AND ESTATE TAXATION

Valuation Discounts

A significant incentive for using an LLC is the leveraging made possible by valuation discounts for gifting purposes. The gift tax value of transferred property is its fair market value as of the date of the gift, and the property transferred is the Membership interest, not the underlying LLC assets. Accordingly, the significant limitations inherent in LLC interests can justify transfer-tax saving valuation discounts. This issue is described in detail in Chapter 19.

Lack of Control Discount

Generally, a transferee of a minority Membership interest in an LLC has no power to control the LLC's management. A buyer would have paid less for a noncontrolling interest in an entity than for an outright ownership and control of the underlying assets. Therefore, the gift tax value of the LLC interest should be reduced accordingly.

Although the general concept of a discount for lack of control is well established, until recently the Internal Revenue Service took the position that a minority or lack-of-control discount was not available in a family-controlled entity. The IRS finally agreed that a minority discount was available even though family members as a unit controlled the entity. This ruling involved a simultaneous transfer of a 20 percent stock interest to five children. The IRS concluded that each 20 percent interest was to be valued as a separate asset without regard to family relationships. The benefits of this ruling should extend to LLCs as well.

Lack of Marketability

A partial interest in a family-controlled entity can be extremely difficult, if not impossible, to sell. This lack of marketability should be factored in when determining a gift tax value of a transferred LLC interest. The lack of marketability discount has two components. The first is the absence of a ready market for selling the LLC interest to third-party buyers.

In addition, a Member's inability to withdraw from the LLC (i.e., a "lock-in" discount) must be considered. Both state law and LLC Operating Agreements often restrict a Member's ability to sell, transfer, withdraw, or "put" the Membership interest to the LLC. Such restrictions would clearly reduce the purchase price of an LLC interest sold in an arm's length transaction.

In the context of a family-controlled entity, however, this factor may be affected by one of the more complex provisions of the tax laws: Internal Revenue Code Section 2704(b). This section provides that certain restrictions on transferring interests imposed by the Operating Agreement must be disregarded for gift or estate tax valuation purposes unless they are no more restrictive than those that would otherwise apply under state law.

Several approaches are available to avoid the Internal Revenue Code Section 2704(b) restrictions and thus maximize the marketability discount. For example, the LLC can be formed in a state with favorable statutory provisions. The general rule is that in the absence of any provision in the Operating Agreement to the contrary, a Member may withdraw from the LLC on not less than six months' written notice and receive the fair value of his or her Membership interest which is usually based on the right to share in LLC distributions. For an LLC formed in a state that has adopted this general rule, any limitation in the Operating Agreement on a Member's ability to liquidate such interests is more restrictive than state law and Section 2704(b) would apply.

If a particular state does not follow this general rule, then a Member may withdraw from an LLC at the time or on the occurrence of events specified in the Operating Agreement, but the statute does not expressly allow a Member to withdraw in the absence of a restriction in the Operating Agreement. Therefore, limitations on the ability of a Member to withdraw that are in an Operating Agreement would appear to be no more restrictive than state law and as a result,

Internal Revenue Code Section 2704(b) should not apply. This would allow a large valuation discount.

As an alternative, it may be possible to avoid the complexities of Internal Revenue Code Section 2704(b) by relying on limitations placed on an assignee of a Membership interest. The general rule is that the assignment of a Membership interest does not entitle the assignee to become or to exercise any rights of a Member. An assignee becomes a Member only as provided in the Operating Agreement or on the written consent of all Members. If the assignee is not a Member, the assignee has no statutory right to withdraw from the LLC. Limitations in an Operating Agreement on an assignee's right to withdraw from the LLC thus would not be more restrictive than those under state law.

If Internal Revenue Code Section 2704(b) applies, the valuation discount is reduced. However, it appears that only the lock-in component of the lack of marketability discount would be unavailable. The minority discount and the general lack of marketability discount should remain available.

The Operating Agreement should be structured to minimize the impact of Section 2704(b). In the final analysis, however, the tax and nontax benefits of the LLC still will be available, Section 2704(b) notwithstanding.

Range of Discounts

Because the valuation of interests in closely held entities is very subjective, it is difficult to precisely determine the discount in any given situation. Nevertheless, it should be substantial for any Membership interest.

The tax court typically approves valuation discounts in the range of 20 percent to 50 percent. Although many of these cases involve closely held corporations, the reasoning should be applicable to LLCs as well. Valuation discounts are described in detail in Chapter 19.

ANNUAL EXCLUSION GIFTING WITH FAMILY LLCs

The current federal tax law allows every person to make annual gifts of up to $10,000 to any other person each year without incurring a gift tax. Husband and wife can elect to have one spouse's $10,000 annual exclusion applied to the other spouse's gift. Thus if a husband makes a $20,000 gift to a child, the wife can elect to use her $10,000 annual exclusion so that the entire $20,000 gift is covered by both spouses' annual exclusions. To qualify for the $10,000 annual gift tax exclusion, the gift must be of a present interest. A present interest is defined to be "an unrestricted right to the immediate use, possession, or enjoyment of property or the income of property" (Treas. Reg. § 25.2503-3(b)). The gift of an LLC interest may be a present interest for purposes of the annual exclusion even though a donee may not receive management rights or participate in the determination of when to make distributions from the LLC to its owners.

PLANNING OPPORTUNITY: Peter and Emily own a $2,000,000 piece of real estate and they want to gift LLC Membership interests to their three children. The annual exclusion and spousal gift splitting would permit an annual gift of $20,000 to each child, or an aggregate of $60,000 of Membership interests each year without gift tax consequences. Peter and Emily could contribute the $2,000,000 piece of real estate to an LLC and gift Membership interests in the LLC to the children.

If a valuation discount of one-third can be justified for the gifted LLC Membership interest, a 1.5 percent Membership interest could be given to each child each year. Effectively, an interest allocable to $30,000 of LLC assets (1.5% of $2,000,000) would have a $20,000 gift tax value. Thus, gifts of Membership interests allocable to $90,000 of LLC assets (rather than $60,000) could be transferred to the three children, fully covered by the gift tax annual exclusions, as follows:

1.5% interest (before discounts)	= $30,000
Less: ⅓ discount	(10,000)
Value of gift	= $20,000

No gift taxes would be owed as a result of Peter's and Emily's $10,000 annual gift tax exclusions.

UNIFIED CREDIT

The unified credit for estates of decedents dying after 1992 is $192,800. It is subtracted from the taxpayer's estate and gift tax liability. Generally, the unified credit permits an individual to leave up to $600,000 of assets to any person or persons without paying federal estate taxes on this amount. As an alternative, this credit may be used to offset gift taxes during one's lifetime. To the extent this credit is exhausted during one's lifetime to avoid gift taxes, it is not available to avoid estate taxes. It can be very effectively used to transfer substantial assets out of one's estate. The leveraging effect of using an LLC is even more dramatic when the $600,000 unified credit exemption equivalent is used.

PLANNING OPPORTUNITY: Using the preceding example where Peter and Emily transfer a $2,000,000 piece of real estate to an LLC, they could each transfer a 45% Membership interest to their three children. The value of this transfer before discounts would be $900,000. Again, assuming a one-third discount can be justified, the value of the gift would be decreased to $600,000 and would be fully covered by each spouse's $600,000 unified credit exemption equivalent. This is exemplified as follows:

45% interest (before discounts)	= $900,000
Less: ⅓ discount	= (300,000)
Value of gift	= $600,000

Effectively, Emily and Peter would have transferred $1,800,000 of assets in the aggregate without paying gift taxes due to their combined $600,000 unified credit exemption equivalents.

LLCs COMPARE FAVORABLY TO TRUSTS

Trusts are one of the most common entities used in family estate and business planning. Where interests in family business are going to be given to a child (even one of adult age), parents frequently make the gifts to a trust. When this approach is used, the parent can remove the value of the family business interest from the estate while still assuring that someone other than the child has control over the asset. This person is the trustee who manages the trust, and depending on the provisions in the trust agreement (the legal document the you would have a lawyer draft to state what the trust should do), control the distributions of income to the child. Trusts are used not only to control a child's access to money, but also to help protect the child's assets against divorce and even from creditors.

When properly used, an LLC can offer benefits similar to those of a trust. But an LLC has one very substantial advantage over the use of trusts in family estate and business planning. To realize the benefits of the trust, it must be irrevocable. This generally means that you will have no right to change the trust in the future if circumstances warrant. An LLC is far more flexible since, subject to the various tax restrictions discussed in this chapter, you and the other Members can vote to change the LLC Operating Agreement at any time, and as often as you wish.

An LLC can substitute in some instance for the benefits obtainable through a trust because the Managers of the LLCs, subject to the family partnership rules of Internal Revenue Code Section 704(e) discussed earlier, can control the distributions to be made to the Members. As discussed in Chapter 2 and elsewhere, an LLC can provide substantial benefits in protecting Membership interests from creditors and an ex-spouse by preventing these outsiders from becoming substitute Members.

There may also be an income tax advantage to the use of an LLC rather than a trust for holding interests in a family business. Trust income is taxed very quickly at the highest marginal tax brackets. Broader, and hence more favorable, tax brackets apply to individuals who would own LLC Membership interests in the family business.

SUMMARY

The LLC may be the ideal entity to form a family business. The LLC may be the preferred entity because it provides the tax benefits of a partnership, the limited liability of a corporation and flexibility of control which is important to the senior members of the family.

In the context of family LLCs, it is important to examine the family partnership rules found in Section 704(e) of the Code so that the IRS will not reallocate the LLC's income.

In addition, Section 2704(b) of the Code must be examined in determining the value of a Membership interest in LLC. Membership interest in an LLC may be an ideal vehicle for gift-giving purposes because the donor of the gift may be entitled to take minority and lack of marketability discounts on the gifted Membership interests to enable him or her to gift more than the true value of the gifted interest. This can be a terrific vehicle in estate planning by leveraging the use of one's gift tax annual exclusions and/or unified credit.

13 USING LIMITED LIABILITY COMPANIES IN ESTATE PLANNING

The LLC presents a tremendous opportunity for many taxpayers involved in estate planning. The flexibility and unique combination of characteristics of the LLC make it an ideal entity to use in many estate planning transactions. You don't have to be a Rockefeller to benefit from these. Even if your estate is under the $600,000 estate tax deduction (called the "unified credit") you can still benefit from using an LLC to minimize probate problems and costs, make it easier and cheaper to give gifts to your children or other heirs, and so on. For the wealthy taxpayers, the ability of an LLC to qualify for marketability and other valuation discounts (these topics were introduced in Chapter 12) makes the LLC an ideal vehicle. This chapter will illustrate many of the benefits that the use of an LLC can provide for estate planning.

OVERVIEW OF LLCs FOR ESTATE PLANNING

An LLC is a hybrid entity combining the best forms of corporate and partnership characteristics. A properly formed LLC should provide all Members with limited liability. From a tax perspective, the LLC provides tremendous flexibility since it will generally be treated as a partnership for federal income tax purposes if properly structured. From an estate planning perspective, the LLC is a vital tool since planning for creditor protection or asset protection has become an integral part of many estate plans in our highly litigious society.

Since an LLC is generally treated as a partnership, the Members of an LLC have tremendous flexibility to allocate income and expenses as they desire, as long as those allocations are in accord with the partnership tax rules (such allocations must have "substantial economic effect" under Section 704(b) of the Code and the regulations thereunder; see Chapter 16). The LLC is an opportunity for clients to "have their cake and eat it too."

USES IN ESTATE PLANNING

The combined advantages of limited liability and flexibility in allocations are only two of the LLC's characteristics that help make it a valuable tool in estate planning. The following discussion will highlight a number of applications of an LLC to various estate planning situations.

Ownership and Gift Program for Small Real Estate Investment Property

A common estate planning strategy for many clients is to make gifts of minority interests in a second home or small rental real property. In the past, a typical approach would have been to transfer the property to a general partnership or limited partnership and thereafter gift interests in the partnership to one's children or other desired donees. The partnership technique was used to achieve divisibility of the otherwise indivisible real estate holdings. This avoided the necessity of creating numerous deeds each year to make the necessary transfers.

An LLC offers a substantial advantage in this regard. LLC statutes allow for the appointment of a Manager to manage the property as contrasted with a general partnership where every partner has the right to participate in the management and affairs of the partnership. This is a substantial advantage if a parent is giving minority interests over a period of time and wishes to retain some measure of control over the property. This can also be quite useful even following the parent's complete gift of all of his or her interest in the property because a particular child or family member can be designated as the Manager. In some states a Manager does not have to be a Member; thus, a parent can gift his or her entire Membership interest in the LLC and still remain as the LLC's Manager. This can avoid potential problems (e.g., who should decide whether the property should be sold, refinanced, improved). The control over management that an LLC allows is a critical benefit. In this situation, the "icing on the cake" is that the family members will also have limited liability in the LLC as part of the same transaction.

CAUTION: Be very careful if you are the parent making the gifts and wish to remain the sole Manager. If either the Operating Agreement or your conduct makes it appear that you have reserved excessive control or rights (e.g., to allocate almost arbitrarily between the children the income from the property), the IRS may challenge the transaction and pull the value of the LLC's assets back into your estate.

PLANNING OPPORTUNITY: If Pa and Ma have a limited liability company in which each of them are 50 percent Members, they could set up two classes of Membership. Class A would be voting Membership interests and represent 1 percent of the total equity of the LLC. Class B would be nonvoting Membership interests that would represent 99 percent of the equity of the entity. Pa and Ma could then gift the 99 percent Class B interest to their children and/or trusts for their primary benefit. Pa and Ma would continue to control the entire entity as the sole owners of the 1 percent Class A voting Membership interest. In this way, they could determine what salaries and bonuses they are entitled to, whether the property should be sold, whether distributions should be made and all other company decisions. This would effectively transfer their entire equity interest in the LLC to their children and/or trusts for their benefit while Pa and Ma still would retain full control over the entity. They would also be entitled to reduce the value of the gift due to lack of control and marketability discounts.

A common transaction involves gifting a family vacation home to the children over several years. In the past, rather than execute a multitude of deeds each year, the property would be transferred to a family general partnership and the partnership interests would be assigned each year in amounts designed to effect gifts of $10,000 (or $20,000 where joint gifts were used) so there would be no gift tax because of the $10,000 annual gift tax exclusion. A similar approach can and should be used with an LLC as the ownership vehicle, with the benefits of limited liability, a statutory definition of a Manager, and so forth.

Ownership of More Significant Real Estate Used in a Family Business

A common planning technique has been to separate business real estate from the family operating business, transfer the real estate to another entity, and make gifts of minority interests in that real estate entity to younger generations. This transaction is typically followed by a lease of the real estate to the family business. The rental payments received by the LLC from the family business can then be used to fund educational payments and other needs of the younger family members. When real estate or other significant assets are to be acquired for business operations, it is crucial that proper planning take place to protect these assets. Generally, you should not acquire real estate in the same entity that is being used for the operating business. If the operating business encounters problems such as being unable to maintain a profitable business, or encounters a devastating lawsuit, the creditors and/or judgment holders of the corporation will be able to satisfy their claims out of the assets of the business, which would include the real estate or other significant assets.

The best approach is to have the real estate owned separately from the operating business in some form of limited liability entity, which would then lease the real estate to the operating entity. Generally, until the advent of the LLC, this entity has either taken the form of an S corporation or limited partnership with the corporate general partner. The determination of which entity to use will depend largely on the tax ramifications of each alternative. From a tax standpoint, it is important to own the real estate in an entity that will permit the tax benefits of owning the real estate to flow through to the individual entrepreneurs.

If there are more than one piece of real estate or other significant assets, the best planning is to have a separate entity for each piece of real estate or significant asset. For example, if two warehouses are used in the business, then separate limited liability entities should own each of the warehouse premises. Each entity would then lease the premises owned by it to the entity operating the business. Thus, if there is a problem with one piece of real estate (e.g., tort liabilities, environmental hazards), the liabilities of that real estate will not negatively impact the other piece of real estate. Having multiple entities will add complexity to the business structure; however, this enhances the liability protection of the business owners.

In many cases, these separate limited liability entities have been structured as S corporations insulate them from potential liability of the business property (e.g., environmental problems). There are several difficulties in utilizing an S corporation. For one, there can be only one class of stock in an S corporation. Therefore, a distribution of income to one shareholder can only be made if there was a simultaneous pro rata distribution to the other shareholders. This scenario frequently was disruptive to the estate planning because parents would typically want distributions for their share but not want to make corresponding distributions to their children's shares. In addition, only a special type of trust can hold stock in an S corporation. The trust would require mandatory distributions of income each year to the child and could be only held for one beneficiary's benefit during the term of the trust.

Another significant disadvantage with regard to real estate is that in an S corporation losses flow through to the individual shareholder's tax returns, but can only be utilized to the extent of a shareholder's basis in his or her stock plus loans made to the corporation by that shareholder. If an S corporation borrows monies, the shareholder receives no credit in his or her basis for such borrowings and therefore is limited in utilizing deductions on his or her tax return. In a partnership or an LLC, the individual partners or Members are entitled to take losses on their tax returns to the extent of their basis in their partnership or Membership interest plus their allocable share of company liabilities.

EXAMPLE: If an S corporation acquires a building for $500,000 and the shareholders make no capital contributions to the S corporation, but rather the S corporation borrows $500,000 that is personally guaranteed by the shareholders, the shareholders would not be entitled to deduct any losses on their individual tax returns because they have no basis in their stock and are not entitled to take losses against the liabilities of the S corporation even if they personally guarantee them. On the other hand, if the entity were a partnership or an LLC, the partners or Members would be entitled to deduct losses up to their allocable share of the liabilities of the entity so that they would be permitted to take another $500,000 in deductions allocated among the Members and partners on their tax returns.

In most other instances, they have been structured as family limited partnership arrangements. Under this structure, an S corporation would typically be formed to be the general partner and the limited partnership itself must be formed. This required two separate legal entities and all the attendant complications, costs, organizational documents, and annual tax filing requirements. It was also prudent to fund the corporate general partner in order to reduce the risk that the IRS would tax the limited partnership as a corporation resulting in double taxation. This funding element exposes more assets of the family members to liabilities of the limited partnership.

EXAMPLE: If a limited partnership is structured with a corporate general partner and no individual general partners, the corporate general partner would need to be funded to help ensure that it will be taxed as a partnership. If the partners of the partnership contributed $10 million, then the corporate general partner would need to have a net worth of $1 million. Therefore, an additional $1 million of assets is exposed to the claims of the partnership's creditors.

In these types of transaction, the LLC offers a simplified method of obtaining the key objective of limited liability and pass-through of income to the lower age family members.

The LLC eliminates most of the structural problems of the S corporation. There is tremendous flexibility in who can be a member as well as no problems with the prohibition against two classes of stock in an S corporation. Compared with limited partnerships, it streamlines the structure by only requiring one entity. It also eliminates the funding requirement of the corporate general partner, thereby exposing less assets to the claims of creditors.

A common technique in such transactions has always been to argue for the most substantial minority interests discount and/or lack of marketability discount possible on the real estate interests transferred by gift to the children and/or other donees. It is not certain how the courts will treat an LLC with respect to minority and lack of marketability discounts. The limitations on participation in management and control, which are typical of the limited partner, are not quite identical to that of a Member of an LLC. However, just as with a limited partnership, the contractual arrangements between the parties (an Operating Agreement with respect to the LLC and a Limited Partnership Agreement with respect to the limited partnership) can provide substantial restrictions and limitations on the donee's ability to participate in management operations and transfer his or her Membership interest. Therefore, contractually similar positions should be achievable, and the courts likely will recognize the same application of discounts for gifted interests in these family LLCs.

Care must be taken to assure that the Manager's powers in an LLC are not so broad as to prevent the technical completion of the gift, or to otherwise pull the asset transferred back into the parent's/donor's estate.

EXAMPLE—SAMPLE CLAUSE: Consider the following language: "Notwithstanding anything in this Operating Agreement to the contrary, should any provision of this Operating Agreement, or any act of the Parties, result in a violation of the family partnership provisions of Internal Revenue Code Section 704(e) and the regulations and cases thereunder, the Manager may amend this Agreement, or take any other actions reasonably necessary to prevent such violation, or to correct such violation."

The clause shown in the Example gives the Manager the right to make changes necessary for the transaction to be respected for tax purposes. The relevant section of the tax law permits a child, for example, to receive a gift of an LLC Membership interest, and for this to be respected for tax purposes, as long as certain requirements are met. The child must truly own the interest in the LLC and capital must be a material income-producing factor for the LLC. In a real estate LLC, for example, the property (capital) will be the only income-producing factor unless the parent is providing substantial services. This rule also requires that the parent be paid reasonable compensation for any services such parent provides to the LLC. Where services will be provided, the Operating Agreement should try to assure a payment of a fair compensation for such services.

In summary, an LLC will afford limited liability to the owners of real estate (where such real estate is owned by the LLC) and expose fewer assets to potential liabilities than utilizing a limited partnership with a corporate general partner. The LLC is much more streamlined than a limited partnership with a corporate general partner and should entitle the donor gifting LLC Membership interests to the same type of discounting features available for a limited partnership while allowing the donor to control the LLC as the Manager.

Closely Held Operating Businesses

A substantial number of closely held businesses are organized as S corporations. In fact, since the 1986 Tax Reform Act repealed the *General Utilities* doctrine, few closely held operating businesses have been organized in any other manner. (The effect of the repeal of the *General Utilities* doctrine is that a C corporation selling appreciated assets must recognize a gain on the sale, which was not the case before such repeal. There is likely to be a second tax on liquidating the corporation and distributing the corporation's assets to its shareholders.) Primary objectives of using the S corporation structure have been to obtain limited liability and to avoid the double taxation. The latter "benefit" of avoiding double taxation was a fallacy in many cases since the owners could withdraw most, if not all, the profits from a closely held C corporation as salary and avoid double taxation. In such a scenario, however, there is the risk that the IRS could claim a portion of the compensation is unreasonable and reclassify such unreasonable compensation as a dividend. The unreasonable compensation portion would be subject to double taxation. In addition, on liquidation of the C corporation, there would be a double taxation, whereas an S corporation (which is an S corporation from inception) would have only one level of taxation on liquidation. Another benefit of using an S corporation is the avoidance of an accumulated earnings tax. This is a second tax on the C corporation's accumulated earnings, which the IRS deems to be, in effect, dividends that should have been paid its shareholders.

For the estate planner, S corporations have created substantial problems and complexities. Where S corporation stock is owned by someone who wishes to transfer by gift shares to a trust for the benefit of a child as part of an estate plan, the Qualified Subchapter S Trust (QSST) rules would have to be addressed. These rules present substantial complications because multiple beneficiaries and trusts that accumulate income would not be permitted as S corporation shareholders. To be a QSST, a special election would need to be filed by the beneficiary of the trust within seventy-five (75) days of receipt of the stock by the trust. Under the election, the beneficiary would state that he or she will report all income, losses, and credits attributable to the stock owned by the trust in his or her individual tax return. Tax advisers frequently neglect to file this election. If such failure occurs, the results can be dire as the S election is terminated by such failure. In the event of the death of a shareholder, issues may arise as to the period of time for which an estate can hold S corporation stock without causing the termination of the corporation's S election. See Chapter 2.

In addition to these estate planning complications, there are numerous operating difficulties in the S corporation context. For instance, different classes of stock (other than classes that differ only with respect to voting rights) cannot be issued. Thus, the traditional recapitalization or different tiers of ownership with different rights which are often favored in many estate planning techniques cannot be used with S corporation. In addition, if these were gifts of stock to children and the donor wanted to make distributions of income to himself or herself, the corporation would be required to make a proportionate distribution of income to the children to avoid running afoul of the prohibition against two classes of stock in an S corporation.

The LLC provides a useful alternative to the preceding scenario where more than one owner is involved in the entity. An LLC can provide the same limited liability and the flow-through tax treatment that the S corporation provides. Yet, the many restrictions applicable to the S corporations, such as the limited number of shareholders, the limited types of trusts that could own the stock, and the one class of stock requirements are not applicable. Therefore, the LLC creates a substantial advantage over the use of S corporations, particularly where the value of the donor's estate will grow to a substantial size and complex estate planning techniques are necessary to reduce estate taxes.

NOTE: Many business owners are reluctant to make outright transfers of ownership interests to children and other family members for fear of the child getting divorced, dying, not being mature enough to manage the asset, incurring creditor problems, facing tax liens, and/or filing bankruptcy. Therefore, they generally opt to transfer the ownership interest into a trust. With an S corporation, this trust must be carefully tailored to meet stringent IRS requirements. The trust can only be set up for the benefit of one beneficiary and must provide for mandatory distributions of income. There is limited flexibility in structuring the trust to avoid many of the problems mentioned earlier. With a limited liability company, the trust can be drawn with a wide variety of provisions to deal with the various scenarios previously mentioned.

CAUTION: LLCs are not currently recognized in all states. Therefore, an LLC should not be utilized if business is to be conducted in a state that does not have LLC legislation in effect.

Operating Agreement—Buy-Sell Agreements

A truly important component of gifting of a Membership interest to a child or any other relative is to have properly structured buy-sell provisions in the Operating Agreement. At the very least, this agreement should cover such issues as the ability of the donee to transfer his or her interest, the death of the Member, sales in violation of the agreement, and involuntary transfers of the Member's interest such as incident to a divorce or bankruptcy.

The following three buy-sell provisions can be used as a structure when there is a gift of a Membership interest to a child:

1. *Voluntary Transfers.* The child would not be permitted to transfer his or her Membership interest without the consent of a majority in interest of the remaining Members. This provision ensures that the LLC will not have the corporate characteristic of free transferability of interest. It has the further benefit of limiting the child's ability to transfer his or her interest. The provision could further state that if the child receives a bona fide offer, then the child is to offer the Membership interest back to the LLC first and the remaining Members second. The LLC and then the remaining Members would have an option to buy the child's Membership interest at the lesser of the bona fide offer price or 50 percent of an agreed-on value (or formula value). The rationale behind this provision is to give the limited liability company or the remaining Members the option to buy the Membership interest at the lower of these two prices.

The terms of the buyout by the LLC or the remaining Members could be either the terms of the bona fide offer or a 10-year note providing for the lowest rate of interest to avoid the imputation of interest by the Internal Revenue Service, whichever the purchaser party (the LLC or the remaining Members) desires.

For example, if the agreed-on value of the member's interest is $100,000 and the child receives an offer for $200,000 payable in the form of a 5-year note calling for 10 percent interest, then the LLC would have the option to buy the child's interest at $50,000 (50% of the $100,000.00, agreed-on value) and either over the 5 years with 10 percent interest or 10 years with the lowest rate of interest to avoid imputation of interest by the IRS, whichever the LLC or remaining Members desire.

2. *Involuntary Transfer or Sale in Violation of the Agreement.* If the Member's interest falls into the hands of a creditor or judgment holder or the child sells an

interest in violation of the agreement, then the LLC first and the remaining Members second could have options to buy the child's interest at the lower of what is actually paid for the Member's interest or 50 percent of the agreed-on value. The terms can be whatever the terms of the purchase are (if any) or the 10-year note with the lowest rate of interest to avoid imputation of interest by the IRS. Even if the LLC or the remaining Members do not exercise their options to purchase the child's Membership interest, the transferee of the child's Membership interest will not be permitted to participate in the management of the LLC.

3. *Death of the Child.* If the child were to die, then the LLC first and the remaining Members second could have options to buy the child's Membership interest at the agreed-on value (or formula price). This purchase can be funded with life insurance. If it is funded with life insurance, then the agreement can provide that to the extent of the life insurance funding, all the proceeds would be used to buy the child's Membership interest. To the extent of any shortfall, then the remaining purchase price could be paid over 10 years with the lowest rate of interest to avoid imputation of interest by the IRS.

Unique Flexibility of the LLC Facilitates Estate Planning

The flexibility that an Operating Agreement can provide allows the head of a family (a parent) who may be planning a gift program to retain control over the company's management, restrict the sale of Membership interests to third parties, and to determine the rights of the Members to distributions. When compared with a general partnership for estate planning purposes, the LLC is a clear winner. The tax consequences should generally be the same, but limited liability can be obtained with little extra effort.

Comparison of LLCs to Trusts

One of the most commonly used estate planning tools is the transfer by the donor of an asset or business to an inter vivos trust. If the trust is a "grantor trust," the grantor (the person who creates the trust) will be taxed on all the trust's income. In contrast, by using an LLC, there is an allocation of income to all the Members so long as the family partnership rules of Code Section 704(e) are complied with. If the trust is not a grantor trust, the income of the trust will be taxed to the trust and thus subject to the applicable tax rates for trusts. It may be desirable to have the income realized by the trust to be taxed at individual rates and not at the trust rates. To achieve this, the trustee will be required to distribute the income to the beneficiaries. This causes the income to be taxed to the beneficiaries at their respective tax rates. However, you may not want your children to receive a distribution of income. LLCs avoid these difficulties since the income recognized by the LLC is passed through to its Members, causing the income to be taxed at the Member's individual rates without having to distribute the income to all or certain Members.

A popular estate planning tool is the irrevocable trust. Although there are many benefits of this popular tool, there are a few important restrictions. This type of trust cannot be amended to deal with the changing environment (e.g., change in relationships). LLCs can deal with a changing business environment better than a trustee who has strict fiduciary restrictions. Another advantage that an LLC has over an irrevocable trust is that the donor may retain managerial control over transferred assets.

LLCs Are Useful to Avoid Ancillary Probate

An interest in an LLC is deemed to be personal property. This can be important for a nonresident, since the ownership of intangible personal property should not subject the estate of a nonresident decedent to ancillary probate proceedings to effect the transfer of an LLC interest. This will also affect the manner of property transferring an LLC interest as a gift (or for other purposes).

Consequences of Death on LLC Ownership

The death of a Member of an LLC will generally cause the termination of the LLC unless all the remaining Members (or some other allowable percentage) agree to continue and unless the Operating Agreement provides otherwise. Assuming that the LLC is continued, then the Member's executor or administrator may exercise all the Member's rights for the purpose of settling the estate or administering his or her property, including any power under an Operating Agreement of an assignee.

VALUATION OF TRANSFERRED LIMITED LIABILITY COMPANY INTERESTS

When valuing an asset for estate or gift tax purposes, the value is the asset's fair market value at the time of the gift or the time that the item can be included in the decedent's estate. The fair market value is the value at which a purchaser would pay for the interest to a seller, neither being under any compulsion to buy or sell, each with reasonable knowledge of the relevant facts.

Valuation Discounts

As noted in Chapter 19, a significant incentive for using an LLC in an estate planning context is the significant leveraging made possible by valuation discounts. The two primary types of discounts are lack of control/minority discounts and lack of marketability discounts. These discounts range from 20 percent to 50 percent. Chapter 19 will focus on the use of discounts in detail.

Code Sections 2701 and 2704

Internal Revenue Code Section 2701 was enacted to prevent a donor from transferring an asset to a partnership while retaining distribution or liquidation rights that would cause a decrease in the value of the gift. This section should also apply to the gift of a Membership interest in an LLC. This provision provides that where a donor transfers an equity interest in a partnership (or in an LLC) to a member of the donor's family, the gift would have a greater value for gift and estate tax purposes than it would otherwise have had. This depresses the value of the donor's retained interest in the same enterprise. To accomplish this goal, the subtraction method of valuation in determining the value of the gift is used. An exception to this Code section is found where the interest retained by the donor is of the same class as the gifted interest. The impact of Internal Revenue Code Section 2704(b) also imposes restrictions on transferring an interest and the amount and availability of the lack of marketability discount. Chapter 19 focuses on this provision.

GRATs AND LLCs

A common estate planning technique for the wealthy is to use techniques to make large gifts at discounted rates. The Grantor Retained Annuity Trust (GRAT) is one such technique. GRATs can be used with gifts of securities, interests in family businesses (Chapter 12), and even other assets. A GRAT, in simple terms, can be illustrated as follows. Parent has a substantial estate and wishes to reduce it through a large gift to child. Parent makes a gift of $1 million of securities into a special trust called a GRAT. If the gift had been made outright to the child, the gift would have been valued at the $1 million fair value of the securities and the parent would have had to pay a substantial gift tax. If the gift is instead made to a GRAT, the parent could reserve the right to receive the income from the GRAT for a period of years, say 3, 5, 10, or even more years. The more years for which the parent reserves the right to receive the income from the gift, the longer the child will have to wait to receive the benefit of the assets, and hence the lower the value of the gift for gift tax purposes. If the parent reserved a right to income for a sufficient number of years, the value of the gift could be reduced to $600,000 or less. This could enable the parent to use the parents' unified credit and not pay any current gift tax cost.

When planning for GRATs, gifts of LLC Membership interests could be used. Membership interests in the LLC can be given to the GRAT. The income from the LLC's assets would fund the payment of the income stream to the parent. On the end of the term of the GRAT, the LLC Membership interests could then be distributed to the child.

SUMMARY

The LLC entity is an estate planning vehicle as well as a form of business entity. If an LLC is structured so that it is taxed as a partnership, the Members of the LLC will have the flexibility to make allocations of income and expenses as long as they follow certain criteria set forth in the Code and Regulations.

If senior family members desire to gift a portion of investment real estate, they could gift Membership interests in an LLC that owns the real property instead of gifting a direct interest in the property. The donor would be able to take discounts on the gifted interest for minority interests and lack of marketability and would not be required to execute a new deed when each gift is made.

In addition, the LLC provides substantial benefits relating to the gifting of ownership interests over the S corporation. If a donor wishes to make a transfer to a trust for the donee's benefit, there are specific restrictions on the types of trusts that can be used if the gifted interest is S corporation stock. These restrictions do not exist in the context of LLCs.

Moreover, a donor of an LLC Membership interest who desires to retain control over the company can accomplish that objective more easily with an LLC than with other business entities.

14 USING LIMITED LIABILITY COMPANIES FOR ASSET PROTECTION

With the emergence of the LLC, an excellent and flexible structure exists for the use of the asset protection planner. The flexibility of an LLC enables the planner to structure the LLC to meet all the client's goals. By using LLCs and properly drafting the Operating Agreement, planners can provide the liability protection typically associated with corporations while also securing the benefits of partnership tax treatment.

ASSET PROTECTION IN GENERAL

Like so many good things, the more you need asset protection, the less likely it is that you are going to get it. Asset protection techniques are of less, if any, value where creditor problems have already occurred. Where lawsuits are already pending, family transfers could be disregarded as fraudulent conveyances. The moral of the story is that one should do asset protection planning before it is truly needed. Asset protection planning in advance of receiving creditors' claims merely out of fear of future creditors and claimants is acceptable for asset protection planning and should not be treated as fraudulent. Accordingly, planning to avoid the risks of possible future creditors, as opposed to probable future creditors, should not be problematic.

EXAMPLE: Mr. A knows that a judgment of $1 million has been obtained against him personally for a loan of which Mr. A is in default for nonpayment. Mr. A then transfers all his assets to an LLC owned by both Mr. A and Mrs. A hoping that the creditor will not be able to take possession of the assets transferred to the LLC. Mr. A hopes that the creditor will be allowed to take only his interest in the LLC—but not as a Member, merely as an assignee—with no management rights. The transfer by Mr. A to the LLC could be disregarded as a fraudulent conveyance because Mr. A already had notice of the judgment against him. If Mr. A transferred his assets to the LLC merely because he was paranoid about the possibility of having a creditor in the future but did not know of any such creditors at the time of the transfer, the transfer should not be disregarded.

TIP: When engaging in this type of planning, have your accountant prepare a personal financial statement. Make a good faith listing of all liabilities and claims. This can help demonstrate that, at the time of the planning, you were solvent and not making any transfers to impede creditors.

More than Asset Protection

Any steps taken to protect one's assets should also be taken for purposes other than solely asset protection. To lend the most credibility to asset protection planning, the actions taken should be consistent with one's overall personal financial and estate planning goals, the diversification of assets, and so forth. A business motive or other nonasset protection motive that can be associated with every asset protection step will give the subject transactions more credibility as nonfraudulent. Where transfers are made pursuant to an overall estate and personal financial plan, and employ commonly used, nonasset protection motivated techniques, the transactions are more likely to be respected. Nonasset protection motives should help deflect challenges that the transferer of the assets had fraudulent intentions when making the transfer.

EXAMPLE: Father transfers real estate to a family limited partnership and retains control over the corporate general partner, thus retaining control over the partnership. The children and father are the limited partners. By transferring the property to a limited partnership, it is not in his individual name to be claimed by creditors. The limited partnership structure permits control by the corporate general partner over the management of the real estate, which is essential to prevent squabbles between the numerous owners (limited partners). Children, as limited partners, cannot participate in management decisions so that the operations remain controlled by father, who is the senior person with the most substantial real estate expertise. As competence is proved by the children limited partners, a particular child may obtain certain rights, and perhaps ownership interests in the corporate general partner, thus facilitating participation in active management. Thus, the family limited partnership can provide a mechanism for transferring ownership interests to the next generation. All these nonasset protection goals are legitimate and can provide important corroboration that the transactions were intended as structured and should be respected.

The Significance of Greater Numbers of Entities

The greater the number of entities involved in the ownership of an asset, the more components into which various interests and rights in that particular asset have to be divided. Having a greater number of entities and contractual relationships makes it more difficult for a creditor to get to that asset. The option of transferring each material asset to its own separate limited partnership, LLC, or other entity in order to insulate each asset, investment, or business from the liabilities of the others, as well as from the personal assets of the owners, should be considered. For example, a single LLC owning several assets can result in all assets being attacked if only one asset becomes subject to a liability or claim. On the contrary, by forming several LLCs, each owning a particular asset, a liability may attach to one asset, but the assets owned by the other LLCs should be insulated from such liability.

EXAMPLE: If LLC A owns real properties X, Y, and Z, and a liability resulting from the LLC's ownership of property X comes into existence, all three properties (as well as any other assets of the LLC) may be available to the creditor, not just property X. However, if LLCs B, C, and D are created to hold real properties X, Y, and Z, respectively, and a liability resulting from LLC C's ownership of real property Y comes into existence, only the assets of LLC C may be available to the creditor, and real properties X and Z should be safely insulated.

If an existing LLC owns several assets and the Members decide to divide the single LLC into several separate and distinct LLCs, the issue arises as to whether the division of the existing LLC will be a termination of the LLC for tax purposes, which can have a number of potentially adverse tax consequences. For example, the LLC tax year will end, which can result in a bunching of taxable income into one year. Where cash is distributed by the LLC on its termination and the amount of such cash exceeds the Member's tax basis in the LLC, gain will be recognized by the Member. A number of other adverse tax consequences can also occur.

The LLC will not be deemed to have terminated where the successor LLCs are considered to be a continuation of the prior LLC. This will occur where the Members of the successor LLCs had interests of more than 50 percent in the capital and profits of the prior LLC. Since in most cases, there will be no significant change in ownership accompanying the restructure, this requirement should usually be satisfied and the LLC should not be deemed to have terminated as a result of the division.

EXAMPLE: A father owns a building and widget manufacturing business. He wishes to restructure the business to facilitate a gift program for estate tax purposes, assure management of the property in a centralized and professional manner, and provide a measure of protection from future unknown creditors or claimants. The building is transferred to an LLC whose interests are to be owned by the family members. The children's interests in the LLC can be owned by trusts for their benefit, rather than by the children directly. The building can be owned by one LLC and the business by a second LLC. A prospective claimant would have to challenge all the entities involved in the various structures to reach all assets. In addition, the other limitations and restrictions on a creditor's ability to attach Membership interests in an LLC, as discussed later in this chapter, would hinder the creditor in collecting any judgment.

Asset Protection and the Importance of Following Details

The best-laid plan is useless if the formalities and details are not adhered to.

EXAMPLE: If an LLC is created, but the owners essentially disregard and ignore the identity of the LLC, it will be more unlikely to withstand a challenge of a claimant creditor than an LLC where the formalities of separate entity status have been carefully respected.

The Requirement of Good Faith Effort

Where asset protection steps are contemplated, one must make a good faith effort to estimate all outstanding claims and reserve in the family business owner/transferor's name adequate assets to reasonably meet those claims and any expected costs.

TIP: Order and save copies of credit reports for both you and your business interests at the time the planning steps are to be implemented. As noted previously, you should have a qualified accountant compile a personal financial statement in accordance with applicable accounting standards to demonstrate solvency before and after any transfers.

Solvency alone may be an insufficient test to meet. Where assets are so depleted that the transaction itself is characterized as constructively fraudulent, the transfer may be set aside.

No transfer should be made with the intent to defraud creditors. No statements should be made, or actions taken, indicating such an intent to defraud.

Asset Protection and Arm's Length Transactions

Extra care must be taken when an arm's length transaction is structured. Where the rights and interests in an asset are divided, each component of the transaction should stand independently and be consummated on terms that can be demonstrated to be arm's length.

EXAMPLE: Real estate is transferred by gift to various trusts for minor children. The rent that the business will pay to the trusts is set by the trusts retaining and paying a qualified local real estate broker for a written appraisal of a fair rental price. A preferable approach may be to have the rent appraisal determined by a certified appraiser, such as a Member of the American Institute of Appraisers (MAI), who would be an arguably more objective party. Further, the trustees of the trust should save the real estate sections from several local real estate and general circulation newspapers to demonstrate the state of the market at the time the transaction was consummated.

Importance of Proper Documentation

The documentation relating to any transaction that is intended to protect assets from future unknown creditors, or between related parties, must be thorough and complete.

EXAMPLE: Where a family member is retained as a consultant by the family LLC, an independent consulting agreement with arm's length terms should be negotiated and signed. The agreement should be a full-fledged agreement with all the provisions that an agreement between unrelated parties would include. It should not be a one-page "quickie." Loans between related parties should be documented with written loan agreements (promissory notes) prepared in the same manner as independent parties would require. This means with all of the protections and provisions an unrelated party would require (e.g., only reasonable grace periods, acceleration clause, reasonable interest rate and payment schedule, and default provisions). If the collateral for a loan is real estate, a mortgage should be recorded. If the collateral is personal property, the appropriate Uniform Commercial Code Financing Statement, Form UCC-1, should be filed where appropriate.

Some Asset Protection Techniques

Some clients will transfer a portion of their assets to an offshore or foreign situs trust (e.g., a trust created outside the United States), or selected assets to a family limited partnership or a family LLC, to secure these assets as a nest egg in the event of a lawsuit or other problems. Other clients will "go all out" and attempt to transfer every asset they own, other than assets deemed exempt under state law, to foreign situs trusts, family LLCs, family limited partnerships, or other "protective" arrangements. Where the nest egg approach is used, rather than an all-out conveyance, asset protection planning is probably an appropriate objective for almost every family business owner with substantial means. Fraudulent conveyance and other issues are less of a concern with the nest egg approach since substantial assets will continue to remain in the hands of the family business owner/transferor.

Limited Partnerships Compared with Other Asset Protection Techniques

Family limited partnerships are typically one of the first entities considered when asset protection concerns are addressed. The decision to use a family limited partnership (or a FLP in conjunction with a foreign situs trust) should only be arrived at after carefully analyzing a broad range of other possible entities, and contractual arrangements, which can be beneficial. In the best of plans, different types and layers of entities and contractual relationships are utilized to build a structure for ownership and operation that is even more impervious to attack.

ASSET PROTECTION AND LLCs

The numerous benefits of a LLC make it an ideal tool for asset protection. If properly structured, an LLC will provide limited liability protection to its owners while providing pass-through partnership tax treatment. Moreover, an LLC may generally conduct any lawful business. Therefore, an LLC may be lawfully used for just about any purpose that could use a limited partnership. An LLC, however, unlike a limited partnership, does not have to have any partner personally liable for the entity's debts (e.g., a general partner).

Since many foreign jurisdictions are familiar with the LLC concept (see the discussion of the historical development of LLCs in Chapter 1), it may even be easier to implement a structure of an LLC and foreign trust than with a family limited partnership and a foreign trust.

SUMMARY

As individuals work throughout their lifetimes and accumulate substantial assets, it makes sense that they would be concerned with taking all steps possible to protect their assets. Accordingly, many successful individuals wish to do asset protection planning.

Asset protection planning generally involves removing assets from the name of one individual and instead having them owned by an entity that may be owned and/or controlled by such individual and/or family members. Having the assets owned by a separate and distinct entity, rather than by the individual, helps create a layer of protection for the assets from the claims of the individual's creditors. It is important, however, that steps taken to transfer the ownership of the assets out of one's name into separate entities also be taken for purposes other than solely asset protection. Such planning actions should be consistent with the individual's financial and estate planning goals, as well as business or other nonasset protection motives.

If steps are taken after the individual becomes aware of claims against him or her, courts may set aside such steps as fraudulent and thus treat the situation as if no transfers out of the individual's personal name have occurred, thus making the assets more reachable by creditors. Therefore, steps for asset protection planning must be taken prior to the knowledge of any claims or potential claims of creditors.

The LLC is an excellent vehicle for asset protection planning. An investor in real property, or a business owner who also owns real property on which the business operates, could transfer the property out of their individual names into an LLC. Each LLC could be owned by the transferor and family members, who would have small Membership interests. The transferor could retain control over the LLC by being its Manager. No Member of the LLC, however, would be personally liable for any of its debts and obligations arising after the transfer to the LLC. Moreover, the Manager would be able to utilize the LLC for valid business succession and/or estate planning purposes, which lends credibility to the transaction.

Ideally, separate major assets should be owned by separate LLCs. In this manner, any liabilities that are associated with one of such assets will not affect the other assets.

15 LOAN TRANSACTIONS AND LIMITED LIABILITY COMPANIES

With the increasing use of LLCs in business and investment transactions, more and more loans will be made by banks and other lenders to LLCs. What special consequences do LLCs have to loan transactions? This chapter will outline some of these issues.

WHAT LENDERS SHOULD REQUIRE FROM LLCs THAT BORROW MONEY

When anyone makes a loan to an LLC, they must take various steps to help assure that they will be repaid:

- The loan documents should include statements (called "representations and warranties") by the LLC that it is properly organized and validly existing under applicable state laws.

- The business purpose of the LLC as set forth in the LLC's Articles of Organization must be broad enough to permit the LLC to borrow funds and to use them for the intended purpose.

- The Operating Agreement should not contain restrictions preventing the loan. Also, any requirements for the approval of the loan in the Operating Agreement must be followed. In addition to the lender requesting representations as to this, the lender should insist on copies of the relevant document to be reviewed by the lender's lawyer. For example, the Operating Agreement could have special approval or voting standards for a loan transaction. The lender wants to be sure that these have been met before releasing any funds.

- Many Operating Agreements specify the amount of capital contribution which each Member will contribute to the LLC. If the lender is relying on the existence of these funds (or other assets contributed), it should be verified that they have in fact been contributed and that the loan documents specify this reliance.

- Since no Member or Manager is personally liable for loans or debts of the LLC, the lender may insist on a personal guarantee from one or all Members unless the LLC's collateral is sufficient.

- One of the advantages to Members of using the LLC entity is the asset protection benefit that a creditor can only receive an assignment of a Member's interest, not become a substitute Member, without approval of the Manager or all other Members (depending on what the Operating Agreement states).

Where a creditor receives only an assignment of a Membership interest, the creditor must report its allocable share of LLC income for tax purposes. If the LLC does not make any distribution to that Member, the creditor has what is called "phantom income"—income that creates a real out-of-pocket cost, but no cash. No lender wants to find itself in this position. Therefore, where a lender wishes to have a security interest in a Membership interest in an LLC to secure repayment of its loan, it must be certain that right is carefully limited to a right to receive actual distributions only, and not to become an assignee of a Membership interest.

- Where a lender loans money to a corporation, it can physically take possession of a shareholder's stock certificate and a stock power signed in blank (a document permitting the lender to transfer the stock if there is a loan default). If the LLC has Membership certificates (some do, many do not) then a similar procedure should be followed to protect the lender's interests.

HOW LOANS AFFECT LLC MEMBERS

From the Members' perspective, there is one very important tax benefit to the Members of an LLC as discussed in prior chapters. In an S corporation, debts of the corporation cannot be allocated to the shareholders. In a limited partnership, recourse financing could only be allocated to the general partner. However, an LLC offers important borrowing advantages over both of these types of entities. Unlike S corporations, LLC debts can be included in the tax basis of Members. Unlike limited partnerships, all Members of an LLC are allocated recourse financing (unless a particular Member personally guaranteed the financing).

SUMMARY

Since LLCs are still relatively new, many types of common commercial transactions will have to adapt to these nuances. Lending funds to LLCs will continue to be more common. Lenders must take care to protect their interests with consideration to the characteristics of an LLC, and not simply to continue using past practices that were designed for corporate borrowers.

Part Four

TAX ISSUES RELATED TO LIMITED LIABILITY COMPANIES

16 TAXATION OF A LIMITED LIABILITY COMPANY

To understand how an LLC will affect your tax situation, you must know the basic principles involved in taxing an LLC. This chapter will provide an overview. Readers who prefer to avoid the tax maze should consult with their accountant.

OVERVIEW OF FEDERAL TAXATION OF A PARTNERSHIP AND ITS PARTNERS

Since an LLC is intended to be taxed as a partnership for federal and state tax purposes, partnership tax rules will apply to the LLC. The following discussion provides a brief overview of some of the basic partnership tax rules of interest to clients investing in LLCs. The following section assumes that the LLC has been structured to be taxed as a partnership.

HOW AN LLC AND ITS MEMBERS ARE GENERALLY TAXED

LLCs are required to complete and file IRS Form 1065, "U.S. Partnership Return of Income," and have a December 31 fiscal year end.

Fixed or guaranteed payments to a Member for services that the Member supplies to the LLC, or for the use of capital, are often treated as if the payments were made to an independent person who is not a Member.

EXAMPLE: Jack is a Member in the Jack and Jill, LLC. Jack provides accounting services to the LLC and receives a regular monthly payment for these services. These payments are treated as if the Jack and Jill, LLC, had paid an independent accountant to do the work, and are therefore deductible by the LLC. The LLC thus obtains the equivalent of a tax deduction for this guaranteed payment. The Member, Jack, would report the payment as ordinary income. This is accomplished by treating the guaranteed payment to Jack as part of Jack's share of the LLC's ordinary income.

Once an LLC's taxable income (or loss) is determined, it must be allocated among the Members so that each one can report his or her share on their tax return. In addition, many specific types of LLC income and deductions must be reported separately to each Member. These include short-term capital gains and losses, long-term capital gains and losses, charitable contributions, alternative minimum tax preference items, medical expenses, and so forth. The IRS Form K-1 that you will receive from any LLC in which you invest will list all the items which must be separately reported. You then report each of these on a different line on your personal income tax return.

The taxable income of an LLC is generally determined in a manner similar to the taxable income of an individual. However, several specific deductions are not permitted to LLCs: personal exemption, charitable contribution, net operating loss, capital loss carryover, foreign taxes, itemized deductions, and so forth.

Since the LLC is in many respects independent of its Members, many tax decisions (called elections), including those concerning the research credit and depreciation, are made at the LLC level. Income and loss are determined at the Member level. Thus, the LLC must choose a tax year, which is generally the same tax year as the majority of its Members.

Another important part of partnership taxation is the Section 754 election. When a Member dies or sells a Membership interest, an LLC may make this election. The "inside" basis of the inheriting or purchasing Member's share of LLC assets is increased or decreased to equal the "outside" basis of that Member's Membership interest. The purchasing or inheriting Member will not include any preacquisition depreciation in the gain on the LLC's sale of the relevant assets, if as a result of the election, the inside basis of the Member's share in assets increases.

EXAMPLE: John and Mary are equal Members in an LLC that holds real property with a fair market value of $1,000, and a basis of $600 (real property value remains constant for the purposes of this example). John dies and leaves his Membership interest to his wife, Susan. Since, under Section 1014 of the Internal Revenue Code, a person acquiring property from a decedent takes a basis in the property based on the fair market value of the property at the time of the decedent's death, Susan's basis in the LLC is $500, or half of the value of the LLC's assets. If a Section 754 election is in effect, Susan can step up her inside basis from $300 to $500. If later the LLC sells its real property for $1,000, Susan realizes no gain. Her share of the amount realized is $500, and her share of the inside basis is $500.

Under a Section 754 election, a step-down basis can also occur. If the fair market value in the preceding example was $600 and the basis was $1,000, Susan's basis would have decreased from $500 to $300. Once an election is made, it can only be revoked with permission from the IRS. While the Section 754 election is available to partnerships and LLCs, S corporations cannot file such an election.

With respect to an LLC, the Section 754 election must:

1. Set forth the name and address of the LLC making the election.
2. Be signed by any one of the Members.
3. Contain a declaration that the LLC elects under Section 754 to apply the provisions of Section 734(b) and Section 743(b) (the enabling Code provisions).

ALLOCATIONS OF LLC INCOME, DEDUCTIONS, AND LOSSES

Once the LLC's income is determined, it must be allocated to the individual Members. The simplest approach is to allocate income, deductions, credits, and so on to each Member in the same proportion as that Member's interest in the LLC. For example, a 12 percent Member would be allocated 12 percent of all LLC items: 12 percent of cash flow; 12 percent of net income or loss; 12 percent of any tax credits (e.g., the research and experimentation, low-income housing, or rehabilitation tax credits), and so on.

Allocations, however, do not have to be made in the exact proportions as each Member's interest in the LLC if the LLC agreement calls for a different method. This flexibility is one of the principal advantages of the LLC form of organization and sets it apart from all the other forms of conducting business. For example, some Members may be given a priority distribution of cash flow. One Member may receive 80 percent of the gain ultimately realized on the sale of certain property (such as land and a building that Member contributed to the LLC). Another active Member may receive 25 percent of the remaining profits on the eventual sale and liquidation of the LLC, although he or she had only a 1 percent interest in the LLC's profits and capital (this could be offered as an incentive fee to the active Member to encourage his or her performance). This freedom to allocate provides an opportunity to devise a distribution and compensation structure to best achieve the family's business goals. A Member's distributive share of income, gain, loss, deductions, and credits is generally determined by the Operating Agreement.

These special allocations cannot be made with total freedom. The special allocation must have what is called "substantial economic effect." Defining this term has proven to be a most complicated task for the Treasury Department, IRS, and courts. In simple terms, it means that the special allocations must be made for more than mere tax reasons. They should have some meaningful economic and nontax impact on the Members making them.

Substantial economic effect requires that there be an economic effect and that such effect be substantial. The economic benefit or burden must be borne by the Member to whom the allocation is made. This requires:

- Members' capital accounts (ledgers reflecting all investments, income, and losses of each Member) must be maintained as required under the tax regulations. This requires, for example, that Member capital accounts must be increased by certain items (money contributed to the LLC, tax exempt income allocated to each Member, allocations of income and gain, etc.); and decreased by certain items (money distributed, loss, deduction, and certain expenditures, etc.).
- On the LLC's liquidation, distributions of LLC property must be made with consideration to each Member's capital account.
- Following this final distribution, Members with negative capital accounts are required to restore (contribute) these amounts, or meet certain other complex requirements.

HOW LLC DISTRIBUTIONS AND LIQUIDATIONS ARE TAXED

One of the first steps in determining the tax consequences of a family business owner's interest in an LLC being sold or liquidated is to determine the tax basis in the Membership interest. The sale of a family Membership interest is generally treated as the sale of a capital asset. The capital gain (or loss) is the difference between the proceeds (called the amount realized) and the Member's adjusted tax basis in his or her LLC interest.

Usually the first item included in the calculation of a Member's tax basis is the cash and tax basis of property the Member contributed to the LLC in exchange for receiving his or her Membership interest. No gain or loss is generally recognized on this type of contribution transaction.

A Member's tax basis (investment) in the LLC is increased by his or her share of LLC taxable income which is allocated to him or her and reported on his or her individual tax return. Basis is also increased by the Member's share of tax-exempt income. When a distribution is made to a Member, his or her tax basis is decreased by the amount of the distribution.

LLC debts may also be included in a Member's tax basis. If none of the Members have any personal liability for a nonrecourse LLC liability (a debt which the lender cannot sue the Members individually to recover on), then the tax laws provide that all the Members can include a portion of such liability in their tax basis (i.e., their investment in the LLC). The proportion that each Member would share in such liability is the ratio in which they share in LLC profits.

Under Section 731(a) of the Code, a Member does not recognize gain on an LLC distribution, except to the extent that any money received exceeds the Member's adjusted basis in his or her Membership interest before the distribution. Under the general rule, a Member does not recognize gain on a distribution of property, but instead takes a basis in the distributed property equal to (1) the basis of that property in the LLC's hands if the distribution is a nonliquidating distribution (i.e., an interim distribution), or (2) the Member's basis in his or her Membership interest if the distribution is a liquidating distribution.

Section 752 of the Code provides rules for determining a Member's share in LLC liabilities. Such rules provide that any increase in the Member's share of liabilities is considered to be a contribution of money by the Member to the LLC and thus would increase his or her basis in the LLC. Any decrease in the Member's share of liabilities is considered by the IRS as a distribution of money by the LLC to the Member and thus would decrease his or her basis in the Membership interest. If this decrease in the Member's share of liabilities is greater than the Member's basis in his or her Membership interest, gain will be recognized by such Member under Section 731(a) of the Code.

New Section 731(c) of the Code, effective for partnership distributions (and LLC distributions) made after December 8, 1994, provides that for purposes of Section 731(a)(1) of the Code, "money" includes "marketable securities" based on their fair market value as of the date of distribution. Accordingly, a Member receiving a distribution of marketable securities generally will have to recognize taxable gain equal to the excess, if any, of the fair market value of the securities over the Member's basis in the Membership interest. Section 731(c) of the Code, however, contains several specific exceptions that restrict the application of the new rules.

The application of the LLC tax rules to distributions and liquidations can be very complex, as the following example illustrates.

EXAMPLE: Say a new Member, Sam, pays $400,000 for a 20 percent interest in an LLC whose sole asset is a building that has appreciated substantially since the LLC purchased it many years ago. The building is on the LLC's books at $500,000, so that Sam's share of it (the inside basis) is $100,000. The LLC is depreciating the building over 39 years. Sam has a problem. He has in effect paid $400,000 for a partial interest in the building but is only getting depreciation based on the LLC's original purchase price of the building, which is much lower. Also, if the building were sold for $2 million (Sam's share being 20 percent, or the $400,000 he paid), the LLC would realize a $1.5 million gain ($2 million less $500,000 basis), Sam's share being $300,000. This is not a reasonable result since Sam's interest in the building only sold for the price he just paid for it. If the LLC's only asset were sold, it would probably liquidate and Sam would get an offsetting capital loss. Unfortunately, some LLCs have multiple assets so liquidation is not guaranteed. The capital loss limitations could also create problems.

If the LLC makes a special Section 754 tax election, Sam can get an adjustment to prevent him from getting taxed on the $300,000 he really did not earn if the building is sold, and he can get a depreciation deduction that more closely reflects his actual investment in the building. The adjustment equals the difference between the $400,000 Sam paid and his $100,000 share of the partnership's basis in the building (the tax regulations use the selling Member's basis in his LLC interest as allocated to the building instead). Since we have assumed the only LLC asset is the building, Sam would then depreciate this amount over 39 years for an additional depreciation deduction on his personal tax return. This would be in addition to his share of the LLC's depreciation deduction (which is included in the calculation of the new Member's share of the LLC's income reported to him on Form K-1).

There is an important exception to the rule that the sale of a Membership interest is treated as the sale of a capital asset. Where a portion of the sale proceeds relate to two special types of assets, a Member may have to report part of his or her gain on the sale as ordinary income. These two special assets are unrealized receivables and substantially appreciated inventory. They are referred to as "hot assets." Unrealized receivables are the right to income that has not been reported under the method of accounting used by the LLC.

EXAMPLE: Medical Associates is an LLC of physicians. It reports income on a cash basis. This means income is only reported when patients pay their bills, not when the medical services are provided. If the LLC is sold, the accounts receivable due from patients who have received services but have not yet paid would be unrealized receivables.

Unrealized receivables also includes certain depreciation recapture and other technical adjustments.

The second category of special assets, substantially appreciated inventory, is much more complicated to define. It includes inventory-type items (the term is much broader than what you would generally consider to be "inventory").

Where you sell or exchange a Membership interest in an LLC, it will be more difficult to avoid ordinary income treatment on your proportionate share of the LLC's substantially appreciated inventory. Prior law permitted the LLC to take steps to help you avoid this adverse tax consequence by acquiring nonappreciated inventory in order to have the LLC fail to meet the technical requirements of having substantially appreciated inventory. Currently, any inventory acquired for this purpose is excluded from the calculations. There also had been an exception that made this rule inapplicable where the LLC's inventory did not exceed 10 percent of its assets (excluding cash). This exception has been repealed.

Members Realize Tax Consequences

Under the Code, no federal income tax is paid by an LLC. Each Member will be required to report on his or her individual federal income tax return his or her distributive share of all items of income, gain, loss, deduction, credit, and tax preference of the LLC for any taxable year of the LLC ending within or with his or her taxable year. This is the result whether or not any actual cash distributions have been or will be made to such Member. Thus, a Member will have to report income and may incur a tax liability as a result of the LLC recognizing business, rental or other income even though the Member may not have received any cash distributions from the LLC.

The preceding approach results in a conduit tax system, with each Member reporting a pro rata share of the LLC's income on his or her tax return, regardless of the actual cash distribution. The result of this could be a Member having to report income on his or her return without a commensurate cash distribution with which to pay the tax. Consideration should be given to this possibility in negotiating and drafting the terms of the Operating Agreement.

Tax Basis in Membership Interest

A Member may deduct a proportionate share of any net losses incurred by the LLC from his or her other taxable income, if any; it is limited, however, to the tax basis of his or her interest in the LLC (and subject to the at-risk rules, passive loss rules, and any other applicable limitations). If a Member's share of LLC losses exceeds the tax basis for his or her interest at the end of any taxable year, such excess loss may be carried over indefinitely and deducted at the end of any succeeding year, to the extent of the tax basis for his or her interest in the LLC.

Generally, each Member's tax basis for his or her LLC Membership interest is equal to the price paid for the interest, plus his or her pro rata share (measured by his or her share of LLC profits) of those liabilities of the LLC to which purchased and constructed property is subject and to which none of the Members have personal liability (known as nonrecourse liabilities).

Such a debt also cannot be in excess of the fair market value of the property burdened by such liabilities. All Members are allocated a portion of such a nonrecourse liability in the same proportion as their share in LLC profits. Each Member's tax basis is increased by his or her pro rata share of LLC taxable income and is reduced (but not below zero) by his or her share of the LLC's taxable loss and by the amount of any distributions (including any reduction in his or her share of LLC nonrecourse liabilities such as the LLC's amortization of such liabilities) during the tax year. If the tax basis of a Member's interest should be reduced to zero, the amount of any distributions (including any reduction in LLC nonrecourse liabilities in excess of his or her share of the LLC's taxable income) for any tax year will be treated as gain from the sale of his or her LLC Membership interest.

Allocation of Net Income and Loss

Broad discretion to accept cash or any type of property or service as a contribution to the LLC is generally permitted. In addition, broad discretion is generally permitted to include in the Operating Agreement any manner of allocation of profits and losses to Members. Therefore, the issues that addressed the allocations of income, gain, and loss in partnership transactions must similarly be addressed in the LLC context.

If the principal purpose of the allocation formula contained in the Operating Agreement with respect to allocating the LLC's income or loss, and gain or loss on a sale or other disposition of LLC property, is the avoidance or evasion of taxes, then such allocation would not be binding on the IRS. The IRS would then reallocate net income and losses among the Members based on their interests in the LLC. The principal factor indicating such a purpose is generally an allocation provision that is without "substantial economic effect." Whether an allocation has "substantial economic effect" was described earlier in this chapter and generally depends on whether the allocation may actually affect the dollar amount of the Member's share of the total LLC income or loss independently of tax consequences.

The allocation must have an economic effect under a capital account analysis, and that effect must be substantial. In fact, an allocation only has economic effect if it is determined to be "substantial" under the Regulations.

Except as otherwise provided, the economic effect of an allocation is substantial if there is a reasonable possibility that the allocation (or allocations) will affect substantially the dollar amounts to be received by the Members from the LLC, independent of tax consequences. The economic effect of an allocation (or allocations) is not substantial if, at the time the allocation (or allocations) becomes part of the Operating Agreement, (1) the after-tax economic consequences of at least one Member may, in present value terms, be enhanced compared with such consequences if the allocation were not contained in the Operating Agreement, and (2) there is a strong likelihood that the after-tax consequences will, in present value terms, be substantially diminished compared with such consequences if the allocation were not contained in the Operating Agreement.

The capital account analysis requirements will be satisfied if the Operating Agreement requires that:

1. The determination and the maintenance of the Members' capital accounts under the rules set forth in the Regulations, including charging losses and crediting profits to the Members, are consistent with the allocations of such items in the Operating Agreement.

2. On the liquidation of the LLC (or any Member's interest therein), liquidating distributions are required to be made in accordance with the positive capital account balances.

3. If a Member has a deficit balance in his or her capital account following the liquidation of his or her interest in the LLC, he or she is obligated to restore that amount to the LLC within the time period required by the IRS. If this is not met, then a rather wild and complex tax rule must be followed (you have to get a tax expert here). The allocation of losses attributable to nonrecourse debt does not cause the sum of the deficit capital account balances of the Members to exceed the minimum gain (the gain that would be recognized on a foreclosure of the property) and the Operating Agreement provides that Members with deficit capital account balances resulting from allocations attributable to nonrecourse debt shall, to the extent possible, be allocated income in an amount no less than the minimum gain at a date no later than the time at which the sum of such deficit capital account balances are reduced below the minimum gain.

If an allocation does not have substantial economic effect and is merely made for the purpose of tax avoidance, it will not be recognized for tax purposes and such deductions would be by the IRS in accordance with the Member's interest in the LLC.

Transferability; Possible Termination of LLC for Tax Purposes

In general, the Code provides that if 50 percent or more of the capital and profit interests in an LLC are sold or exchanged within a single 12-month period, the LLC will terminate for tax purposes. Members could be precluded from making transfers sufficient to trigger such a termination by the provisions of the Operating Agreement. However, where 50 percent or more of the LLC interests are nevertheless sold or exchanged within a single 12-month period, a termination of the LLC for tax purposes would result. In such an event, Members could recognize gain to the extent their pro rata shares of any cash received plus their pro rata share of the LLC's debt exceeded the tax basis for his or her interest in the LLC.

STATE TAX CONSIDERATIONS

There is no consistency among the states that have LLC legislation for the treatment of LLCs for state tax purposes. Some states, such as Florida and Pennsylvania, tax LLCs at the entity level, and other states, such as Texas, tax LLCs with an earned surplus tax. The classification of LLCs in states without LLC legislation is not uniform.

LLC's METHOD OF ACCOUNTING

Generally, the cash or the accrual methods of accounting are permitted for an LLC. However, taxpayers must use the accrual method for C corporations, partnerships with a C corporation partner, and tax shelters. A tax shelter is any enterprise if interests are offered in a registered offering, or a syndicate. A syndicate is anything, other than a C corporation, in which greater than 35 percent of the losses are allocated to limited partners or limited "entrepreneurs." A limited entrepreneur, as defined by Section 464(e)(2) of the code, is a person who is not a limited partner and does not actively participate in the management. LLCs can get around these rulings either by taking the position that these rules do not apply until the business takes losses. For professional practices, this is a viable solution because they rarely take losses. Another possible solution is that due to a Member's active role in management, a Member of an LLC is neither a limited partner nor an entrepreneur. The IRS has ruled that LLCs can use the cash method for accounting purposes.

The LLC will make certain tax elections rather than the individual Members making the elections. For example, the method of accounting will be elected at the LLC level. The Operating Agreement may provide that a particular tax election be used. Alternatively, the Operating Agreement may direct that the determination of which tax elections to make shall be made by the Managers or Members.

Usually, the tax year for an LLC will be a calendar year. This is because LLCs are required to adopt the tax reporting period consistent with the tax reporting period of its Members who hold a majority of the LLC's profits and capital interests, which is the identical rule for partnerships.

SUMMARY

Assuming the LLC is taxed as a partnership, then the LLC will pay no entity level tax and all its income, losses, and credits will flow through to the individual Member's tax return. A host of partnership tax rules apply to an LLC and will bear on the issues such as allocation of income and losses, deductible losses, taxation of the sale or exchange of a Member's interest, and basis of the assets in an LLC on the sale or exchange of a Member's interest.

17 NEW ISSUES, PROBLEMS, AND RISKS

For the numerous reasons discussed in this book, limited liability companies provide an attractive form in which to conduct business or investments. LLCs are relatively new entities, however, and this fact must be kept in mind when analyzing whether or not to use an LLC. Because of the newness of LLCs, state laws are still developing; there is less published guidance in the form of treatises and sample forms; and case law on LLCs is limited. Thus, there are unresolved issues relating to LLCs and risks associated with their use. Many important issues relating to LLCs still require guidance.

These factors must be weighed against the benefits of an LLC when making the ultimate decision whether or not to utilize this entity.

PIERCING THE LLC "VEIL"

Members in an LLC will be liable only to the extent of their investment in the company, thus providing Members with the personal liability protection traditionally associated with corporations. Since the LLC is a relatively new entity and there is very limited case law relating to LLCs, it is logical that the limits to the personal liability protections afforded to Members of an LLC can be analyzed by reviewing the law relating to the liability protection afforded to shareholders of a corporation.

There is a corporate doctrine known as "piercing the corporate veil." This doctrine permits, in certain instances, a claimant to have the courts disregard, or "pierce," the corporate entity, to reach the shareholders' assets personally to satisfy a judgment against the corporation. Courts will pierce the corporate veil when the owners use the corporation as their alter ego, rather than respecting its status as a separate and distinct entity. The piercing of the veil is a term that applies to the legal process of holding a shareholder liable for the acts of a corporation. The courts have established factors (which vary from state to state) to consider when determining whether to pierce the veil. The primary factors can be broken down into four main categories:

1. Fraud by owners.
2. Inadequate capitalization of the entity.
3. Failure to observe company formalities.
4. Mixing of the businesses and finances of the company with the owners, to the extent that there is no distinction between them.

Since the vast majority of LLC statutes do not provide guidance on the concept of "piercing the LLC veil," it is likely that the situations that would result in the piercing of an LLC veil should be very similar to those that pierce the corporate veil.

An LLC should be much easier to operate in accordance with the required LLC formalities since they are so much simpler than those for a corporation. However, care must always be taken to be certain that clients are apprised of the importance of having all documents and contracts signed in the name of the LLC, by the Manager if so required under the Operating Agreement, and to have all necessary tax and annual report filings made. Where additional certificates (Certificate of Amendment, Certificate of Assumed Name, etc.) are required, these too should be properly filed. Leases, licenses, and other ancillary agreements should all be completed in the proper name of the LLC. Time will tell, however, if the law relating to piercing an LLC's veil is the same as the one that currently exists relating to corporations.

EXAMPLES

- State A requires all LLCs formed in that state to file annual reports setting forth the names of its Members and Managers, its registered agent, and registered office. The report must be accompanied by a filing fee. If an LLC formed in State A continually and repeatedly fails to file its annual report, this would be an example of failing to comply with company formalities.
- Where the Members of an LLC cause the LLC's cash receipts to be distributed directly into their individual checking accounts rather than first going into a company account and thereafter having the company issue a check to them, there is further abuse of the company formalities and a better chance a creditor may pierce the LLC veil.

FIDUCIARY OBLIGATIONS OF MANAGERS

Generally

The case law relating to obligations and responsibilities of Managers of an LLC, both to the LLC itself and its Members, is currently lacking but will undoubtedly expand over time. It is very important that the LLC's Operating Agreement sets forth to the greatest extent possible the rights and obligations of the Managers. An Operating Agreement's drafter must not overlook this most important subject, especially in light of the absence of case law.

Most state statutes address a Manager's duty of care and loyalty to the LLC. Generally, a Manager for this purpose could be either Members or Managers, whichever group has management authority. The states that have such statutes vary in their approach to the duty of care and loyalty owned by the management group. Therefore, the state LLC statute should be reviewed to determine what rights and obligations would exist in the absence of such provisions in an Operating Agreement or if no Operating Agreement was in existence.

Duty of Care

Generally, five categories of duty of care standards are provided by various state statutes:

1. Duty to exercise ordinary care.
2. Gross negligence/willful misconduct.
3. Duty to exercise good-faith business judgment.
4. Duty to not act in a reckless manner.
5. Duty of care to LLC as to reliance on information provided by others.

The particular state LLC statute must be reviewed to determine which of the preceding, if any, standards relating to the duty of care exist in that state. Some state statutes will not have an express provision. In those states, it is most likely that the courts would require some degree of duty of care by the management group.

Duty of Loyalty

Generally, three categories of duty of care standards are provided by various state statutes:

1. Duty to account for profits made in connection with the LLC's business.
2. Authorize management to self-deal.
3. Duty of good faith.

Again, the particular state LLC statute must be reviewed to determine which of the preceding, if any, standards relating to the duty of loyalty exist in that state. If a state does not have an express provision, it is most likely that the courts would require some degree of duty of loyalty by the management group.

ONE-MEMBER LLCs

Currently, approximately 20 states authorize the formation of one-Member LLCs. The proposed Uniform Limited Liability Company Act (discussed in Chapter 1) allows for the formation and operation of one-Member LLCs. There is a question as to how a one-Member LLC will be taxed. In Revenue Proceeding (Rev. Proc.) 95-10, where the IRS listed guidelines to follow in order to receive a ruling from the IRS that an LLC will be treated as a partnership for federal tax purposes, the IRS limited such ruling to LLCs that have at least two Members. To date, the IRS has not provided any guidance relating to how one-Member LLCs will be taxed.

There are several possibilities as to the federal tax treatment of one-Member LLCs, which may differ from state treatment of such entities. For federal tax purposes, the following are potential tax treatments of one-Member LLCs:

- Unincorporated organization taxable either as a corporation or as a partnership (as determined by examination of the corporate characteristics provided in the Regulations, with such characteristics discussed in Chapter 18);
- Sole proprietorship.
- Agency relationship.
- Grantor trust.
- Single-member partnership.

Although a certain state law may not permit the formation of a specific entity (e.g., single-member partnership), the classification of an entity for federal tax purposes is not controlled by state law.

It is currently unclear which of the preceding tax treatments will be followed by the IRS. Although it is possible that a one-Member LLC may enjoy pass-through tax treatment, because of the IRS' ruling policy in this area, it is advisable to form an LLC with at least two Members.

SELF-EMPLOYMENT TAXES AND LLCs

The self-employment income of every individual is taxed under the Self-Employment Contributions Act. This tax involves a 12.40 percent tax for old-age, survivor, and disability insurance (which is capped by the contribution and benefit base for an employee's wages) and a 2.90 percent tax for hospital insurance (which is uncapped), totaling a tax 15.30 percent. There is a deduction, however, for one-half ($\frac{1}{2}$) of the self-employment taxes paid. The determination of the benefits a self-employed individual may have in a qualified retirement plan depends on the self-employment income attributable to such individual.

Under Section 1402 of the Code, self-employment income includes a partner's distributive share of net income and loss from a partnership engaged in a trade or business. The term "partnership" for this purpose should include any entity that is classified as a partnership for federal tax purposes. A limited partner in a limited partnership, however, does not include his or her distributive share of partnership income or loss in net income from self-employment, other than specific guaranteed payments to such limited partner under Section 707(c) of the Code. There was a question as to how self-employment income taxes are to apply to LLCs. Should Members be treated more like general partners or limited partners with respect to this issue? The IRS, however, has addressed this issue.

The IRS recently issued Proposed Regulation Section 1.1402(a)-18, relating to self-employment taxes imposed on Members of a limited liability company that is classified as a partnership for federal tax purposes. Pursuant to the proposed regulation, a Member's distributive share of the LLC's income or loss would be subject to self-employment taxes unless both of the following requirements are satisfied:

1. The Member is not a Manager of the LLC in an LLC managed by Managers.
2. The LLC could have been formed as a limited partnership rather than an LLC in the same jurisdiction, and the Member could have qualified as a limited partner in that limited partnership under applicable law.

Pursuant to the proposed regulations, a Manager is a person who alone, or together with others, is vested with the continuing exclusive authority to make the management decisions necessary to conduct the business for which the LLC was formed. All Members of the LLC will generally be treated as Managers if there are no specific designated or elected Members with continuing exclusive authority to manage the LLC.

The regulation will be effective for the Member's first taxable year beginning on or after the date that the regulation is published as a final regulation. Although the regulation is not final, it nonetheless provides useful guidance and some certainty as to the application of the self-employment taxes to Members of LLCs.

As a result of the proposed regulation, there is now important relief for passive investors in LLCs. However, there is still uncertainty regarding coverage in different states. As a result of variations in permitted businesses that limited partnerships can engage in from state to state, Members of an LLC may have differing results as to whether they are subject to self-employment taxes depending on the choice of state of organization. It is also unclear how Members will be treated. An argument can be made that the proposed rule should apply currently. It is probably prudent to treat Members in accordance with the proposed regulation because the Member's status must be determined. Despite the uncertainty with the proposed regulation in general, in the vast majority of cases, the proposed regulation will provide clear guidance with respect to the treatment of a member for self-employment taxes.

LIMITED LIABILITY PARTNERSHIPS

LLCs are currently recognized in all but two states; however, another new business entity, the limited liability partnership, also known as registered limited liability partnership (LLP), is recognized in more than one-half all states with pending LLP legislation in most others. LLPs were discussed in Chapter 9 of this book in the context of professional practices.

An LLP is a general partnership that files a registration form with the appropriate state filing authority. The registration provides information relating to the partnership and its partners, with such information requirements varying from state to state.

At the time this book is being written, the IRS has issued one revenue ruling relating to the tax treatment of LLPs. In Revenue Ruling (Rev. Rul.) 95-55, the IRS ruled that a New York general partnership that registered as a New York registered limited liability partnership will be classified as a partnership for federal tax purposes. Accordingly, there is a good degree of comfort that LLPs will enjoy the same partnership tax treatment as do LLCs.

An LLP retains the entity's original general partnership form, but provides a partial liability shield to the partners. Most state statutes provide that a partner in an LLP is not liable for debts, obligations, and liabilities chargeable to the partnership arising from negligence, malpractice, wrongful acts, or misconduct of employees not under the direct supervision of that partner. The partners in an LLP formed in those states, however, are generally liable for the commercial obligations (i.e., contract liability) and tort liability of the LLP. With the recent development of the LLP, the advantage of the LLC over a partnership has slightly diminished.

By contrast, the LLC provides limited liability to its owners with respect to contractual and tort liabilities of the entity. In certain states where professional LLCs are permitted, however, a Member in a professional LLC will generally not be protected from liability resulting from his or her own malpractice or the malpractice of someone directly under his or her supervision. There are a few states (e.g., Minnesota, Colorado) where partners in an LLP are protected from all the LLP's debts and obligations.

LLPs have been primarily enacted for use by national accounting and law firms. The big six accounting firms have all opted to be LLPs rather than LLCs because LLPs are taxed as partnerships at all state levels, whereas LLCs are taxed by some states at the entity level (e.g., Texas, Florida).

Converting to an LLP is a much more streamlined procedure than converting to an LLC, which necessitates the creation of a new entity. An LLP may be formed by an existing partnership, filing a registration statement. The LLP may be preferred by some people because of the ease of conversion.

The choice as to whether to be an LLP or an LLC also may be limited by certain professional state licensing authorities. For instance, a state LLC statute may expressly permit the formation of a professional LLC to practice law, but the court in that state, which provides the rules regulating the practice of law, may not allow lawyers to practice as LLCs. In such states, lawyers would not be permitted to practice as LLCs.

BANKRUPTCY ISSUES AND LLCs

It is currently unclear how bankruptcy law will be applied to LLCs since the Bankruptcy Code does not address LLCs. The term "corporation," however, has a very expansive definition under the Bankruptcy Code and thus it is highly likely that an LLC will be treated a corporation under bankruptcy law.

The distinction between corporate and partnership treatment under the Bankruptcy Code is important because general partners of a partnership may be held personally liable if the partnership's assets are insufficient to satisfy claims of creditors in a bankruptcy proceeding against the partnership, where shareholders of a corporation will not be subject to such personal liability.

SUMMARY

The limited liability company is a relatively new form of business entity and thus several tax and other related issues have not yet been resolved. Due to the newness of LLCs, case law in this area is lacking, leaving entrepreneurs and professionals in the dark on many issues.

As with corporations, there is also the potential to pierce the veil of an LLC. If an LLC's veil should be pierced, owners would potentially be subject to personal liability for debts, liabilities, and obligations of the LLC. Again, since the case law relating to LLCs is quite limited, most of the analysis relating to piercing an LLC veil would currently come from the law relating to piercing the veil of a corporation.

Many state statutes provide specific rules relating to the fiduciary duty of an LLC's management group, and some state statutes provide no such guidance. It is important for an LLC's Operating Agreement to address this issue to limit uncertainty in this area to the greatest extent possible.

Although some states allow the formation of single-Member LLCs, it is unclear how such entities will be treated for federal tax purposes. Therefore, it is advisable to create two or more Member LLCs.

In addition to LLCs, limited liability partnerships are another new form of business entity. An LLP does not require the formation of a new entity but is merely a general partnership that files a registration statement with the appropriate state filing authority of the state in which the general partnership was formed. Most state statutes relating to LLPs provide that such entity is effective to limit the liability of an owner from the malpractice of his or her coowners, but not against contract and tort liability.

18 CLASSIFYING A LIMITED LIABILITY COMPANY AS A PARTNERSHIP OR CORPORATION—TAX ISSUES

A primary advantage of using an LLC is that it provides the pass-through tax treatment of partnerships. This means that the entity (the LLC) pays no tax. All tax consequences flow through the LLC to your personal tax return (and the tax returns of the other Members). This is a tremendous benefit when compared with corporations that must pay tax on their income and then distribute dividends to their shareholders, who then pay tax a second time on the dividends.

For an LLC to avail itself of this pass-through tax treatment, however, the LLC must be structured to meet specific IRS requirements. A discussion of such criteria follows in this chapter. Since these issues are rather technical, you may wish to review them with your accountant or tax attorney.

CHARACTERIZATION OF AN LLC AS A PARTNERSHIP

Corporate versus Noncorporate Characteristics under the Treasury Regulations

Essential to the purpose of an LLC is to be taxed as a partnership for tax purposes and not as a corporation. If an LLC is not taxed as a partnership, it would be subjected to two tiers of taxation, corporate (the corporate level tax on earnings) and individual (the Members would be taxed personally on receipt of dividends for which the corporation cannot claim a deduction).

The term "partnership" for tax purposes includes a syndicate, group, pool, joint venture, or other unincorporated organization, through or by means of which any business, financial operation or venture is carried on, and which is not a trust or estate or a corporation. The term "partner" includes a member in such a syndicate, group, pool, joint venture, or organization. An organization will be treated as a corporation for federal income tax purposes if it has more of certain corporate than noncorporate characteristics. The six characteristics to consider are:

1. Associates.
2. An objective to carry on business and divide the gains therefrom.
3. Limited liability.

4. Centralized management.

5. Free transferability of ownership interests.

6. Continuity of life.

Partnerships and corporations both have associates, and both share an objective of carrying on business and dividing the gains. Accordingly, the last four of the preceding factors will determine whether an LLC is taxed as a partnership or as a corporation. An LLC must lack at least two of the last four corporate characteristics to be taxed as a partnership. The determination is based on the state statute under which the LLC was formed as well as other factors. These factors have been clarified by the recent ruling by the IRS, Revenue Procedure (Rev. Proc.) 95-10. This recent ruling does not necessarily represent the litigating or audit position of the IRS. However, it is important to structure your LLC within these guidelines. An LLC that does not meet the new requirements will not necessarily fail to be classified as a partnership for federal income tax purposes.

In the following discussion, each factor will be analyzed in the context of IRS rulings, tax cases, and so forth. There is a substantial discussion regarding limited partnerships in this context because the entities have significant similarities and there is a much more extensive body of law for limited partnerships than for limited liability companies.

LIMITED LIABILITY

State statutes permitting the formation of LLCs provide generally that the LLC Members will not be liable for the LLC's debts or other obligations. Members are at risk for the amounts that they have invested in the LLC but are shielded from the LLC's creditors. This provides the corporate characteristic of limited liability since no Member is personally liable for the debts of, or the claims against, the organization.

The IRS generally will not rule that an LLC lacks limited liability unless at least one Member validly assumes personal liability for all (but not less than all) of the LLC's obligations, pursuant to express authority granted in the state LLC statute. In addition, the IRS generally will not rule that an LLC lacks limited liability unless the assuming Members have an aggregate net worth equal to at least 10 percent of the total contributions to the LLC at the time of the ruling request and throughout the LLC's life. When assuming Members do not satisfy the 10 percent safe harbor, the IRS will closely scrutinize the LLC to determine whether the entity lacks limited liability, including whether an assuming Member has, or the assuming Members in the aggregate have, substantial assets (other than the Member's interest in the LLC) that could be reached by a creditor of the LLC. Although it is possible under Rev. Proc. 95-10 to structure an LLC so that it lacks limited liability, there would be no incentive to do so if the LLC is structured to lack at least two of the other three corporate characteristics. In addition, one of the primary reasons to create an LLC is for the liability protection to its Members, which is inconsistent with structuring an LLC to lack limited liability.

If a ruling is requested that an LLC lacks limited liability, or that an LLC with Member-Managers lacks the corporate characteristics of continuity of life or free transferability of interests, there are minimum ownership tests that must be satisfied.

By analogy, a limited partnership subject to a state statute corresponding to the Uniform Limited Partnership Act, is subject to regulations providing for personal liability with respect to each general partner, except as limited by applicable regulations: (Treas. Reg. § 301.7701-2(d)(2)):

> . . . personal liability does not exist . . . with respect to a general partner when he has no substantial assets (other than his interest in the partnership) which could be reached by a creditor of the organization and when he is merely a "dummy" acting as the agent of the limited partners. . . . A general partner may contribute his services, but no capital, to the organization, but if such general partner has substantial assets (other than his interest in the partnership), there exists personal liability. Furthermore, if the organization is engaged in financial transactions which involve large sums of money, and if the general partners have substantial assets (other than their interests in the partnership), there exists personal liability although the assets of such general partners would be insufficient to satisfy any substantial portion of the obligations of the organization. In addition, although the general partner has no substantial assets (other than his interest in the partnership), personal liability exists with respect to such general partner when he is not merely a "dummy" acting as the agent of the limited partners.

Whether or not a general partner has substantial assets in addition to its interest in the typical limited partnership, it often did not act as a mere "dummy" and mere agent of the limited partners in connection with the formation and management of the partnership. Consequently, as a result of actual net worth and/or not serving as a dummy, many limited partnerships do not, according to the terms of the regulation, have the characteristic of limited liability.

The IRS, however, could argue differently. The IRS requirements for issuing an advance ruling on the status of an entity had relied solely on the substantial asset test, to the exclusion of the dummy test.

Most LLCs have limited liability. The implication of this is that an LLC must lack at least two of the remaining three corporate characteristics to be taxed as a partnership: centralized management, free transferability of interests, and continuity of life. In recently published Notice 95-14, the IRS implies that an LLC may have more than two of the four characteristics of a corporation and still be taxed as a partnership.

CENTRALIZED MANAGEMENT

Centralized management exists if any person or group has continuing and exclusive authority to conduct the business of the entity. Persons who have such authority may or may not be members of the organization and may hold office as a result of a selection by the members from time to time, or may be self-perpetuating in office. In addition, centralized management can be accomplished by the election to office, by proxy appointment, or by any other means that has the effect of concentrating in a management group continuing exclusive authority to make management decisions. Whether an LLC lacks centralized management or not depends on how it is structured. If an LLC is structured like a corporation, and management is in the hands of a group of Members or Managers, then it is most likely that the LLC has centralized management. In Rev. Proc. 95-10, the IRS confirmed with prior rulings that Member-managed LLCs generally lacked centralized management. However, the ruling also provides that even Manager-managed LLCs may lack centralized management if the Member-Managers all together own at least 20 percent of the LLC interests, and Members who are Managers are not controlled by the other Members. Even if the LLC meets the 20 percent test, however, the IRS will examine the facts and circumstances to determine the lack of centralized management, particularly Member control of the Member-Managers, whether direct or indirect. Neither periodic elections nor the Members' right to remove Member-Managers will cause the IRS to rule that the LLC lacks centralized management.

In Rev. Proc. 89-12 dealing with partnerships, the IRS set forth rules to be used in determining when a partnership lacks centralized management. If the limited partnership interest exceeds 80 percent of the total interest in the partnership, the partnership will not lack centralized management.

The IRS has ruled that an LLC had centralized management because 3 out of 25 Members were designated as Managers. The IRS has also held that a Colorado LLC possessed centralized management when the LLC was managed by five Members, who were also Managers, because the Colorado statute requires an LLC to be managed by Managers. On the other hand, the IRS ruled that an LLC lacked centralized management where management was reserved to all the Members in proportion to their Membership interests.

A limited partnership subject to a statute corresponding to the Uniform Limited Partnership Act generally does not have centralized management, but centralized management ordinarily will exist in a limited partnership if substantially all the interests in the partnership are owned by the limited partners. There is no published authority as to what is considered "substantially all" of the interests in a partnership for this purpose.

In summary, depending on the structure of the LLC, it may be deemed to have the corporate characteristic of centralization of management or it may not. As a general rule, if Members manage their LLC in relative proportion to their interests in the LLC and do not select Managers, then it will not have centralization of management. If Members manage their LLC by representation that is not pro rata or appoint Managers, then it will likely be deemed to have the corporate characteristic of centralized management.

FREE TRANSFERABILITY OF OWNERSHIP INTERESTS

For an organization to possess the corporate characteristics of free transferability of interests, a member of the organization must have the ability to transfer his or her interests in the organization to a person who is not a member, and must be able to do so without the consent of the other members. If the transfer must be approved by the other members, or if the transferee receives only the right to share in profits, free transferability does not exist. The typical limited partnership agreement specifically provides that no limited partner may transfer his or her interest other than by testamentary disposition or pursuant to the operation of the laws of descent and distribution, except where the prior written consent of the general partner is obtained. Pursuant to the regulations, the corporate characteristic of free transferability generally does not exist in most limited partnerships with such a provision in their limited partnership agreement.

The IRS has set forth in various rulings certain requirements that must be satisfied before it will issue a ruling that a limited partnership will be treated as a partnership for federal income tax purposes. Revenue Proceeding 74-17 also provides that the rules stated therein are not intended to be restatements of the law nor are they intended to be criteria for the audit of returns.

Regarding free transferability of interests in LLCs, in a Manager-managed LLC the required consent to a transfer to avoid free transferability may be limited to a majority of the nontransferring Member-Managers provided that certain ownership requirements are met. Also in Rev. Proc. 95-10, if an LLC's Members designate a Manager or Managers and the Operating Agreement provides that each Member, or those Members owning more than 20 percent of all interests in the LLC's capital, income, gain, loss, deduction, and credit, does not or do not have the power to confer on a non-Member all the attributes of a Member's interest in the LLC without the consent of not less than a "majority" of the nontransferring "Member-Managers," the Service will generally rule that the LLC lacks free transferability of interests.

PLANNING TIP: There is a planning opportunity here in that it is possible to remove certain Members from the consent process by not having such Members serve as Member-Managers.

One issue not addressed in Rev. Proc. 95-10, however, is what happens if there is only one Member-Manager and such Member-Manager desires to transfer its interest as a Member to a non-Member. In this scenario, there are no other Member-Managers to consent to the transfer. It would appear that by default, the transferring Member-Manager would have to obtain the consent of the other Members (who are not Member-Managers), but the IRS did not provide guidance on this issue.

If, instead, the LLC's Members do not designate one or more Members as Managers (or if the LLC requests a ruling under these conditions rather than those in the preceding paragraph despite the presence of Member-Managers) and the Operating Agreement provides that each Member, or those Members owning more than 20 percent of the LLC's capital, income, gain, loss, deduction and credit, do not have the power to confer on a non-Member all the attributes of the Member's interests in the LLC without the consent of not less than a "majority" of the nontransferring "Members," the Service will generally rule that the LLC lacks free transferability of interests.

For purposes of satisfying the majority standard for free transferability of interests as set forth in the preceding two paragraphs, one of the following four standards may be used:

1. The majority in interest standard set forth in Rev. Proc. 94-46 (discussed later in this chapter regarding continuity of life).
2. A majority of the capital interests in the LLC.
3. A majority of the profits interests in the LLC.
4. A majority determined on a per capita basis.

The Service will not rule that the LLC lacks free transferability of interests unless the power to withhold consent to the transfer constitutes a "meaningful restriction" on the transfer of the interests. Under Revenue Procedure 95-10, a power to withhold consent to a transfer is not a meaningful restriction if the consent may not be unreasonably withheld.

In one IRS revenue ruling regarding LLCs, the IRS ruled that a Wyoming LLC had no free transferability where transfer of voting and management rights required unanimous consent of all Members, although economic interests were freely assignable.

CONTINUITY OF LIFE

The absence of "continuity of life" is one of the characteristics that LLCs rely on for their tax treatment as a partnership. Continuity of life does not exist if a dissolution of the entity results from the death, insanity, bankruptcy, retirement, resignation, or expulsion of any Member without any further action on the part of the entity. The IRS has provided guidance on whether an entity will be found to have continuity of life and thus be taxed as a corporation. An entity created to exist for a specific period may not necessarily be found to have a limited life. Statutes in most states provide that an LLC will terminate either with the expiration of a period stated in the Articles of Organization, or upon the death, insanity, bankruptcy, retirement, resignation, or expulsion of any Member. In most states, the LLC can continue on a unanimous vote of the remaining Members. An LLC may also continue its existence even by a majority vote. The IRS ruled that a Wyoming LLC lacked continuity of life because, on the death, dissolution, or other departure of any Member, it required the unanimous consent of all remaining Members to continue the LLC.

Under Rev. Proc. 95-10, if an LLC's Members designate a Manager or Managers from among their number and the Operating Agreement provides that the death, insanity, bankruptcy, retirement, resignation, or expulsion of any Member-Manager causes a dissolution of the LLC without any further action of the Members, the Service will generally rule that the LLC lacks continuity of life, unless the LLC can be continued by the consent of not less than a "majority in interest of the remaining Members." For this purpose, all the Member-Managers must be subject to the specified dissolution event.

EXAMPLE: If A, B, and C are Member-Managers of the LLC, it must be provided that a dissolution with respect to A, B, or C will dissolve the LLC, and not a dissolution event with respect to only one of the named Managers. Therefore, if a dissolution event applies to A and B, but not C, continuity of life will be found to exist.

This provision of Rev. Proc. 95-10 provides a planning opportunity if clients do not want the LLC to dissolve on the occurrence of a dissolution event with respect to certain Members. Such Members should not serve as Managers.

If, instead, the LLC's Members do not designate one or more Managers and the Operating Agreement provides that the death, insanity, bankruptcy, retirement, resignation, or expulsion of any Member dissolves the LLC without any further action of the Members, the Service generally will rule that the LLC lacks continuity of life, again unless the LLC can be continued by the consent of not less than a "majority in interest of the remaining Members." For this purpose, all the Members must be subject to the specified dissolution events.

For purposes of satisfying the "majority in interest" standard for continuity of life in the preceding two paragraphs, the most recent revenue procedure states that Rev. Proc. 94-46, which provides a safe harbor for determining a "majority in interest" for continuity of life in the context of limited partnerships, will apply. Applying Rev. Proc. 94-46 to LLCs, continuity of life will not exist where, after a dissolution event, the remaining Members owning a majority of the profits, interests, and capital interests agree to continue the LLC.

EXAMPLE: If A, B, C, and D each own a 25 percent interest in both the LLC's profits and capital, and A dies, the LLC will dissolve unless two of the remaining three Members agree to continue the LLC. If only B in this example desires to continue the LLC, the LLC will be dissolved because B represents only one-third of the profits and capital interests owned by all the remaining Members (B, C, and D).

The IRS will not rule that an LLC lacks continuity of life if the Operating Agreement provides that less than all the listed dissolution events dissolves the LLC, unless the taxpayer clearly establishes in the ruling request that the event or events selected provide a "meaningful possibility of dissolution." Revenue Procedure 95-10 does not provide examples of what would constitute a "meaningful possibility of dissolution." For example, if an LLC has two Members, both of which are corporations, and the Operating Agreement provides that only the death or insanity, but not bankruptcy, resignation, retirement, or expulsion, of a Member dissolves the LLC, continuity of life will likely be found to exist.

The terms of the governing agreement are crucial to the continuity of life analysis. For example, in the typical limited partnership, the partnership agreement would provide that the partnership will be dissolved in the event of the bankruptcy of the general partner, but that in certain circumstances the limited partners may elect to continue the business of the partnership. In addition, the limited partnership law of most states under which the partnership was formed generally correspond to the Revised Uniform Limited Partnership Act and consequently the partnership would generally lack continuity of life.

Implications of the Provisions of the Operating Agreement to Proper Characterization

Practitioners drafting LLC Operating Agreements for their clients should keep the four material corporate characteristics in mind and take care to qualify the LLC for tax treatment as a partnership. Since, for practical purposes, most LLCs will have both limited liability and centralized management, caution must be taken to ensure that the LLC avoids free transferability of interests and continuity of life.

SUMMARY

One of the primary reasons for using an LLC is to obtain the taxation treatment that partnerships receive. The IRS has issued specific guidelines that must be followed for an entity to be taxed as a partnership rather than a corporation. Specifically, an LLC will be taxed as a partnership if it lacks at least two of the following four corporate characteristics: (1) limited liability, (2) centralized management, (3) free transferability of interest, and (4) continuity of life. In determining whether or not the entity lacks any of these corporate characteristics each such characteristic must be reviewed in the particular context. As a general rule, the LLC will need to be structured to not have the corporate characteristics of free transferability of interest and continuity of life. In some circumstances, it may also be structured to avoid the corporate characteristic of centralization of management.

19 VALUATION, MINORITY DISCOUNTS, LACK OF MARKETABILITY DISCOUNTS, AND LIMITED LIABILITY COMPANIES

It is important to properly value interests in real estate partnerships (general or limited), LLCs, and other types of business entities (such as C corporations, S corporations, trusts, etc.) when conducting many types of family business transactions. Valuations must be made where financing, tax planning, or estate planning are contemplated. A determination of the value of an interest in a business entity that is not publicly traded requires the consideration of numerous factors including the entity's economic outlook, earnings, goodwill, dividend paying capacity and other relevant factors.

A significant issue in determining the value of an interest in a business entity is whether and to what extent a discount to reflect the interest's lack of control and its lack of marketability is applicable. This chapter will survey how to value an interest in a limited liability company, limited partnership, or closely held corporation. This chapter will also examine the discounts that apply to an interest in an entity. Because an LLC is taxed like a partnership (if properly structured), the discussion regarding partnerships and minority and lack of marketability discounts also relates to LLCs. Case law analyzing the valuation of closely held businesses is also relevant, since courts have held that the rules applicable for valuing interests in closely held businesses apply to the valuation of interests in closely held partnerships.

VALUATION

Date of Valuation

Assets are generally valued at their fair market value. For estate tax purposes, the date of valuation is either the date of death or the alternate valuation date, which is six months later. For gifts of family property or real estate or business interests, the date of the actual transfer is the date of valuation.

EXAMPLE: Where a sale of a family business occurs, the property sold will be valued on the date of the closing and the value of a gift of an interest in a closely held business entity is measured on the date of the gift.

Valuation Defined

Fair market value is generally defined as the price that a willing buyer would pay to a willing seller, both persons having reasonable knowledge of all the relevant facts and neither person being under a compulsion to buy or to sell. Where the item being valued is an interest in a family partnership or an LLC where there is no market for the interest, an appraiser must examine other factors to determine the value of the interest. Three basic methods are used to value interests in business entities: (1) the cost approach; (2) the income approach; and (3) the market analysis approach.

The Cost Approach

The cost approach values property based on an analysis of the cost needed to replace or reproduce the property. The replacement amount is reduced by depreciation. This method is commonly used to value real estate, where the property is unique and the market is limited. It is also used to value holding companies whose assets are likely to establish the value of the business entity. Since a family limited partnership that holds real estate is similar to a holding company, this method would be appropriate in valuing interests in these partnerships.

Replacement cost may not provide an accurate assessment of how much a willing buyer would pay for the business interest since it does not reflect the investor's potential return on the investment or the risk faced by the investor.

The Income Approach

The income approach to valuation determines the fair market value of an asset based on the present value of the income that the property will produce (or is expected to produce) in the future. The income stream is projected into the future for a reasonable amount of time (such as five years). The projected income is inserted into a mathematical formula that results in the fair market value of the asset. A capitalization or discount rate is applied that reflects the type of income stream and an appropriate rate of return for the perceived risks. This approach is effective in valuing income-producing real estate (such as an office building) and business interests.

Market Analysis Approach

The market analysis approach derives the value of an asset from the price actually paid for the asset. The sale must have occurred within a reasonable time before or after the valuation date. Additionally, the sale must be an arm's-length transaction. Bona fide offers that were not accepted may be considered as well. Sales prices of the same or similar property are also relevant in determining a property's fair market value.

Revenue Ruling 59-60 Eight-Point Guidelines

The eight-factor guidelines for establishing the fair market value of an interest in a closely held company developed in Revenue Ruling (Rev. Rul.) 59-60 incorporates each of the three major approaches to valuation. The eight factors include:

1. The nature of the business and history of the company.
2. The economic outlook for the nation and for the particular industry.
3. The book value of the stock or interest in the company or partnership and the financial condition of the business.
4. The company or partnership's earning capacity.
5. The business entity's dividend paying capacity.
6. Evidence of goodwill or other intangible value.
7. The amount of stock valued.
8. The prices of stocks of publicly traded businesses in similar lines of business; and all other relevant factors affecting fair market value.

Each of these factors will be examined in detail in this chapter. Although Rev. Rul. 59-60 only specifically addresses the valuation of interests in closely held corporations, the ruling's analysis is also applied in the context of partnerships and will surely have applicability to LLCs.

Nature and History of the Business and Real Estate

By reviewing the history of a business and considering the nature of the business (its stability, growth rate, and diversity of operations), the appraiser can evaluate the degree of risk an individual takes in investing in the entity. This risk affects the worth of the property to the investor. Where the property valued is real estate, the historical rental income and expense history of the building, including its stability and its growth or decline are critical to the valuation for the same reason. Changes in demographics and developments in the local economy that the building or business serves should all be analyzed in a historical perspective with consideration given to potential future earning capacity and appreciation.

Economic Outlook

An appraisal of the value of a closely held business, partnership, or LLC should consider the current and prospective economic conditions of the business with regard to the national economy and the business's specific industry. In examining a business entity's economic outlook, an analysis of the prospective competition faced by the business is relevant, as is the company's current position with respect to its competitors. Where real estate is the subject of the appraisal, the appraiser should examine the tenants, the leases, and the economic outlook for the real estate. Factors such as high vacancy rates, oversupply of inventory, and falling lease rentals in a recessionary economy will decrease the value of the real estate.

Book Value and Financial Condition

Cash flow generated by the business should be calculated to determine the cash position and riskiness of the business interest valued. The practices of the business in question (specifically the policies of funding growth and improvements through operations as opposed to financing), all of which are fully controlled by the Manager of an LLC, are specifically relevant to valuation. In valuing a family real estate or business holding entity, large cash reserves or portfolio investments not reasonably required for working capital needs should be separately valued as part of the underlying family business valuation.

Earnings

An LLC's prospective and recent earnings, and the Members' ability to realize such earnings are a factor in valuing an interest in the business. An appraiser should consider the profits and losses realized by the LLC for a representative period prior to the valuation (such as five years). The appraiser should distinguish between operating income and investment income in order to predict the business entity's potential future income. Costs and expenses incurred by the business are also relevant in valuing an interest in the business.

Dividend/Distribution Paying Capacity

For closely held businesses or real estate properties, cash flow distributions should be considered. In valuing a closely held business, the dividend/distribution-paying capacity of the business entity is relevant, rather than the dividends or distributions actually paid in the past by the entity. Rev. Rul. 59-60 noted that evidence of dividends paid by a closely held business in the past may only measure the shareholders' needs or their desire to avoid income taxes and not the ability of the business to make distributions.

Goodwill

For a family-controlled business, goodwill can be the most significant asset, depending on the characteristics of the business. It is also the most difficult asset to value. Rev. Rul. 59-60 provides that goodwill is based on the earning capacity of the business, and any intangible value there is can be measured by the amount by which the value of the tangible assets exceeds the net book value of the assets. In the context of a family business, the issue as to whether the goodwill can be transferred to a third-party purchaser must be addressed. Goodwill is not considered when evaluating real estate.

Size of the Ownership Block to Be Valued

The size of the interest in the entity being valued can affect the value of the interest because of the interest's potential lack of control. An investor will be less willing to invest in a business in which he or she will have little control, and an interest in a business that represents control over that business has an added element of value.

Market Value of Interests in Similar Entities or Properties

The value of comparable properties or interests in similar businesses is relevant in determining the value of a business interest. Section 2031(b) of the Code provides that in valuing unlisted securities, the value of securities of a corporation engaged in the same or a similar line of business should be considered when the comparable corporation's securities are listed on an exchange. The value of comparables is traditionally the key element in valuing interests in a real estate entity.

Other Factors

Rev. Rul. 59-60 provides that any other factors that are relevant to the value of the asset or business entity valued should also be considered by an appraiser. For example, if the business interest is subject to an Operating Agreement, the effect of any restrictions contained in the agreement relating to the transfer of a Member's Membership interest is relevant to the interest's value.

Where an agreement is an arm's length agreement executed for valid business reasons, the restrictions contained in the agreement should be considered in determining the value of an interest in the family business governed by that agreement. In the context of family LLCs, however, certain restrictions that may be contained in the Operating Agreement may be ignored in valuing minority interests due to Chapter 14 of the Internal Revenue Code.

A series of decisions in the gift and estate tax context agree that restrictions on transfer must be considered in determining value as long as the agreements serve a bona fide business purpose. Such a restriction may affect both the initial value given to the business and any discount for lack of marketability considered. Courts have specifically noted that the limited partnership agreement (and thus by analogy the Operating Agreement) may prevent a limited partner from compelling the liquidation of the partnership and may expressly prohibit any involvement in the daily management of the partnership affairs. A limited partner's (Member's) restriction on compelling a liquidation invariably excludes liquidation values in valuing a limited partnership interest (Membership interest).

A typical provision in an Operating Agreement provides that nonmanaging Members have no right to participate in the company's management in any fashion. Another common restriction is that no Member has the right to force a distribution or partition of the real property held by the LLC. These provisions significantly restrict the right of a Member to control the return to be realized, or the results of the LLC. One of the few rights that Members may have under an Operating Agreement is to approve the liquidation of the LLC. However, often this right may only be exercised by a minimum of three-fourths of all of the Membership interests. Each of these restrictions may reduce the value of the business entity and any interest therein.

In *Harwood v. Commissioner* (82 T.C. 239 (1984)), the donor transferred an interest in a family partnership to her children in exchange for a note. The children subsequently formed trusts for the benefit of their children to which they transferred limited partnership interests in the family partnership. The family partnership agreement contained a restrictive clause entitling the partnership to buy out withdrawing partners at book value under certain circumstances. The court held that although the terms of the partnership agreement were not binding for gift tax purposes, the restrictive clauses did have a depressing effect on the gifts' value. The fact that all of the parties to the partnership agreement were lineal descendants, thus, related parties, did not dissuade the court from taking restrictive provisions into account in determining that the agreement depressed the value of the stock.

Certain restrictions may be virtually ignored for purposes of valuation. For example, little if any weight is given to a right of first refusal contained in a shareholder or partnership agreement where the agreement does not fix a price. Additionally, as described later in this chapter, certain restrictions on the ability of an interest holder to liquidate the entity are ignored for valuation purposes under Section 2704 of the Code.

VALUATION DISCOUNTS

In valuing Membership interests in LLCs, shares of a closely held corporation, fractional interests in real estate or partnership interests in a partnership, discounts, such as those reflecting the lack of marketability or lack of control associated with a business interest, can significantly affect the value of interests transferred.

Minority Discount

The concept of a minority discount is that the sum of the parts is worth less than the whole. An undivided minority interest is worth less than the allocable share of the entire value of the entity as a result of the restrictions and limitations that affect the minority interest. The minority interest discount is designed to reflect that a Member, shareholder, or partner who owns less than a majority of the voting interest in the entity has no meaningful control over the day-to-day and long-range managerial and policy decisions of the business. This inability to control the entity depresses the value of the interest so that a buyer would pay less to acquire it. The discount also reflects the interest holder's inability to obtain his or her pro rata share of the entity's net assets by forcing a liquidation.

Depending on each case's specific facts and circumstances, combined discounts in the range of 20 percent to 50 or more percent are not uncommon. To strengthen the argument for a sizable minority interest discount, the Operating Agreement should place maximum restrictions on the abilities of Members (or anyone who obtains an interest in the LLC) to transfer their interest or liquidate the entity, taking into account Code Section 2704(b) limitations, as discussed later in this chapter.

Courts apply minority interest discounts in the context of partnership interests. If the interest being valued is a limited partnership interest that does not have the power to be involved in management decisions, a minority interest discount is applicable. In one case (*Moore*, 62 TCM 1128 (1991)), the court stated:

> Courts have long recognized that the shares of stock of a corporation which represent a minority interest are usually worth less than a proportionate share of the value of the assets of the corporation. [Citations omitted] . . . The minority discount is recognized because the holder of a minority interest lacks control over corporate policy, cannot direct the payment of dividend, and cannot compel a liquidation of corporate assets. [Citations omitted] . . . Although these cases deal with minority interests in closely held corporations, we see no reason for a different rule for valuing partnership interests in this case . . . The critical factor is lack of control, be it as a minority partner or as a minority shareholder."

Similarly, if a Member of an LLC does not have management control, a minority discount may be applied in determining the value of the Member's interest.

Minority Interest Discount Factors

In determining the appropriate discount for a minority interest, a crucial factor is the rights possessed by the holder of the LLC Membership interest. Rights are afforded through applicable state law, the Articles of Organization, and any existing Operating Agreement. Courts examine factors including the interest holder's:

- Ability to share in the LLC's profits and losses.
- Ability to manage and control the LLC's assets.
- Ability to compel the payment of distributions.
- Authority to be paid salaries.
- Power to admit new Members.
- Ability to withdraw from the LLC.
- Authority to dissolve the LLC.
- Power to institute lawsuits to resolve conflicts among the Members.

An LLC Member may be prohibited from participating in management if the Operating Agreement vests management in a few selected individuals, who may or may not be Members. A limited partnership interest is prohibited by statute from participating in the management of partnership operations. Similarly, holders of a relatively small interest in a closely held corporation do not have the power to control management policy. Thus the value of a Membership interest in an LLC, shares of a closely held corporation, or of a limited partnership interest is commonly discounted. The rationale for the discount is that the perceived investment risk is greater where the investor cannot control the company's course of conduct.

Historically, in valuing partnership interests, whether the minority interest discount applies frequently depends on the ability of the owner of the partnership interest to force the liquidation of the partnership or to compel the partnership to purchase the partnership interest at its liquidation value, allowing the interest holder to recover his or her investment in the entity. For example, in *Estate of Watts v. Commissioner* (823 F.2d 483 (11th Cir. 1987)), the court determined that the interest holder's inability to compel liquidation justified a 35 percent discount from the value of the interest for federal estate tax purposes.

Transfers to Family Members

An analysis of the factors described previously does not complete the determination of whether a minority interest discount is applicable to the transfer of a non-controlling interest in a family LLC. Until 1993, the IRS took the position that a minority interest discount was generally not permitted with respect to transfers of stock or partnership interests among family members if, at the time of the transfer, the family controlled the entity. Prior to 1993, minority interest discounts were applied in the context of a family-run entity only where there was substantial documented discord among the family members that could indicate that the family members would act independently and adversely to each other. Thus, a 13 percent interest in a family partnership would be worth 13 percent of the fair value of the partnership's property, and not something less after a discount. Courts disagreed with the IRS position and permitted fractional discounts.

In Revenue Ruling 93-12, the IRS reversed its position and ruled that "a minority discount will not be disallowed solely because a transferred interest, when aggregated with the interests held by family members, would be part of a controlling interest." This ruling does not conclude the discount analysis, however. An appraiser must also examine the interaction between the state law under which the entity is organized and Section 2704 of the Code. Even when a minority interest discount is applicable under federal estate and gift tax valuation principles, the portion of the minority discount based on the interest holder's inability to liquidate the LLC, corporation, or partnership to obtain his or her pro rata share of the entity's assets will not be applied when certain interactions exist between state law and Section 2704 of the Code.

Section 2704 prohibits a minority discount based on restrictions on an interest holder's inability to compel a liquidation of his or her interest (or the entire entity) where the subject interest is transferred to a member of the interest holder's family when that family has control over the entity. For Section 2704 to apply, the liquidation restriction must be more restrictive than the limitations that apply under state law, and either (1) the restriction by its terms must lapse at some designated time after the transfer; or (2) the transferor (or the transferor's estate) and members of his or her family must have the power to remove the restriction on liquidation immediately after the transfer. Section 2704(b) does not apply to a "commercially reasonable" restriction on liquidation that arises as part of a financing with an unrelated party or to a restriction that is "not more restrictive than the limitations that would apply under state law generally applicable to the entity in the absence of the restriction" (Treas. Reg. 25.2704-2(b)). Section 2704(b) is also not applicable if the consent of a nonfamily member is required to remove the restriction. If Section 2704(b) does apply, a significant portion of the minority interest discount that would otherwise have been available based on the interest holder's inability to liquidate is lost.

In the context of family LLC Membership interest, any limitation placed on a Member's ability to liquidate his or her Membership interest that is more restrictive than the provisions under state law will be disregarded in determining the value of a Membership interest if Section 2704(b) applies. In some states, the Articles of Organization must set forth the LLC's termination date and the Members are not allowed to direct the liquidation of their Membership interests before the end of the LLC's term unless the Operating Agreement specifies otherwise. In those states, Section 2704(b) will not affect the valuation of Membership interests because the Members could not compel the liquidation of their interests prior to the expiration of the LLC's term under state law. In other states, where the law does not require that the Articles of Organization contain the LLC's termination date and a Member can withdraw from the LLC after giving notice, any restrictions on this withdrawal right contained in an Operating Agreement would be disregarded under Section 2704(b) in valuations where Section 2704(b) applies. Accordingly, in the context of an LLC, any restrictions on the ability of a Member to liquidate his or her interest in an LLC that are more restrictive than state law will be disregarded in determining the value of a transferred LLC Membership interest for estate or gift tax purposes where Section 2704(b) is applied.

Relationship between Discounts for Minority Interest and Lack of Marketability

Although the two discount concepts are closely related, and may overlap, courts recognize that the discount for lack of marketability and the minority interest discount are distinct. While the minority interest discount focuses on a Member's ability to effect the profitable distribution of his or her own particular Membership interests, the marketability discount is designed to reflect that there is no ready market for Membership interests in a closely held LLC. The marketability discount also reflects that investors prefer investments that have access to a liquid secondary market and that can be easily converted into cash.

The distinction between the two discounts is illustrated by situations where only one discount applies. For example, in one case transferability restrictions caused the tax court to apply a 40 percent marketability discount in valuing a 62 percent interest in a real estate investment company. Even controlling shares in a nonpublic corporation may suffer from lack of marketability because of the absence of a ready private placement market and the fact that flotation costs would have to be incurred if the corporation were to publicly offer its stock. Conversely, a minority discount may apply to the valuation of minority interests in a publicly traded company where a lack of marketability discount would be inapplicable.

Although the two discounts are analytically distinct, some factors may affect both discounts. For example, lack of control and the size of the holding being valued may affect the interest's marketability.

Lack of Marketability Discount

The marketability discount reflects that a willing buyer would not consider property for which there is no ready public market to have the same value as property that is freely tradable in the open market. As the court stated in *Central Trust Co. v. United States* (305 F.2d 393 (Ct. Cl. 1962)), "It seems clear that . . . an unlisted closely-held stock of a corporation in which trading is infrequent and which therefore lacks marketability, is less attractive than a similar stock which is listed on an exchange and has a ready access to the investing public." The discount for lack of marketability applies to the valuation of partnership interests as well as to the valuation of closely held corporations. Discounts for lack of marketability range from 10 percent to over 50 percent. Accordingly, Membership interests in LLCs should also be subject to a lack of marketability discount.

Generally, courts consider several broad factors in determining the applicability and amount of a marketability discount. If there is no established market for the interest valued, the marketability discount is greater. In the context of a family LLC, there is no active market for minority interests in closely held, nonsyndicated, real estate LLCs. In a properly drawn Operating Agreement, the minority Member has no right to force the liquidation of the LLC. The sole right of the minority Membership interest holder is to sell the membership interest pursuant to the Operating Agreement. This limitation on the minority interest holder's ability to retrieve his or her other share of the LLC reduces the value of the holder's interest. The fact that few markets exist to sell LLC Membership interests in either public or private LLCs affects the value of the interests.

In *Bernard Mandelbaum et. al. v. Commissioner* (69 TCM 2852 (1995)), the Tax Court designed a method of determining the appropriate marketability discount for an interest in a family-owned business. The court began by examining the average marketability discount (as set forth in published studies) for a public corporation's transfer of restricted stock (35 percent) and the average discount for an initial public offering (45 percent). The court used these amounts as benchmarks of the marketability discount. The court proceeded in determining that a 30 percent marketability discount was applicable based on an analysis of the following factors:

- *Financial Statement Analysis.* The court noted that investors normally consider the company's financial statements as a significant factor for determining the worth of the company's stock. Factors such as the company's earnings, revenue, and net worth affect the marketability of an interest in the entity.
- *Business Entity's Dividend/Distribution Policy.* The likelihood that an investor will receive a fair rate of return on his or her investment should be

considered in determining the value of an interest in a company. The *Mandelbaum* case focused on the business entity's dividend paying *capacity* as opposed to its dividend paying *history*.

- *Holding Period for the Business Interest.* The length of time that an investor must hold his or her investment before the investor can retrieve that investment from the entity is critical to a valuation of an interest in a business. The longer the member must hold his or her interest before being able to sell or otherwise dispose of the interest is relevant to a determination of the value a potential buyer would pay for an interest in the business entity.

- *Company's Redemption Policy.* This factor is only applicable in the case of a corporation.

- *Costs Associated with Making a Public Offering.* This factor is relevant in determining the value of unlisted stock. The effect of this factor is based on whether the buyer must bear the cost of registering the purchased stock and whether the buyer has the ability to minimize his or her registration costs.

- *Nature of the Company, Its History, Its Position in the Industry, and Its Economic Outlook.* These factors are relevant in determining the worth of an interest in the entity.

- *Company's Management.* The strength of the management of a business entity affects the value of an interest in that entity.

- *Amount of Control in Transferred Interest.* An interest in a business entity that gives the investor control over the entity is worth more to an investor and is therefore more easily transferable than a noncontrolling interest in that entity.

- *Restrictions on Transferability.* Restrictions contained in Operating Agreements affect the transferability of the interest in the entity and the value of that interest.

A discount for lack of marketability should not be rejected simply because a controlling interest in the business was involved. In claiming a discount for lack of marketability on gifts of Membership interests in family LLCs, donors will have to make their claim without regard to their inability to force a liquidation of the LLC. Because of previous taxpayer abuses, Chapter 14 of the Code now prohibits consideration of any restrictions that limit a Member's ability to liquidate his or her Membership interest in valuing a transfer among family members if the donor and his or her family control the LLC and the restriction can be removed, if the donor and his or her family choose to do so. Therefore, it is essential that donors ensure that there are sufficient other restrictions on any such Membership interests to bolster the lack of marketability discount.

SUMMARY

Factors such as the partnership or LLC's earning capacity, economic outlook, and book value should be considered when valuing interests in partnerships or LLCs for purposes of evaluating collateral for a loan; for determining the amount of a gift or bequest for federal gift, estate, or generation-skipping transfer tax purposes; for structuring a buy-sell agreement; or for other purposes. Once the value of the interest has been determined based on all the relevant factors, the appraiser must consider whether the value can be discounted to reflect the interest's lack of marketability and/or lack of control (e.g., minority discounts).

EPILOGUE

WHAT DOES THE LIMITED LIABILITY MEAN FOR YOU?

The LLC is one of the newest, most flexible, and perhaps most useful of all business entities available. In time, it will likely revolutionize the manner in which business and investment transactions are organized by replacing many of the more common types of entity. In the years to come, however, many businesses and investments will remain organized as S corporations, family (and other) limited partnerships, and so forth. Initially, what the LLC will mean for you is a bit more complexity in the choice of how you should structure a particular business, investment, or other transaction. However, with competent legal, tax, and accounting advice, this complexity will enable you to make the best choice. The characteristics of the LLC structure may result in your saving taxes, avoiding ancillary probate, obtaining protection from creditors, simplifying your tax and financial matters, or even gaining other benefits. Use this book as a guide to help you obtain the best use, for the most reasonable cost, of your professional advisers in making this decision. Good luck.

APPENDIX A

Limited Liability Company Statutes in the United States

The following tables present a summary of the LLC laws in each state. LLCs are, relative to other types of legal entities, quite new. As a result changes should be expected to occur. As the tax and legal rules mature, even some of the basic rules summarized in this Appendix could change. Therefore, it is essential that you consult with an attorney in your state before organizing an LLC.

TIP: If your LLC may operate in a state other than where you reside, be certain the lawyer you hire is qualified to assist you with that other state. Ask your lawyer whether an attorney in the other state should also be retained.

Alabama

State Statute. The Alabama LLC Act, Ala. Code §§ 10-12-1 through 10-12-61, became effective October 1, 1993.

Formation. Articles of Organization must contain the following information: name; duration, if less than perpetual; purpose; registered agent and office; names and mailing addresses of the initial Members; reservation of right to admit new Members; right to continue following act of dissociation or dissolution; whether there will be a Manager(s); and any additional matters.

Minimum Number of Members. Two.

Default Rules. The following are examples of default rules provided by the Alabama LLC Act. Unless otherwise provided in the Articles of Organization or Operating Agreement:

- Members will manage the LLC.
- The LLC's profits and losses will be apportioned on the basis of the pro rata value of the contributions of each Member.
- A Member on 30 days' notice can withdraw from the LLC.
- Unanimous consent of the Membership is required for a person who wants to become a Member.
- A Membership interest is not assignable.
- An assignment does not dissolve the LLC.
- An assignee only obtains a financial interest in the LLC.
- An assignor does not lose his or her Membership interest in the entity.
- The unanimous vote of the Members is required for an assignee to become a Member.
- An assignor is not released from his or her obligations to the LLC.
- The full assignment of a Member's interest is an act of dissociation.

State Classification.   An LLC will be classified in the same manner as it is classified for federal income tax purposes.

State Entity Level Tax.   None.

Alaska

State Statute.   The Alaska Limited Liability Company Act, Alaska Stat. §§ 10.50.010 through 10.50.990, became effective July 1, 1995.

Formation.   Articles of Organization must contain the following information: name; purpose; duration if less than perpetual; whether there will be a Manager(s); registered agent and office; and any additional matters.

Minimum Number of Members.   Two.

Default Rules.   The following are examples of default rules provided by the Alaska LLC Act. Unless otherwise provided in the Articles of Organization or Operating Agreement:

- Members will manage the LLC.
- Members share equally in allocations and distributions.
- If a Member has no power to withdraw from the company by voluntary act, the Member may withdraw at any time by giving 30 days' written notice.
- Action requires the unanimous consent of the Members.
- A Member is able to assign his or her interest without restriction except that the assignee will not have any right to participate in LLC's management.

State Classification.   An LLC will be classified in the same manner as it is classified for federal income tax purposes.

State Entity Level Tax.   None.

Arizona

State Statute.   The Arizona Limited Liability Company Act, Ariz. Rev. Stat. Ann. §§ 29-601 through 29-857, became effective September 30, 1992.

Formation.   Articles of Organization must contain the following information: name; the latest date on which the LLC is to dissolve; registered agent and office; a statement that there are or will be two or more Members at the time the entity is formed; and whether management is by Members or Managers, and the name and address of those who are to participate in management.

Minimum Number of Members.   Two.

Default Rules.   The following are examples of default rules provided by the Arizona LLC Act. Unless otherwise provided in the Articles of Organization or Operating Agreement:

- Members will manage the LLC.
- The LLC's profits and losses will be apportioned among its Members and classes of Members according to the relative capital contributions that they have made or promised to make in the future.
- A majority vote of the Managers or Members is required to (a) make decisions, (b) authorize distributions, (c) repurchase a Member's interest, (d) file notices of winding up, and (e) authorize nonmandatory amendment of the LLC's Articles of Organization.
- The Members' unanimous vote is required to (a) authorize activities outside the company purpose, (b) issue an interest in the LLC, (c) approve a plan of merger or consolidation, and (d) change the form of management the Articles of Organization authorizes.

State Classification.   For all state and local taxes, except state income tax, an LLC is treated as a limited partnership. For state income tax purposes, an LLC will be classified in the same manner as for federal income tax purposes.

State Entity Level Tax.   None.

Arkansas

State Statute.   The Arkansas Small Business Entity Tax Pass Through Act of 1993, Ark. Code Ann. §§ 4-32-101 through 4-32-1316, became effective April 12, 1993.

Formation.   Articles of Organization must contain the following information: name; the latest date on which the LLC is to dissolve; registered agent and office; and whether there will be a Manager(s).

Minimum Number of Members.   One.

Default Rules.   The following are examples of default rules provided by the Arkansas LLC Act. Unless otherwise provided in the Articles of Organization or Operating Agreement:

- The right to manage the affairs of the LLC rests with the Managers.
- Members must fulfill their contribution promises even when unable to do so.
- Compromising an obligation to contribute to the LLC requires an unanimous vote of the Members.
- Unanimous consent of the Membership is required for new Members to be admitted.

State Classification.   Arkansas' past record of tax suggests that an LLC will be classified in the same manner as it is classified for federal income tax purposes.

State Entity Level Tax.   None.

California

State Statute.   The California Limited Liability Company Act, Cal. Corp. Code §§ 17000 through 17705, became effective September 30, 1994.

Purposes.   California is the only state that does not permit an LLC to be formed for a limited purpose. A California LLC may engage in any lawful business activity except banking, insurance or trust.

Formation.   Articles of Organization must contain the following information: name; the latest date on which the LLC is to dissolve; purpose (which may not be a limited purpose); registered agent and office; whether the LLC is to be managed by Managers and not by all its Members if the LLC is to be managed by Managers; and any other matters.

Minimum Number of Members.   Two.

Default Rules.   The following are examples of default rules provided by the California LLC Act. Unless otherwise provided in the Articles of Organization or Operating Agreement:

- Members will manage the LLC.
- Allocations and distributions are shared equally among the Members.
- If a Member has no power to withdraw from the company by voluntary act, the Member may withdraw at any time by giving 30 days' written notice.
- Consent of all Members is required for company action.
- A Member's interest is assignable without restriction except that the assignee will not have any right to participate in management of the company.

State Classification.   An LLC will be classified in the same manner as it is classified for federal income tax purposes.

State Entity Level Tax.   There is an annual $800 minimum franchise tax and maximum gross receipts tax of $4,000.

Colorado

State Statute.   The Colorado Limited Liability Company Act, Colo. Rev. Stat. §§ 7-80-101 to 7-80-913, became effective April 18, 1990.

Formation.   Articles of Organization must contain the following information: name; the latest date on which the LLC is to dissolve; registered agent and office; names and addresses of initial Manager(s); and principal place of business.

Minimum Number of Members.   One.

Default Rules.   The following are examples of default rules provided by the Colorado LLC Act. Unless otherwise provided in the Articles of Organization or Operating Agreement:

- Managers and Members can conduct business and lend money with the LLC.
- Only a Manager can incur debt or liability.
- Distributions will be made on the basis of the value of the contributions made by each Member to the LLC.
- A Member is only entitled to receive cash distributions.

State Classification.   Colorado treats all LLCs as pass-through entities. All Colorado LLCs must file a partnership income tax return.

State Entity Level Tax.   None.

Connecticut

State Statute.   The Connecticut Limited Liability Company Act, P.A. 93-267, became effective October 1, 1993.

Formation.   Articles of Organization must contain the following information: name; the latest date on which the LLC is to dissolve; whether there will be a Manager(s); and purpose of the LLC.

Minimum Number of Members.   Two.

Default Rules.   The following are examples of default rules provided by the Connecticut LLC Act. Unless otherwise provided in the Articles of Organization or Operating Agreement:

- All Members must agree to compromise the required capital contribution.
- Profits and losses and distributions will be apportioned according to a Member's basis of value as shown on the LLC's books.
- The LLC can only distribute cash and a Member only has the right to receive cash as a distribution.
- A Member who allows a lien to be filed, or gives a security interest or pledges his or her interest, does not surrender Membership rights.
- A Member can withdraw from the LLC on 30 days' notice.
- New Members can be admitted by a majority in interest.

State Classification.   An LLC will be classified in the same manner as it is classified for federal income tax purposes.

State Entity Level Tax.   None.

Delaware

State Statute.   The Delaware Limited Liability Company Act, Del. Code Ann. §§ 18-101 through 18.1107, became effective October 1, 1992.

Formation.   The Certificate of Formation must set forth the following information: name; registered agent and office; and a specific date of dissolution, if desired.

Minimum Number of Members.   Two.

Default Rules. The following are examples of default rules provided by the Delaware LLC Act. Unless otherwise provided in the Articles of Organization or Operating Agreement:

- The Manager or Member may conduct numerous forms of business dealings with the LLC.
- Specific factors causing a Member to lose his or her Membership in the LLC will apply by default. These Membership-terminating factors include filing of bankruptcy; assignment for the benefit of creditors; and debtor protection court pleading.
- Managers or Members can withdraw on six months' notice.
- Members are obligated to perform their promises to contribute property or cash or to perform services even if they are unable to perform because of death, disability, or other reason.
- Members, in proportion to their capital interests, will share in the profits and losses of an LLC.
- On withdrawal from the LLC or when receiving distributions, a Member will receive the fair value of his or her interests in a reasonable time. Payment will be made in cash. The Member has the same status against the LLC as a creditor.
- Membership interests are assignable in whole or part.
- An assignee is not liable for the liabilities of the assignor Member unless or until he is authorized by the Company Agreement or he becomes a Member.
- An assignee cannot participate in management.

State Classification. An LLC will be classified in the same manner as it is classified for federal income tax purposes.

State Entity Level Tax. There is a $100 tax on domestic and foreign LLCs.

District of Columbia

State Statute. The District of Columbia Limited Liability Company Act, D.C. Code Ann. §§ 29-1301 through 29-1375, became effective July 23, 1994.

Formation. Articles of Organization must contain the following information: name; the latest date on which the LLC is to dissolve; and registered agent and office.

Minimum Number of Members. Two.

Default Rules. The following are examples of default rules provided by the District of Columbia LLC Act. Unless otherwise provided in the Articles of Organization or Operating Agreement:

- No Manager, Member, employee, or other agent of an LLC shall have any personal obligation for any debt, obligations, or liabilities of an LLC, whether such debts, obligations, or liabilities arise in contract, tort, or other act of an agent, Manager, Member, or employee of the LLC.
- Members shall manage the LLC.
- The Members of an LLC shall vote in proportion to their respective interests in the profits of the LLC.
- Decisions concerning the affairs of the LLC shall require the consent of those Members with voting rights holding at least a majority of the interests and profits of the LLC.
- A Member is obligated to the LLC to perform any enforceable promises to contribute property or cash or to perform services. If a Member dies and does not make the required contribution of property or services, at the option of the LLC, such Member is obligated to contribute cash equal to that portion of the value of the stated contribution that has not been made.

- If a Member is unable to perform any enforceable promise to perform services because of disability or death, such Member or such Member's successor or assign shall have the option of either:

   Contributing cash equal to that portion of the value of a stated contribution that the Member had promised to make in services but had failed to make.

   Forfeiting the Member's interest in the LLC.

- Profits and losses shall be allocated on the basis of value, as stated in the LLC records, of the contributions made by each Member to the extent they have been received by the LLC and have not been returned.

- A Member, regardless of the nature of such Member's contribution, has a right to demand and receive a distribution from an LLC in cash only.

- A Member shall not be required to accept (in lieu of the Member's share of a pro rata cash distribution) a distribution of any asset in-kind from an LLC to the extent that the percentage of the asset that would otherwise be distributed to such Member would exceed the percentage that such Member's membership interest bears to all Membership interests in the LLC.

- A Member may resign from an LLC on not less than six months' prior written notice to the LLC or to each member at such Member's address on the books of the LLC.

- Except as provided in the statute, a Member's financial rights associated with his or her interest in the LLC is assignable in whole or part.

State Classification. An LLC will be classified in the same manner as it is classified for federal income tax purposes.

State Entity Level Tax. There is a 10 percent tax on D.C. source income earned by unincorporated businesses.

Florida

State Statute. The Florida Limited Liability Company Act, Fla. Stat. §§ 608.401 through 608.514, became effective in 1982. The Act was substantially rewritten by the 1993 Legislature. The new Act became effective in October 1993.

Formation. Articles of Organization must contain the following information: name; duration; mailing address of the principal office of the company; name and address of the LLC's registered agent; reservation of right to admit new Members; right to continue following dissolution; whether there will be a Manager(s); and any additional matters.

Minimum Number of Members. Two.

Default Rules. The following are examples of default rules provided by the Florida LLC Act. Unless otherwise provided in the Articles of Organization or Operating Agreement:

- All capital contribution commitments must be performed by a Member.
- Management of an LLC rests with the members in relative proportion to their capital accounts.
- Members cannot admit new Members without the unanimous vote of the Members.
- When the LLC is managed by Managers, only Managers can obligate the LLC; when the LLC is managed by Members, only Members can contract LLC debts.
- A Member, before withdrawing from the LLC, must give six months' written notice.
- A Member cannot assign his or her LLC interest, in whole or part, without the approval of a majority of the nonassigning Members.
- The unanimous consent of the Members is required for an assignee to become a Member.

State Classification.   Florida taxes LLCs as "artificial" entities, and they are subject to an entity level tax.

State Entity Level Tax.   The LLC is subject to a 5.5 percent artificial entity tax.

Georgia

State Statute.   The Georgia Limited Liability Company Act became effective March 1, 1994.

Formation.   Articles of Organization must contain the following information: name; and the latest date on which the LLC is to dissolve.

Minimum Number of Members.   One.

Default Rules.   The following are examples of default rules provided by the Georgia LLC Act. Unless otherwise provided in the Articles of Organization or Operating Agreement:

- The unanimous consent of the Members is required for the admission of additional Members.
- A person who ceases to be a Member has no management rights in the LLC.
- All LLCs are Member-managed.
- A Member is not entitled to receive an in-kind distribution.
- Members' interests are assignable in whole or part.
- The unanimous vote of the Members is required for an assignee to become a Member.
- A Member, on six months' written notice to the LLC, can withdraw.

State Classification.   An LLC will be classified in the same manner as it is classified for federal income tax purposes.

State Entity Level Tax.   The LLC pays 5 percent withholding tax on behalf of nonresident Members' distributive shares of LLC income.

Idaho

State Statute.   The Idaho Limited Liability Company Act, Idaho Code §§ 53-601 through 53-672, became effective July 1, 1993.

Formation.   Articles of Organization must contain the following information: name; registered agent and office; address of the registered office; the latest date on which the LLC is to dissolve; and whether there will be a Manager(s).

Minimum Number of Members.   One.

Default Rules.   The following are examples of default rules provided by the Idaho LLC Act. Unless otherwise provided in the Articles of Organization or Operating Agreement:

- Managers make decisions by majority vote.
- A Member is liable for his or her contributions to the LLC and this obligation cannot be compromised without the unanimous consent of the Membership.
- Distributions must be paid in cash to a Member unless an in-kind payment is authorized in the Operating Agreement.
- Assignments of Membership interests are permitted.
- A person who receives a pledge of a Member's Membership interest is not an assignee.
- Assignees can become Members only with the unanimous consent of the Members.
- Assignees have no right to participate in management.
- An assignor is not released from his or her liability to the LLC.
- A Member who assigns his or her entire interest in the LLC loses Membership in the entity.

- Unanimous consent of the Membership is required for a person to become a Member.
- Members, on 30 days' notice may withdraw.

State Classification.   An LLC will be classified in the same manner as it is classified for federal income tax purposes.
State Entity Level Tax.   None.

Illinois

State Statute.   The Illinois Limited Liability Company Act became effective January 1, 1994.
Formation.   Articles of Organization must contain the following information: name; purpose; registered agent and office; whether there will be a Manager(s); the latest date on which the LLC is to dissolve; address of the LLC's principal office; name and address of each organizer; and any additional matters.
Minimum Number of Members.   Two.
Default Rules.   The following are examples of default rules provided by the Illinois LLC Act. Unless otherwise provided in the Articles of Organization or Operating Agreement:

- A Member may transact business and lend money to the LLC.
- New Members must have the unanimous consent of existing Members to be admitted.
- All decisions of Members must be approved by the Members owning a majority vote of the book value of Membership interests.
- Membership interests in the profits are assignable in whole or part.

State Classification.   An LLC will be classified in the same manner as it is classified for federal income tax purpose.
State Entity Level Tax.   The LLC pays a 1.5 percent tax on partnerships.

Indiana

State Statute.   The Indiana Business Flexibility Act, Ind. Code §§ 23-18-1-1 through 23-18-13-1, became effective July 1, 1993.
Formation.   Articles of Organization must contain the following information: name; registered agent and office; the latest date on which the LLC is to dissolve; whether there will be a Manager(s); and any additional matters.
Minimum Number of Members.   One.
Default Rules.   The following are examples of default rules provided by the Indiana LLC Act. Unless otherwise provided in the Articles of Organization or Operating Agreement:

- Members have the power and authority to manage the LLC.
- Governing decisions are by majority vote when there is more than one Manager.
- Absent a unanimous vote of the Membership, the LLC cannot reduce the obligation of a Member to repay a distribution or make a capital contribution.
- A Member cannot be required to receive a distribution in-kind rather than cash.
- A vote of all Members is required for admission of Members.
- Members' interests are assignable.
- The unanimous consent of the Members is required for an assignee to become a Member.
- A Member, on 30 days' notice, may withdraw from the LLC.

State Classification.   An LLC will be classified in the same manner as it is classified for federal income tax purposes.

State Entity Level Tax.   None.

Iowa

State Statute.   The Iowa Limited Liability Company Act, Iowa Code §§ 490A.100 through 490A.1601, became effective September 1, 1992.

Formation.   Articles of Organization must contain the following information: name; duration, if not perpetual; registered agent and office; address of principal office; and any additional matters.

Minimum Number of Members.   Two.

Default Rules.   The following are examples of default rules provided by the Iowa LLC Act. Unless otherwise provided in the Articles of Organization or Operating Agreement:

- Members will manage the LLC.
- Members can withdraw on six months' notice.
- Managers will be elected by majority vote of the Members.
- Managers can be removed by a majority vote of the Members with or without cause.
- Decisions by Managers will be made by majority vote.
- Members vote in proportion to their contributions to the LLC's capital.
- A unanimous vote is needed to approve:

    Dissolution and winding up.

    The sale, lease, exchange, mortgage, pledge, or other transfer of all or substantially all of the LLC's assets.

    Amendment of the Articles of Organization or Operating Agreement.

- Members will share the LLC's profits and losses in proportion to their capital interests.
- Interests of the Membership are assignable in whole or part.
- A Member ceases to be a Member on assignment of his or her entire Membership interest.
- The unanimous consent of the existing Members is required for the assignee to become a Member.

State Classification.   An LLC will be classified as a partnership under federal classification guidelines.

State Entity Level Tax.   None.

Kansas

State Statute.   The Kansas Limited Liability Company Act, Kan. Stat. Ann. §§ 17-7610 through 17-7652, became effective July 1, 1990.

Formation.   Articles of Organization must contain the following information: name; the latest date on which the LLC is to dissolve; purpose; registered agent and office; whether there will be a Manager(s); reservation of right to admit new Members; and the right to continue the LLC.

Minimum Number of Members.   Two.

Default Rules.   The following are examples of default rules provided by the Kansas LLC Act. Unless otherwise provided in the Articles of Organization or Operating Agreement:

- Management of the LLC rests with the members, with each Member having one vote.
- Members can transact business and lend money with the LLC.
- The allocation of gain, income, loss, deduction, or credit will be allocated to Members in proportion to the right to share in distributions to the LLC.

State Classification.   A Kansas LLC is taxed as a corporation for state franchise taxes.

State Entity Level Tax.   The LLC is subject to franchise tax on net capital accounts.

Kentucky

State Statute.   The Kentucky Limited Liability Company Act, KRS Chapter 275, §§ 1 through 93, was enacted March 29, 1994.

Formation.   Articles of Organization must contain the following information: name; registered agent and office; address of the principal office; whether there will be a Manager(s); statement that there are two or more Members; specific date of dissolution; and any additional matters.

Minimum Number of Members.   Two.

Default Rules.   The following are examples of default rules provided by the Kentucky LLC Act. Unless otherwise provided in the Articles of Organization or Operating Agreement:

- Members manage the company.
- There will be only one class of Members.
- Management action requires a majority of Members on a per capita basis.
- Approval of action requires only a simple majority of the Members on a per capita basis.
- The Members share equally in allocations and distributions.
- A Member's interest is assignable without restriction, except that the assignee will not have any right to participate in Management of the company.
- Consent of all Members is required for admission of members, whether they take their interest directly from the company or by assignment.
- If a Member has no power to withdraw from the company by voluntary act, the Member may withdraw at any time by giving 30 days' written notice.

State Classification.   An LLC will be classified in the same manner as it is classified for federal income tax purposes.

State Entity Level Tax.   None.

Louisiana

State Statute.   The Louisiana Limited Liability Company Act, La. Rev. Stat. Ann. §§ 12:1301 through 12:1369, became effective July 7, 1992.

Formation.   Articles of Organization must contain the following information: name; purpose; and any additional matters.

Minimum Number of Members.   Two.

Default Rules.   The following are examples of default rules provided by the Louisiana LLC Act. Unless otherwise provided in the Articles of Organization or Operating Agreement:

- Voting is by plurality vote of the members.
- Silence permits management to be removed with or without cause.

- Silence results in management by the Members.
- When voting requirements of Managers/Members are not established, each Manager has one vote and decisions are made by majority vote.
- If a Member's obligation to pay capital contributions because of death, disability, or other reason is not limited, then the payment must be made.
- The vote to compromise a capital contribution must be unanimous.
- Allocation of profits and losses will be equally among the Members.
- The withdrawing Member is entitled to his or her fair market value share of distributions within a reasonable time. All payments must be in cash and not in kind.
- Failure to control/limit the assignability, pledge, or encumbrance of membership interests in the Articles or the Operating Agreement results in the assignability and pledge or encumbrance of Membership interests. Pledge or encumbrance of a Member's interest does not cause him or her to lose Membership status.
- Unanimous consent of Membership is required for an assignee to become a Member or participate in the management of an LLC.

State Classification.   An LLC will be classified in the same manner as it is classified for federal income tax purposes.

State Entity Level Tax.   None.

Maine

State Statute.   The Maine Limited Liability Company Act, Me. Rev. Stat. Ann. Tit. 31, §§ 601 through 762, became effective January 1, 1995.

Formation.   Articles of Organization must contain the following information: name; registered agent and office; whether there will be a manager(s); and any additional matters.

Minimum Number of Members.   One.

Default Rules.   The following are examples of default rules provided by the Maine LLC Act. Unless otherwise provided in the Articles of Organization or Operating Agreement:

- Members manage the LLC.
- There will be only one class of Members.
- Management action requires a majority of Members on a per capita basis.
- Unless otherwise provided for in the statute, approval of action requires only a simple majority of the Members on a per capita basis.
- The company is not obligated to indemnify an employee or agent.
- A Member's successor is obligated to the company to pay his or her obligation for contributions.
- Members share equally in allocations and distributions.
- A withdrawing Member is not entitled to receive any distributions, now or later.
- A Member's interest is assignable without restriction, except the assignee will not have any right to participate in management of the company.
- Consent of all Members is required for admission of Members, whether they take their interest directly from the company or by assignment.
- If a Member has no power to withdraw from the company by voluntary act, the Member may do so at any time by giving 30 days' written notice.

State Classification.   An LLC will be classified in the same manner as it is classified for federal income tax purposes.

State Entity Level Tax.   None.

Maryland

State Statute.   The Maryland Limited Liability Company Act, Md. Code Ann. §§ 4A-101 through 4A-1103, became effective October 1, 1992.

Formation.   Articles of Organization must contain the following information: name; the latest date on which the LLC is to dissolve; principal agent and office; purpose; and any additional matters.

Minimum Number of Members.   Two.

Default Rules.   The following are examples of default rules provided by the Maryland LLC Act. Unless otherwise provided in the Articles of Organization or Operating Agreement:

- Each Member is an agent of the LLC.
- Oral Operating Agreements are permitted.
- All Members will vote in proportion to their interests in the profits of the LLC and management decisions will be made by majority vote.
- Members can do business with the LLC.
- Members must make promised capital contributions to the LLC. Required contributions can be compromised only with the unanimous consent of the Members or pursuant to terms of the Operating Agreement.
- The interests of the LLC are assignable.
- A Member has the right to withdraw on six months' written notice.
- Merger is permitted.
- An LLC dissolves when a person ceases to be a Member or at the time of the entry of a decree of judicial dissolution, except as provided by the unanimous consent of the Members.
- The remaining Members may wind up an LLC.

State Classification.   All LLCs are treated as pass-through entities; all Maryland LLCs must file a pass-through entity income tax return.

State Entity Level Tax.   The LLC pays 5 percent withholding tax on behalf of nonresident Members' distributive shares of LLC income.

Massachusetts

State Statute.   The Massachusetts Limited Liability Company Act, The Acts and Resolve of 1995, Chapter 281, was enacted January 1, 1996.

Formation.   Articles of Organization must contain the following information: name and address; latest date on which the LLC is to dissolve; principal agent and office; name and address of the managers, if any; name of any other person authorized to execute documents; general character of business; purpose; and any additional matters.

Minimum Number of Members.   Two.

Default Rules.   The following are examples of default rules provided by the Massachusetts LLC Act. Unless otherwise provided in the Certificate of Incorporation or Operating Agreement:

- The decision of Members who own more than fifty percent of the unreturned contributions shall be controlling.
- Management shall be vested in the Members.
- A Member is obligated to perform any promise to contribute cash or property or to perform services to the LLC.
- A Member has no right to demand and receive any distribution from an LLC in any form other than cash.
- An LLC interest is assignable, in whole or in part.

- An assignment entitles the assignee to share in profits and losses.
- Until an assignee becomes a Member, the assignee shall have no liability as a Member.

State Classification.   All LLCs are taxed as partnerships.
State Entity Level Tax.   None.

Michigan
State Statute.   The Michigan Limited Liability Company Act became effective June 1, 1993.
Formation.   Articles of Organization must contain the following information: name; purpose; registered agent and office; whether there will be a Manager(s); and duration.
Minimum Number of Members.   Two.
Default Rules.   The following are examples of default rules provided by the Michigan LLC Act. Unless otherwise provided in the Articles of Organization or Operating Agreement:

- All Members must comply with promises to contribute to the LLC.
- Unanimous consent of the Membership is required for Members to be excused from performing contributions promised to the entity.
- A Manager or Member entitled to participate in a decision to make a distribution is presumed to have assented to a distribution once he or she files a written dissent with the company.
- Members manage the LLC. However, management rights can be enlarged or restricted in the Operating Agreement.
- A majority vote of the Members elect managers.
- Managers can be terminated without cause.
- Unless contracted, an assignee has no liability as a Member solely as a result of the assignment.
- A Member, on 90 days' written notice, may withdraw from the LLC.

State Classification.   An LLC is subject to state income taxes.
State Entity Level Tax.   The LLC pays 2.3 percent of a specified LLC tax base.

Minnesota
State Statute.   The Minnesota Limited Liability Company Act became effective January 1, 1993.
Formation: Articles of Organization must contain the following information: name; registered agent and office; name and address of each organizer; duration of the LLC; and the power to enter into a business continuation agreement.
Minimum Number of Members.   Two.
Default Rules.   The Minnesota LLC Act lists 18 statutory provisions that may be modified in the Articles of Organization.

- Members vote in proportion to their contributions to the capital of the LLC.
- The profits and losses of an LLC will be shared by the Members in proportion to their value of their capital interests.

State Classification.   An LLC will be classified in the same manner as it is classified for federal income tax purposes.
State Entity Level Tax.   There is no entity level tax, but there is an annual flat fee for farming partnerships.

Mississippi

State Statute. The Mississippi Limited Liability Company Act became effective July 1, 1994.

Formation. Articles of Organization must contain the following information: name; duration, if less than perpetual; registered agent and office; whether there will be a Manager(s); and any additional matters.

Minimum Number of Members. Two.

Default Rules. The following are examples of default rules provided by the Mississippi LLC Act. Unless otherwise provided in the Articles of Organization or Operating Agreement:

- A Member may transact other business and lend money to the LLC and, subject to other applicable law, has the same rights and obligations with respect thereto as a person who is not a Member or Manager.

- An LLC shall indemnify a Manager, Member, or other person who is wholly successful, on the permits or otherwise, in the defense of any proceeding to which he or she was a party because he or she is or was a Manager, Member, or agent of the LLC against reasonable expenses incurred by him or her in connection with the proceeding.

- One or more LLCs may merge with or into one or more domestic or foreign LLCs with such LLC or foreign LLC being the surviving organization.

- Written consent of all Members is required for a person acquiring an LLC interest directly from the LLC.

- Members manage the LLC.

- Each Member of an LLC shall be entitled to one vote on any matter entitled to be voted on by the Members.

- Unless otherwise provided in the statute, any action required or permitted to be taken by the Members of an LLC must be by a majority vote of the Members.

- Subject to the consent of all Members at the time, a person ceases to be a Member on his or her death or the entry of an order by a court of competent jurisdiction adjudicating the person incompetent to manage his or her person or estate.

- If a Member has no power to withdraw by voluntary act from an LLC, the Member may do so at any time on giving 30 days' written notice.

- A withdrawal by a Member before the expiration of that term is a breach of the Certificate of Formation in situations where the LLC is for a definite term or particular undertaking.

- Members elect the Manager.

- Any action required or permitted to be taken by the Managers of an LLC may be taken on a majority vote of the Managers.

- Profits and losses must be apportioned on the basis of the value, as stated in the LLC records, of the contributions made by each Member to the extent that they have been received by the LLC and have not been returned.

- Distributions must be made on the basis of the value of the contributions made by each Member to the extent that they have been received by the LLC and have not been returned.

- Regardless of the nature of his or her contribution, a Member has no right to demand and receive any distribution from an LLC in any form other than cash.

- An interest of the LLC is assignable in whole or in part.

- On assignment of the Member's entire LLC interest, a Member ceases to be a Member.

- The Manager, or if management of the LLC is not vested in a Manager, and the Members who have not wrongfully dissolved an LLC, may wind up the LLC's affairs.

State Classification.   An LLC is presumed to be a partnership unless classified otherwise for federal income tax purposes.

State Entity Level Tax.   None.

Missouri

State Statute.   The Missouri Limited Liability Company Act, Mo. Rev. Stat. §§ 347.010 through 347.735, became effective December 1, 1993.

Formation.   Articles of Organization must contain the following information: name; purpose; registered agent address; whether there will be a Manager(s); the latest date on which the LLC is to dissolve; the right to continue following a Member's withdrawal; and name and address of each organizer.

Minimum Number of Members.   One.

Default Rules.   The following are examples of default rules provided by the Missouri LLC Act. Unless otherwise provided in the Articles of Organization or Operating Agreement:

- Managers need not be Members of the LLC.
- The unanimous vote of the Membership is required to:

    Issue an interest in an LLC or to admit a new Member.

    Approve a merger or consolidation.

    Change management from Member-managed to Manager-operated or vice versa.

    Authorize activity outside the scope of the purpose of the LLC.

    Affect a Member's contribution to the LLC.

- Decisions on any matter connected with the business or affairs of the LLC requires a majority vote of the membership.
- All Managers and Members can do business with and lend money to the LLC.
- Distributions to the Members are controlled by a majority vote.
- Assignments of Membership interests can be made in whole or part.
- If an assignee becomes a Member, the assignor is still liable for his or her obligations to the LLC.

State Classification.   An LLC will be classified in the same manner as it is classified for federal income tax purposes.

State Entity Level Tax.   None.

Montana

State Statute.   The Montana Limited Liability Company Act became effective October 1, 1993.

Formation.   Articles of Organization must contain the following information: name; the latest date the LLC is to dissolve; address of the principal place of business; registered agent and office; a statement as to whether the company will be managed by Members or Managers; whether there will be a Manager(s); if a professional LLC, a statement of the services it will render; and any additional matters.

Minimum Number of Members.   One.

Default Rules.   The following are examples of default rules provided by the Montana LLC Act. Unless otherwise provided in the Articles of Organization or Operating Agreement:

- To compromise an obligation to contribute to the LLC requires the unanimous vote of the Members.
- Each Member must be repaid his or her capital contributions and then each Member shares equally in distributions.
- The unanimous consent of the Membership is required to admit new Members.

State Classification. An LLC is treated as a partnership for state tax purposes.
State Entity Level Tax. None.

Nebraska

State Statute. The Nebraska Limited Liability Company Act became effective September 9, 1993.

Formation. Articles of Organization must contain the following information: name; duration, not to exceed 30 years; purpose; address of the principal office; registered agent; total amount of cash or property contributed; the right to admit new Members; the right to continue following act of dissolution; whether there will be a mAnager(s); and any additional matters.

Minimum Number of Members. Two.

Default Rules. The following are examples of default rules provided by the Nebraska LLC Act. Unless otherwise provided in the Articles of Organization or Operating Agreement:

- Management of the company rests with the Members in proportion to their capital contributions.
- Two-thirds of the Membership must approve a Member withdrawing property.
- To continue the business following an act of dissolution, at least two-thirds of the Membership must approve the plan of continuation.
- The assets of the LLC are shared by Members in relation to the capital account.

State Classification. An LLC will be classified in the same manner as it is classified for federal income tax purposes.
State Entity Level Tax. None.

Nevada

State Statute. The Nevada Limited Liability Company Act, Nev. Rev. Stat. §§ 86.010 through 86.571, became effective October 1, 1991.

Formation. Articles of Organization must contain the following information: name; duration; purpose; registered agent and office; provision discussing the management of the company; the right to continue; the location of records; and any additional matters.

Minimum Number of Members. Two.

Default Rules. The Nevada LLC Act contains the following default rule. Unless otherwise provided in the Articles of Organization or Operating Agreement:

- Members, when they retain management rights, can incur obligations and bind the company for debt.
- Members vote in proportion to their contributions to the capital of the LLC.

State Classification. Nevada does not have an income tax for partnerships or corporations. However, LLCs are subject to franchise taxes, must obtain a business license and pay an annual fee of $25 per Nevada employee.
State Entity Level Tax. None.

New Hampshire

State Statute. The New Hampshire Business Flexibility Act, N.H. Rev. Stat. Ann. §§ 304-C:1 through 304-C:85, became effective July 1, 1993.

Formation. Articles of Organization must contain the following information: name; purpose; registered agent and office; latest date on which the LLC will dissolve; and whether there will be a Manager(s).

Minimum Number of Members. Two.

Default Rules. The following are examples of default rules provided by the New Hampshire LLC Act. Unless otherwise provided in the Articles of Organization or Operating Agreement:

- Except the Act, an LLC can indemnify its Managers and Members.
- A majority of Managers and Members decide business matters.
- Management is reserved to the Members.
- Members who are Managers have the rights and powers of both positions.
- A Member is responsible for his or her capital contributions to the LLC; this obligation can be compromised only by the unanimous vote of the Membership.
- Members are entitled to interim distributions.
- Except as provided in other documents, an assignee has no liability as a Member solely as a result of the assignment.
- The LLC's term is 30 years.
- A vote of all the Members is required for admission of Members.
- The unanimous consent of the Members is required for an assignee to become a Member.

State Classification. An LLC will be classified in the same manner as it is classified for federal income tax purposes.

State Entity Level Tax. The LLC pays 5 percent on dividends and interest of the partnership, and 7 percent on business profits.

New Jersey

State Statute. The New Jersey Limited Liability Company Act became effective January 26, 1994.

Formation. Articles of Organization must contain the following information: name; statutory agent; registered office; a statement that the LLC has at least two Members; and duration—if nonstated, LLC will terminate in 30 years.

Minimum Number of Members. Two.

Default Rules. The following are examples of default rules provided by the New Jersey LLC Act. Unless otherwise provided in the Articles of Organization or Operating Agreement:

- The LLC is managed by Members.
- Members are liable to perform their capital obligations to the company even when performance is impossible.
- Members can forgive the failure to perform member obligations to the LLC only with the unanimous consent of the Members.
- Distributions will be made in proportion to the agreed value of paid contributions.
- A Member is entitled to receive distributions prior to winding up of the LLC or his retirement.
- A Member may resign on six months' written notice.
- A Member has no liability after three years for improper distributions.

State Classification. An LLC will be classified in the same manner as it is classified for federal income tax purposes.

State Entity Level Tax. None.

New Mexico

State Statute. The New Mexico Limited Liability Company Act became effective June 17, 1993.

Formation. Articles of Organization must contain the following information: name; registered agent and office; the latest date on which the LLC is to dissolve; and a provision on the management by nonmember Managers.

Minimum Number of Members. One.

Default Rules. The following are examples of default rules provided by the New Mexico LLC Act. Unless otherwise provided in the Articles of Organization or Operating Agreement:

- Silence with respect to use of Managers results in Members managing the LLC.
- Except when specific matters are delegated to a particular person, Managers or Members make decisions by majority vote.
- To remove a Member, the vote or consent of all Members is necessary.
- Unless approved by all Members, no Member has the right to withdraw any part of his or her contribution to capital.
- The unanimous vote of the membership is required for an assignee to become a Member.
- An individual must have the written consent of all Members to obtain a Membership interest from the entity.
- A Member can withdraw on 30 days' written notice when the LLC has perpetual existence.

State Classification. New Mexico will tax an LLC as a partnership.

State Entity Level Tax. None.

New York

State Statute. The New York Limited Liability Company Law became effective October 24, 1994.

Formation. Articles of Organization must contain the following information: name; county; date of dissolution; office and agent for service of process; a statement whether management of the LLC is vested in a Manager; any limit on the grant of limited liability; and any additional matters.

Minimum Number of Members. One.

Default Rules. The following are examples of default rules provided by the New York LLC Act. Unless otherwise provided in the Articles of Organization or Operating Agreement:

- Members manage the LLC.
- There will be only one class of Members.
- Management action requires a vote of a majority of the Members' profits interest.
- Any or all Managers may be removed by a majority in interest vote.
- On giving six months' written notice, a Member may withdraw and demand a return of the "fair value" of his or her interest within a reasonable time period.
- After an event that terminates the continued Membership of a Member, a vote to continue the company requires the consent of a majority in interest of all other remaining Members.

State Classification. An LLC will be classified in the same manner as it is classified for federal income tax purposes.

State Entity Level Tax. The LLC pays $50 per Member annually up to a maximum fee of $10,000.

North Carolina

State Statute. The North Carolina Limited Liability Company Act, N.C. Gen. Stat. §§ 57C-1-101 through 57C-10-06, became effective October 1, 1993.

Formation.   Articles of Organization must contain the following information: name; the latest date on which the LLC is to dissolve; the name and each address of each person who executes the Articles; registered agent and office; and notice when all Members are not participants in management.

Minimum Number of Members.   Two.

Default Rules.   The following are examples of default rules provided by the North Carolina LLC Act. Unless otherwise provided in the Articles of Organization or Operating Agreement:

- Unanimous consent of the Membership is required for admission of new Members.
- All LLCs are Member-managed.
- A Member is not entitled to receive a noncash distribution.
- The unanimous vote of the Members is required for an assignee to become a Member.
- On six months' written notice, a Member may withdraw.

State Classification.   An LLC will be classified in the same manner as it is classified for federal income tax purposes.

State Entity Level Tax.   None.

North Dakota

State Statute.   The North Dakota Limited Liability Company Act, N.D. Cent. Code §§ 10-32-01 through 10-32-155, became effective April 12, 1993.

Formation.   Articles of Organization must contain the following information: name; address of the principal executive office; registered agent and office; name and address of each organizer; the LLC's period of existence; statement about the right to give a "dissolution avoidance consent" to continue the business; and right to enter into a "business continuation agreement."

Minimum Number of Members.   Two.

Default Rules.   The following are examples of default rules provided by the North Dakota LLC Act. Unless otherwise provided in the Articles of Organization or Operating Agreement:

- Members vote in proportion to their contributions to the capital of the LLC.
- The profits and losses of an LLC will be shared by the Members in proportion to their capital interest.

State Classification.   An LLC will be classified in the same manner as it is classified for federal income tax purposes.

State Entity Level Tax.   None.

Ohio

State Statute.   The Ohio Limited Liability Company Act, Ohio Rev. Code Ann. §§ 1705.01 through 1705.58, became effective July 1, 1994.

Formation.   Articles of Organization must contain the following information: name; duration; address; and any additional matters.

Minimum Number of Members.   Two.

Default Rules.   The following are examples of default rules provided by the Ohio LLC Act. Unless otherwise provided in the Articles of Organization or Operating Agreement:

- The management of an LLC rests with its Members in proportion to their contributions to the capital of the company as adjusted from time to time to reflect any additional contributions or withdrawals by the Members.

- A person who is both a Manager and a Member of an LLC has the rights and powers of Manager and is subject to the liabilities and restrictions of a Manager.

State Classification.   An LLC will be treated as a corporation for state tax purposes only if the company is classified for federal tax purposes as an association taxable as a corporation.

State Entity Level Tax.   None.

Oklahoma

State Statute.   The Oklahoma Limited Liability Company Act became effective September 1, 1992.

Formation.   Articles of Organization must contain the following information: name; duration; purpose; and principal agent and office.

Minimum Number of Members.   Two.

Default Rules.   The following are examples of default rules provided by the Oklahoma LLC Act. Unless otherwise provided in the Articles of Organization or Operating Agreement:

- Silence with regard to the use of Managers results in at least one Manager being required.

- Managers will make decisions by majority vote.

- Interests of the Members are assignable in whole or part.

- An assignee is not liable for the liabilities of the Member unless or until he or she becomes a Member.

State Classification.   An LLC will be classified in the same manner as it is classified for federal income tax purposes.

State Entity Level Tax.   None.

Oregon

State Statute.   The Oregon Limited Liability Company Act became effective January 1, 1994.

Formation.   Articles of Organization must contain the following information: name; registered agent and office; notice address; whether there will be a Manager(s); name and address of each organizer; and duration, if less than perpetual.

Minimum Number of Members.   Two.

Default Rules.   The following are examples of default rules provided by the Oregon LLC Act. Unless otherwise provided in the Articles of Organization or Operating Agreement:

- The LLC is managed by the Members.

- Managers are elected and terminated by majority vote of the Members.

- On six months' notice, a member can withdraw.

- Members have no right to distributions in kind.

- The unanimous vote of the Membership is required for a new Member taking his or her interest from the LLC or an assignee becoming a Member.

State Classification.   An LLC will be classified in the same manner as it is classified for federal income tax purposes.

State Entity Level Tax.   None.

Pennsylvania

State Statute.   The Pennsylvania Limited Liability Company Act, 15 Pa. Cons. Stat. Ch. 89, became effective February 5, 1995.

Formation.   Articles of Organization must contain the following information: name; purpose; office and agent for service of process; whether there will be a Manager(s); and any additional matters.

Minimum Number of Members.   One.

Default Rules.   The following are examples of default rules provided by the Pennsylvania LLC Act. Unless otherwise provided in the Articles of Organization or Operating Agreement:

- All the Members of the LLC will manage the company.
- A majority of the Managers or Members of an LLC shall be required to decide any matter.
- A majority vote of all Members is required for admission of new Members who take directly from the company.
- Voting is by Members on a per capita basis, and not in proportion to their profits interest or capital contributions.
- The LLC will have only one class of Members.
- A Manager shall serve for the shorter of:

    One year plus the time needed to elect and qualify a successor.

    The Manager's resignation, removal, or death.

State Classification.   Pennsylvania taxes LLCs as corporations, even when they are recognized and taxed as partnerships at the federal level.

State Entity Level Tax.   The LLC will be taxed as a corporation except for restricted professional companies.

Rhode Island

State Statute.   The Rhode Island Limited Liability Company Act became effective September 21, 1992.

Formation.   Articles of Organization must contain the following information: name; a statement that the LLC has at least two Members; registered agent and office; the latest date on which the LLC is to dissolve; and a statement of intent for purposes of federal income taxation.

Minimum Number of Members.   Two.

Default Rules.   The following are examples of default rules provided by the Rhode Island LLC Act. Unless otherwise provided in the Articles of Organization or Operating Agreement:

- Members vote in proportion to their contributions to the capital of the LLC.
- Interim distributions will be distributed on the basis of the value of the capital contributions made by each Member to the extent that such contributions have not been returned.
- The profits and losses of an LLC will be shared by the Members in proportion to their capital interests.

State Classification.   An LLC will be taxed as a general partnership for state tax purposes.

State Entity Level Tax.   None.

South Carolina

State Statute.   The South Carolina Limited Liability Company Act, SC Code Ann. §§ 33-43-101 to 33-43-1409, became effective June 16, 1994.

Formation.   Articles of Organization must contain the following information: name; specific date of dissolution; registered agent and office; whether there will be a Manager(s); and name and signature of each organizer.

Minimum Number of Members.   Two.

Default Rules.   The following are examples of default rules provided by the South Carolina LLC Act. Unless otherwise provided in the Articles of Organization or Operating Agreement:

- Members manage the business affairs of the LLC.
- An LLC must maintain at its principal place of business:

    A writing setting out the amount of cash, if any, and the statement of the agreed value of other property or services, if any, contributed by each Member and the times at which or events on the happening of which any additional contributions are to be made by each Member.

    A writing stating events, if any, on the happening of which the LLC is to be dissolved and its affairs wound up.

    Other writings prepared pursuant to a requirement, if any, in any Operating Agreement.

- Only with the unanimous consent of the Members can an obligation of a Member to make a contribution be compromised.
- An assignment of an LLC interest does not entitle the assignee to participate in the management and affairs of the LLC or to become or exercise any rights of a Member or dissolve the LLC.
- Until the assignee of an LLC interest becomes a Member, the assignor continues to be a Member and to have the power to exercise any rights of a Member, subject to the other Members' right to remove the assignor pursuant to the statute.

State Classification.   An LLC is classified as either a partnership or a corporation according to state law.

State Entity Level Tax.   None.

South Dakota

State Statute.   The South Dakota Limited Liability Company Act became effective July 1, 1993.

Formation.   Articles of Organization must contain the following information: name; duration; purpose; registered agent and office; description and amount of capital contributions; additional contributions; right to admit new Members; right to continue; and discussion of management.

Minimum Number of Members.   Two.

Default Rules.   The following are examples of default rules provided by the South Dakota LLC Act. Unless otherwise provided in the Articles of Organization or Operating Agreement:

- Members manage the LLC in proportion of their capital contributions.

State Classification.   An LLC is not subject to state income tax regardless of the federal tax classification.

State Entity Level Tax.   None.

Tennessee

State Statute.   The Tennessee Limited Liability Company Act, Tenn. Code Ann. §§ 48A-1-101 through 48A-47-603, became effective June 21, 1994.

Formation.   Articles of Organization must contain the following information: name; office and agent for service of process; name and address of each organizer; statement of at least two Members; statement as to management; reservation of power to expel a Member; reservation of right to continue by less than a unanimous vote; and any additional matters.

Minimum Number of Members.   Two.

Default Rules.   The following are examples of default rules provided by the Tennessee LLC Act. Unless otherwise provided in the Articles of Organization or Operating Agreement:

- Members do not have preemptive rights.
- An LLC does not have the right to expel a Member.
- Management is not by the Members of voting in proportion to their profit interests.
- The LLC will have only one class of Members.
- A majority vote of the Members, without regard to their capital or profit interest, is required for action of management in a Member-managed LLC.
- After an event that terminates the continued membership of a Member, a vote to continue the company requires the consent of all the remaining Members.

State Classification.   An LLC will be classified in the same manner as it is classified for federal income tax purposes.

State Entity Level Tax.   The LLC must pay $50 per Member annually with a $3,000 cap.

Texas

State Statute.   The Texas Limited Liability Company Act, Tex. Rev. Civ. Stat. Ann. Art. 1528n, became effective August 26, 1991.

Formation.   Articles of Organization must contain the following information: name; duration; purpose; registered agent and office; and provision discussing management.

Minimum Number of Members.   One.

Default Rules.   The following are examples of default rules provided by the Texas LLC Act. Unless otherwise provided in the Articles of Organization or Operating Agreement:

- The company is run by Managers who need not be residents of Texas.
- If the regulations are silent, written consent of all Members is required for admission of new Members.
- Management is not by the Members voting in proportion to their profit interests.
- The LLC will have only one class of Members.

State Classification.   Texas is not a conformity state as are most other states that allow LLCs. Rather, Texas imposes a franchise tax on all LLCs.

State Entity Level Tax.   The LLC pays a tax of .25 percent of capital and 4.5 percent of earned surplus.

Utah

State Statute.   The Utah Limited Liability Company Act, Utah Code Ann. §§ 48-2b-101 through 48-2b-156, became effective July 1, 1991.

Formation.   Articles of Organization must contain the following information: name; duration; purpose; registered office and agent; whether there will be a Manager(s).

Minimum Number of Members.   Two.

Default Rules.   The following are examples of default rules provided by the Utah LLC Act. Unless otherwise provided in the Articles of Organization or Operating Agreement:

- The written consent of all Members is required for a prospective Member.
- Management of the company rests with the Members in proportion to their capital contribution.
- Continuation requires unanimous consent of the remaining Members within 90 days of the event causing dissolution.

State Classification. An LLC will be classified in the same manner as it is classified for federal income tax purposes.

State Entity Level Tax. None.

Virginia

State Statute. The Virginia Limited Liability Company Act, Va. Code Ann. §§ 13.1-1000 through 13.1-1073, became effective July 1, 1991.

Formation. Articles of Organization must contain the following information: name; duration; registered agent and office; and address of principal office.

Minimum Number of Members. Two.

Default Rules. The following are examples of default rules provided by the Virginia LLC Act. Unless otherwise provided in the Articles of Organization or Operating Agreement:

- Managers manage the LLC.
- The operating Agreements do not have to be written.
- A majority vote of the Members will fill a vacancy in management.
- Managers can be removed by a majority vote of Members with or without causes.
- The liability of a Manager to the company cannot exceed the greater of $100,000 or the amount of cash compensation paid during the 12 months immediately preceding the Act or omission.

State Classification. An LLC will be classified in the same manner as it is classified for federal income tax purposes.

State Entity Level Tax. None.

Washington

State Statute. The Washington Limited Liability Company Act became effective October 1, 1994.

Formation. Articles of Organization must contain the following information: name; the latest date on which the LLC is to dissolve; registered agent and office; principal place of business; whether there will be a Manager(s); name and address of each person executing the Articles of Organization; and any additional matters.

Minimum Number of Members. Two.

Default Rules. The following are examples of default rules provided by the Washington LLC Act. Unless otherwise provided in the Articles of Organization or Operating Agreement:

- Except as otherwise provided by the statute, the debts, obligations, and liabilities of an LLC, whether arising in contract, tort, or otherwise, shall be solely the debts, obligations, and liabilities of the LLC; and no Manager or Member of an LLC shall be obligated personally for any such debt, obligation, or liability of the LLC solely by reason of being a Member or acting as a Manager of the LLC.
- A Member, on 30 days' written notice to the other Members, may withdraw from the LLC at any time.

- The LLC must have a written document setting the financial relationships between the LLC and the Members and between the various individual Members.
- The affirmative vote, approval, or consent of more than ½ by number of the Managers shall be required to decide any matter connected with the business or affairs of the LLC.
- A Member has the status of, and is entitled to all remedies available to, a creditor of an LLC with respect to the distribution at the time the Member becomes entitled to receive a distribution. A Limited Liability Company Agreement may provide for the establishment of a record date with respect to allocations and distributions by an LLC.
- An assignment entitles the assignee to share in profits and losses, to receive distributions and to receive allocation of income, gain, loss, deduction, or credit or similar items to which the assignor was entitled, to the extent assigned.
- A Member ceases to be a Member and to have the power to exercise any rights or powers of a Member on assignment of all of his or her LLC interest.

State Classification.   An LLC will be taxed as a partnership.
State Entity Level Tax.   None.

West Virginia

State Statute.   The West Virginia Limited Liability Company Act, W. Va. Code §§ 31-1A-1 through 31-1-1A-69, became effective March 15, 1992.

Formation.   Articles of Organization must contain the following information: name; duration, which cannot be perpetual; registered agent and office; address of LLC's principal place of business; purpose; and name and address of organizer(s).

Minimum Number of Members.   Two.

Default Rules.   The following are examples of default rules provided by the West Virginia LLC Act. Unless otherwise provided in the Articles of Organization or Operating Agreement:

- Members manage the LLC.
- The Operating Agreements do not have to be in writing.
- A vacancy in management will be filled by a majority vote of the Members.
- Managers can be removed by a majority vote of Members with or without cause.
- A Member, on six months' written notice to each Member, may resign.

State Classification.   An LLC will be classified in the same manner as it is classified for federal income tax purposes.
State Entity Level Tax.   None.

Wisconsin

State Statute.   The Wisconsin Limited Liability Company Act became effective January 1, 1994.

Formation.   Articles of Organization must contain the following information: a statement of intent for purposes of federal income taxation; name; registered agent and office; whether there will be a Manager(s); name and address of each organizer; and name of drafter.

Minimum Number of Members.   Two.

Default Rules.   The following are examples of default rules provided by the Wisconsin LLC Act. Unless otherwise provided in the Articles of Organization or Operating Agreement:

- There is a conclusive presumption that a Manager or Member has not breached or failed to perform a company duty.

- The unanimous vote of the Members is required for assignees to become Members.

State Classification.   An LLC will be classified in the same manner as it is classified for federal income tax purposes.

State Entity Level Tax.   If the LLC is taxed as a partnership, the LLC is subject to a temporary surcharge of up to $9,800.

Wyoming

State Statute.   The Wyoming Limited Liability Company Act, Wyo. Stat. §§ 17-15-101 through 17-15-136, became effective in 1977.

Formation.   Articles of Organization must contain the following information: name; duration; purpose; registered agent and office; amount of capital contributions of the Members; any additional contributions; right to admit new Members; right to continue; and statement on the management of the company.

Minimum Number of Members.   Two.

Default Rules.   The following are examples of default rules provided by the Wyoming LLC Act:

- Unless otherwise provided in the Articles of Organization or Operating Agreement, the ability to contract or incur debt or liability for the Company is restricted to Members, if there are no Managers, or Managers, when Managers are authorized.

State Classification.   There is no Wyoming state income tax at either the personal or corporate level. Therefore, classification of an LLC for state income tax purposes is irrelevant.

State Entity Level Tax.   None.

APPENDIX B

Sequence of States' Adoption of Limited Liability Companies Laws

At the time this book was written, 48 states and the District of Columbia had passed LLC acts. It is likely that the remaining states will follow. For historical interest, the progression of adoption is as follows:

1977   Wyoming

1982   Florida

1990   Colorado, Kansas

1991   Nevada, Utah, Texas, Virginia

1992   Arizona, Delaware, Illinois, Iowa, Oklahoma, Minnesota, Maryland, Louisiana, Rhode Island, West Virginia

1993   Alabama, Arkansas, Connecticut, Georgia, Idaho, Indiana, Michigan, Missouri, Montana, Nebraska, New Hampshire, New Jersey, New Mexico, North Carolina, North Dakota, Oregon, South Dakota, Wisconsin

1994   Alaska, California, District of Columbia, Kentucky, Maine, Mississippi, New Jersey, New York, Ohio, Pennsylvania, South Carolina, Tennessee, Washington

1995   Massachusetts

APPENDIX C

Comparison of Business Entities

Table C.1 summarizes key characteristics of each of the different types of entity that you may consider for organizing your business or investment. The ability to view key items in a few pages can help you understand the main differences before you read a particular chapter of the book, or serve to summarize a portion of the book that you have just completed. When doing so, however, remember that the generalizations necessary to prepare this chart could obscure a nuance that is critical to your particular situation.

The entities summarized are generally those that provide the often vital element of limited liability.

CAUTION: The limited liability of a corporation, limited partnership, or LLC is not guaranteed. If you personally guarantee a bank debt (or any liability for that matter), the fact that a corporation or LLC is the primary obligor (the actual borrower responsible) will not relieve you of your liability. If you fail to respect the identity and formalities of the entity, limited liability benefits may be lost. For example, if you organize a corporation and have no minutes, no bylaws and never issue stock, a court may refuse to respect the corporation and find you personally liable. If you use a corporation, LLC, or other entity and commingle personal and business funds, a similar result may occur.

These entities include:

- *C Corporation.* This is an entity organized under your state's corporation law. Each shareholder should not be held liable for acts of the corporation. For tax purposes, however, the corporation is taxable as a separate entity from its owners. This can result in a two-tier tax—the corporation pays tax on its income and the shareholders then pay tax on the dividends distributed to them.

- *S Corporation.* This is an entity organized under your state's corporation law exactly like a C corporation. However, for federal tax purposes (some states and local governments recognize the S corporation tax status, others do not, and some in a modified format), the corporation itself is generally not taxed. Instead, the S corporation acts like a conduit for income and expenses to flow through to the individual owners.

- *Limited Partnership.* This is an entity organized under your state's limited partnership law. Every limited partnership must have at least two types of partners: general partner who is fully liable for all partnership debts and liabilities and limited partners who are not liable for partnership debts or liabilities except to the extent of their investment in the partnership. There are exceptions. In Table C.1, the general partner is assumed to be an S corporation (as previously described). The result

Table C.1. Comparison of Business Entities

	C Corporation	S Corporation	General Partnership	Limited Partnership with a Corporate General Partner	Limited Liability Company
Statutes permitting formation	All states.	All states.	All states.	All states.	48 and District of Columbia.
Limitations on minimum number of owners	None.	None.	At least 2.	At least 2.	Usually at least 2.
Limitations on maximum number of owners	None.	Cannot have more than 35.	None.	None.	None.
Limitations on who can be an owner	None.	Individuals other than nonresident aliens, certain trusts, and estates.	None.	None.	None.
Allowable business purposes	Any, unless otherwise provided by statute.	Generally, same as C corporation.	Any for profit business unless otherwise provided by statute.	Same as general partnership.	Same as C corporation, but some states exclude certain activities.
Capital structure limitation	None.	Only one class of stock is permitted (classes that differ in respect to voting rights only are permitted).	None.	None.	None.
Formation of entity	Formal filing required.	Same as C corporation.	No.	Same as C corporation.	Same as C corporation.
Creation documents	Articles or Certificate of Incorporation.	Same as C corporation.	Partnership Agreement.	Certificate of Limited Partnership.	Articles of Organization or Certificate of Formation.
Personal liability of owners	None.	Same as C corporation.	All parties jointly and severally personally liable.	General partner liable. Limited partners not so.	None.
Default management structure	Board of directors.	Same as C corporation.	All partners participate.	General Partner.	Member managed in most states.

Ownership participation in management	Shareholders elect directors.	Same as C corporation.	All partners may participate in the entity's management.	Only General partner. Limited partners risk liability by participating in management.	Depends on whether management is by Members or Managers.
Governing Agreement	Shareholders Agreement and Bylaws	Same as C corporation	Partnership Agreement	Same as general partnership	Operating Agreement
Voting rights of owners	Generally, pro rata to number of shares. May have voting and non-voting shares.	Generally, pro rata to number of shares. May have voting and non-voting shares.	Per capita or pro rata unless modified by partnership agreement.	As provided in Partnership Agreement.	Varies by each state, but generally pro rata unless modified by Operating Agreement.
Basic ownership unit	Share of stock.	Same as C corporation.	Partnership interest.	Same as general partnership.	Membership interest.
Rules for allocating profits and losses	Pro rata to number of shares (unless varied by other class(es) of stock).	Pro rata to number of shares.	Per capita unless modified by partnership agreement.	Pro rata to capital contributions less returned capital contributions.	Same as limited partnership unless modified by Operating Agreement.
Undistributed income of company	No current tax to owners.	Current tax to owners.	Current tax to owners.	Current tax to owners.	Current tax to owners.
Character of income and loss	Determined at entity level.	Same as C corporation.	Same as C corporation.	Same as C corporation.	Same as C corporation.
Deductibility of company's losses	No deduction to owners but entity may use current loss to offset unrelated income in certain instances.	Subject to certain limitations, losses pass through to owners on per share basis and are deductible against unrelated income.	Same as limited partnership.	Subject to certain limitations discussed below, losses pass through to owners according to their distributive shares and are deductible against unrelated income.	Same as limited partnership.
Flexibility of loss allocations	N/A	None.	Same as limited partnership.	Maximum flexibility since losses may be allocated by agreement to those members who will most benefit from tax deductions as long as allocations have "substantial economic effect."	Same as limited partnership.

(Continued)

Table C.1. (continued)

	C Corporation	S Corporation	General Partnership	Limited Partnership with a Corporate General Partner	Limited Liability Company
Basis limiting deduction of losses	N/A	Owners' deductions are limited first by their bases in stock and then their bases in any direct loans to entity (basis does not include share of entity debt).	Same as limited partnership.	Owners' deductions are limited by their bases in their membership interests (basis includes their share of entity debt).	Same as limited partnership.
At-risk limitation on deductibility of losses	N/A	Loss deduction is limited by allocable share of at-risk amount, which includes amount contributed to entity, debt to extent the owner is personally liable, and qualified nonrecourse financing with respect to real estate.	Same as limited partnership, except that all general partners are generally at risk with respect to partnership recourse loans.	Same as S corporation except general partner is the only at-risk partner with respect to recourse partnership loans unless there are guarantees running from a limited partner to a general partner.	Same as S corporation.
Passive activity limitation on deductibility of losses	N/A	After the basis and at-risk limitations are applied, owner's loss deductible if active income if owner "materially participates." Income will be passive if owner does not "materially participate."	Same as S corporation.	Same as S corporation with question as to whether limited partner will be treated as S shareholder or as more restricted limited partner (more likely to be treated as S shareholder).	Same as S corporation.
Federal tax returns required to be filed	Form 1120	Form 1120S	Same as limited partnership.	Form 1065 with K-1 to members.	Same as limited partnership. (Unless set up to be taxed as a corporation (1120).)

Entity-level federal tax (assuming limited liability company and limited partnership are structured so that they will be taxed as a partnership for federal tax purposes)	Yes.	Usually not, but yes if passive income exceeds 25% of gross receipts and entity has earnings and profits. Moreover, usually not, but a built-in gains tax is imposed on sale or disposition of assets within 10 years of when corporation was C corporation and made an S election.	No.	No.	No.
Taxable year	Generally, calendar year or any fiscal year.	Generally, a calendar year.	Same as limited partnership.	Calendar year or fiscal year of the majority in interest partner or, if none, the principal partners or, if none, any other fiscal year for which the limited partnership establishes a business purpose; a fiscal year of September through November may be adopted even without a business purpose if the S corporation makes a Section 444 election and the required payments to compensate Service for cost of deferral.	Same as limited partnership.
Permissible accounting methods	Generally must use accrual unless entity is professional service corporation or small business with gross receipts of less than $5 million.	Same as C corporation.	Same as limited liability company.	Same as limited liability company.	May elect cash or accrual; tax shelters required to use accrual method.

(Continued)

Table C.1. (continued)

	C Corporation	S Corporation	General Partnership	Limited Partnership with a Corporate General Partner	Limited Liability Company
Fringe benefits	Shareholder-employees receive tax qualified fringe benefits without restrictions of pass-through entities.	Greater than 2% owner-employees are generally ineligible for tax-free fringe benefits.	Same as limited liability company.	Same as limited liability company.	Owners are generally not considered employees so limitations apply.
Employment taxes	FICA tax is payable by both corporation and employee.	Same as C corporation.	General partner distributive share is subject to self-employment tax.	General partner distributive share is subject to self-employment tax; limited partner distributive share is not subject to the tax under Section 1402(a)(13).	Members generally subject to self-employment tax unless: (1) the Member is not a Manager in a Manager-ruled LLC, and (2) the entity could have been formed as a limited partnership.

is that all individual owners (i.e., the limited partners and the shareholder/owners of the S corporation general partner) can achieve limited liability.

- *Limited Liability Company.* This is an entity formed under your state's (assuming your state is not one of the few remaining holdouts as this book is written) limited liability company statute. For tax purposes, an LLC can be taxed as a partnership (which is almost always the intent and which is generally the result) or a corporation (i.e., analogous to a C corporation).

The table, for comparison purposes also illustrates one entity where there is no limitation on the liability of the owners, a general partnership. This is then only appropriate to use for simple transactions where large claims or liabilities are unlikely.

CAUTION: Too often, people assume that if they buy insurance they needn't worry about acquiring the limited liability benefit of an entity. While insurance is essential, and securing adequate insurance coverage should be one of the first steps taken in planning any transaction, don't minimize the important protection an entity can provide. Insurance limits can be exceeded. Policies contain limitations, restrictions, and exclusions. The old maxim: "Better safe than sorry" provides the right approach.

For simplicity, Table C.1 omits many other types of entities, including professional corporations (a special type of C corporation or S corporation for certain licensed professional practices), limited liability partnerships (a variation of an LLC used by some professional practices), and trusts. Depending on your particular situation, one or more of these other approaches may be appropriate.

CAUTION: It's always best to seek the professional guidance of an accountant and business lawyer before selecting the entity for any particular business or investment.

GLOSSARY

Accelerate Expenses. The payment of certain expenses prior to December 31, rather than after December 31. This common year-end tax planning step can give you the tax benefit of a deduction a year earlier than if you had waited until January 1 or later to pay the expense. An example of this is to pay your estimated state taxes by December 31, rather than by the following January 15 when it is often due. An LLC, as a pass-through entity, can be used in this type of planning.

Accrual Method. A system of accounting. The tax laws provide sets of rules for determining when you can claim a deduction and when you must report income. There are two major sets of rules. The simplest, which is used by individuals, is called the cash method of accounting. Under the cash method of accounting, you generally report income for tax purposes when you receive it and generally deduct expenses for a year in which you pay them. Under the accrual method of accounting, which is used by many businesses, partnerships, corporations, and so forth, income is reported and expenses deducted in the year to which they relate rather than the year when paid.

Accumulated Earnings Tax. A penalty tax charged against a corporation that retains an excessive amount of profits beyond the reasonable needs of its business, rather than distributing those profits to its owners. An LLC that is taxed as a partnership will not face this problem.

Acquisition Costs. Costs incurred when buying a business or property that have to be added to (capitalized as part of) your cost (adjusted basis) in the property. For example, the cost of a title insurance report, legal fees, transfer taxes, accounting fees, and so forth may all have to be added to your cost in the property. If the property is an investment property, and not your home, carefully evaluate the acquisition costs to find expenses that you can deduct currently. Plan how you allocate the total acquisition cost between land, building, furniture, and other assets you purchased since land can't be written off (depreciated), buildings can be, and furniture can be written off (depreciated) quickest of all.

Adjusted Basis. Roughly speaking, your investment, for tax purposes, in certain property. The cost you pay to buy or build a building (or any other asset), plus costs to improve it. If you have a casualty loss, it reduces your adjusted basis. Adjusted basis is used to calculate depreciation (multiply it by the appropriate depreciation percentage) and to determine the taxable gain or loss when you sell property (subtract adjusted basis from your net sales proceeds to determine your gain). If you're subject to the alternative minimum tax, your assets may have different adjusted basis for the regular tax and the alternative minimum tax. Your adjusted tax basis in your LLC is determined based on your investment, reduced by income distributed, increased by certain loans taken out by the entity (where your LLC is taxed as a partnership), and so forth. Your adjusted basis in your LLC interest will determine the amount of gain or loss on your sale of the interest.

Adjusted Gross Income. All your income from whatever source (wages, rents, dividends, profits from a business, and so forth) less certain deductions (trade or business expenses, depreciation on rental property, allowable losses from sales of property, alimony payments, and so forth). Adjusted gross income, (sometimes called AGI) is important for calculating the amount of medical expenses and casualty losses that you can deduct. A modified version of adjusted gross income is used in determining how much Social Security is taxed. The $25,000 special allowance to deduct rental expenses when you actively participate is based on modified adjusted gross income, which is adjusted gross income increased by any passive activity losses, certain Social Security payments, and individual retirement account (IRA) deductions. This is important in assessing the value to an investment in the low-income housing credit.

Alternative Minimum Tax (AMT). A second parallel tax system that many wealthier taxpayers will have to consider when calculating their tax. The alternative minimum tax (or AMT) is calculated by starting with your taxable income calculated according to the regular tax rules. Add certain tax preference items and adjustments required by the AMT. Only certain itemized deductions are allowed. Next, subtract an exemption amount. The result is multiplied by either a 26 percent or 28 percent rate for individuals. If the tax due exceeds the tax you owe under the regular tax system then you must pay the larger alternative minimum tax.

Amount Realized. The money and the fair market value of any property you receive when you sell property. It also includes the amount of any liabilities that the buyer takes responsibility for.

Annual Exclusion. The amount of $10,000 per year to any other person without incurring any gift tax. There is no limit on the number of people you can make these gifts to in a year. To qualify for this exclusion, a gift must be a gift of a present interest, meaning that the recipient can enjoy the gift immediately. This can present problems when you make gifts to trusts. This exclusion can be doubled to $20,000 per person, per year, if you're married and your spouse consents to join in making the gift. This is called gift-splitting. A common gift and estate planning technique is to transfer property that would not otherwise be divisible into $10,000 units, such as real estate, to an LLC, and then gift $10,000 interests each year to your children or other heirs.

Articles of Organization. The initial document filed with a state to form or organize your LLC (also called Certificate of Formation). It includes basic provisions concerning the duration, nature, owners, management, and so on of the LLC and becomes a matter of public record.

Asset Protection. The process of taking steps to minimize the risk of creditors or other claimants being able to reach your assets. This can include setting up a different entity, such as an LLC, for each property or business. Thus, if one particular property is subject to a suit (e.g., a tenant is hurt on one rental property), the claimant will be limited to the assets from that particular property or entity. This can prevent a domino effect against your other assets. An LLC, just like a limited partnership, offers important benefits in the area of asset protection.

At-Risk Rules. Rules limiting the amount of tax losses that can be deducted from a business or investment to the amount you have at risk in that investment. The at-risk amount includes the cash and fair market value of any property you have invested in the business. The at-risk amount (your deduction limit) also includes debts for which you are personally liable.

Basis. Taxpayer's investment for tax purposes.

Beneficiary. A person who receives the benefits of a trust or of transfers under a will. An LLC is intangible property. Thus, if you own an interest in an LLC that owns real property, the intangible or business disposition clauses of your will may govern instead of the real property disposition clauses. You may wish to be careful and have the will explicitly state where the LLC interest is to be given.

Bequest.   Property transferred under your will.

Blue Sky Laws.   State security laws that govern the right to sell interests in a security, among other matters. Anytime you are forming an LLC where more than a handful of active and knowledgeable investors are involved, always consult with a securities attorney to be certain you are not subject to any blue sky, federal, or other security or reporting requirements.

Buy-Sell Agreements.   Contractual arrangements governing the transfer of ownership interests (LLC Membership, corporate stock, or partnership interests) in a closely held business. These often rely on insurance to provide the necessary funds.

Calendar Year.   A reference to the twelve month period ending December 31 that many entities are required to use as their tax year.

Capital Expenditure.   A payment to buy, build or improve an asset (property you own) that will last for more than one year. Capital expenditures generally can't be deducted in the year paid. Instead, they must usually be added to your investment (adjusted basis) in the asset and then be written off (depreciated) over a period of time. Examples of capital expenditures include the costs to organize your LLC (but a special amortization period may be available; check with your accountant), the costs to construct a new building, add a new roof, and so forth.

Capital Gain.   The gain from selling a capital asset. The gain usually equals the amount realized (sales price) less your investment (adjusted tax basis) in the property. Capital gains receive favorable tax treatment in that the maximum rate is set at 28 percent while the maximum tax rate on ordinary income is 39.6 percent. Capital losses can only be deducted in any year up to the amount of capital gains plus $3,000. Your sale of your LLC, depending on the circumstances, may qualify as a sale of a capital asset that is taxed at favorable capital gains rates. Special rules apply for capital gains realized on investments in qualified small business stock, which permit 50 percent of the capital gain to be excluded, but this may not be available to an LLC.

Capitalize.   To add expenses that are not deductible to a person's investment (adjusted basis) in a property.

Cash Basis Method.   A method of determining when income must be reported and when expenses can be deducted. It is used by most individual taxpayers. Certain partnerships (including LLCs taxed as partnerships), corporations, and other taxpayers may not be able to use the cash method. Under the cash method, income is generally reported in the year when you receive the money, and expenses are usually deducted in the year you pay the expense.

Cash Flow.   Cash generated by a business or investment. Since an LLC is a pass-through entity, each owner will have to report on his or her personal tax return an allocable share of LLC income, even if the LLC doesn't have adequate cash flow to make a distribution of that income.

C Corporation.   A regular corporation that pays federal taxes on its net income. A C corporation can be contrasted with an S corporation, which generally does not pay corporate level taxes; instead, its shareholders (owners) pay tax on their pro rata share of the S corporation's income.

Centralized Management.   One of four characteristics that distinguish an entity taxed as a partnership (flow-through income and loss to the owner) and an association taxable as a corporation (the corporate entity pays tax and then the owner pays tax on distributions received—called "double taxation"). Centralized management is a corporate (not partnership) characteristic. If all Members of the LLC are permitted to manage the LLC, there is no centralized management. Where only one Member is named the Manager, centralized management generally exists.

NOTE: The exact names of the certificates described in this Glossary may differ from state to state.

Certificate of Alternate Name. A legal document that may need to be filed if your LLC will operate under a different or additional name than the name under which it was formed. The laws vary significantly from state to state. A filing may be required in your state, county, both or even elsewhere. Check with a local attorney.

Certificate of Amendments. A legal document filed to register a change made in the Certificate of Formation. It is often necessary, or prudent, to amend the Articles of Organization by filing a Certificate of Amendment, which then also becomes part of the public record on your LLC. For example, if your state requires that the business purpose of the LLC must be specified, and this changes, a Certificate of Amendment may be necessary to file.

Certificate of Cancellation. A legal document that must be filed when you wish to terminate and liquidate your LLC.

CAUTION: On termination, there will also be special tax filings with the IRS and state and local tax authorities.

Certificate of Merger and Consolidation. A legal document that must be filed where a partnership, corporation or LLC is to be merged with an LLC.

CAUTION: There are also tax filing requirements. You may also need permission of a landlord, lender, or anyone else with whom the LLC or other entity has contractual arrangements.

Certificate of Reservation of Name. A legal document used in some states to reserve a name for an LLC. It may be less expensive and simpler to just file the Articles of Organization and form the LLC. Ask a local attorney.

Closely Held Business. A family business or a business owned by relatively few individuals. An LLC can be an excellent entity to own the particular business, or even key assets (e.g., equipment or a building to rent back to the business).

Continuity of Life. One of the four characteristics that distinguish an entity taxed as a partnership and an association taxable as a corporation.

Contribution. Property transferred to an LLC in exchange for a membership interest in the LLC. This type of transfer is often referred to as a contribution of property to the LLC. Special tax rules will affect this transfer. Generally, you will not have taxable gain on the contribution of property to an LLC in exchange for a membership interest.

Corporation. A legal entity separate and distinct from the individuals who own it (called shareholders). Corporations can be S corporations and C corporations.

Credit Shelter Trust. A trust designed to utilize your $600,000 unified credit exemption equivalent. Often the same as a bypass trust because such a trust is not included in (bypasses) your surviving spouse's estate. An interest in an LLC can be one of the assets bequeathed into a credit shelter trust.

Decedent. A person who dies. A decedent's assets are disposed of by will, or if no will exists by the intestacy laws of the decedent's state.

Deferral of Estate Tax.   A provision of estate tax law. Where a sufficient portion of your estate comprises assets in a closely held and active business, your estate may qualify to pay the estate tax attributable to these assets over approximately a 14-year period instead of within nine months of death. The fact that the business interest is owned by an LLC (or other entity) will not necessarily disqualify it for this favorable estate tax provision.

Deferral of Income.   A common tax planning technique near December 31. By not recognizing income until the next year, the taxpayer may postpone payment on the income for another full year. Examples of income deferral include delaying the sale of stocks or property until January, selling property on the installment method and not receiving cash until the next year, and so forth. Since an LLC taxed as a partnership is a flow-through entity, this type of planning is possible.

Depreciation.   The writing off of an asset's cost over its useful life or using methods prescribed by the tax laws. Depreciation is based on the idea that property wears down over time from exposure to the elements, physical wear and tear from use, and so forth. Depreciation of assets held by your LLC will be passed to your personal tax return and deducted there as part of the results you realize in that given tax year from your LLC.

Depreciation Convention.   An assumption or rule used by accountants for tax purposes. To simplify depreciation calculations, depreciation is not calculated on a daily basis for years when property is bought or sold. Instead certain rules, called conventions, are used. For furniture and equipment (personal property), a mid-year convention is generally used. This results in taxpayers getting one half year of depreciation no matter when during the year the property is bought or sold. Depreciation write-offs for real estate are calculated using a mid-month convention so that one half month of depreciation is claimed no matter which day during the month the property was purchased or sold.

Depreciation Method.   An accounting rule for calculating the depreciation of assets over time. To calculate depreciation, certain prescribed approaches, called depreciation methods, must be used. The straight line method results in deducting equal or ratable amounts of an asset's cost over the asset's useful life or depreciation (recovery) period. For example, a machine costing $1,000 for which a depreciation period is 10 years would be depreciated at a rate of $100 in each year. The rate of depreciation using the straight line method is 10 percent ($100 annual depreciation divided by the $1,000 asset cost). The 200 percent (or double) declining balance method of calculating depreciation uses a rate twice the straight line rate, or 20 percent in our example. The 150 percent declining balance method uses a rate that is one and one-half times as fast as the straight line method, or 15 percent in our example. Where an LLC owns an asset, the LLC (through its Tax Matters Member) must decide which depreciation method and elections to make for tax purposes.

Discount.   A discount on the value of a gift of a minority (less than controlling) and/or lack of marketability interest in an LLC may sometimes be claimed. This can enable the donor to give a greater percentage interest in the LLC as a gift in any year under the $10,000 annual exclusion without, for example, using any of the donor's unified credit.

Distribution.   The parceling out of profits or other assets to members of an LLC. As an owner of an LLC, you may receive distributions of cash or even property. However, your tax results are not limited to the amount you receive as a distribution where the LLC is taxed as a partnership. You will be taxed on your pro rata portion of LLC income or loss.

Donee.   A person who receives a gift.

Donor.   A person who makes a gift.

Election.   In accounting, the choice of a particular method for calculating taxes. The tax laws provide for optional treatment of many different items. Often the taxpayer must make an election (usually by filing a statement or checking a box on the tax return) as to which optional method will be used. An LLC, as a separate tax reporting entity, must make its own tax elections. The Tax Matters Member of your LLC will likely have control over all these decisions.

Elective Expensing. The option of immediately writing off property in certain circumstances. The cost of furniture and equipment must be written off over seven years using the 200 percent declining balance method of depreciation. If certain requirements are met, however, you may be able to write off up to $17,000 of certain furniture and equipment (personal property) immediately. This election is made by the LLC on its tax return for assets it purchased.

Estate Tax. A tax that may be due on the death of a taxpayer, as a result of the transfer of wealth to family and others. Exclusions are provided for transfers to the taxpayer's spouse, charities, and so forth. The tax rate for the estate tax can reach as high as 55 percent. A once-in-a-lifetime credit is permitted that enables you to pass property worth up to $600,000 to others (not including spouses) without having to pay a Federal estate tax.

Estimated Tax. Income taxes paid by certain individuals on a quarterly basis to avoid underpayment penalties. Your expected income (or loss) from your LLC investments must be considered in making these calculations.

Fair Market Value. The price at which an item can be sold at the present time between two unrelated people, neither under compulsion to buy or sell. Where a gift is made of an interest in an LLC, it must be valued at its fair market value. This may, however, be permitted to reflect a minority (lack of control) and/or lack of marketability discount.

Family Limited Partnership, or FLPs. A limited partnership owned by a family for purposes of transferring some of the value of the business or real estate to the younger generation and possibly involving them in the management of the business as well.

Fiscal Year. A tax year other than the calendar year used by a particular taxpayer. LLCs are subject to limitations on when they can use a tax year other than the calendar year.

Free Transferability. A key characteristic in distinguishing the taxation of an LLC as a partnership or as an association taxable as a corporation. Where interests in your LLC can be freely transferred without restriction, it is more like a corporation than a partnership. The LLC's Operating Agreement could include restrictions so that, for example, the Manager, or 75 percent of the Members, may have to approve a transfer. Also, where the transfer is not approved, the person acquiring the interest is merely a substitute assignee and not an actual Member. Thus, certain important attributes of ownership may not be passed where the approval process is not obtained.

General Partner. An owner of a partnership who is personally liable for all partnership debts and may be permitted to participate in the management of the partnership. Every limited partnership must have at least one general partner. Often this general partner is a corporation to avoid any one individual being personally liable.

General Partnership. A partnership that has only general no limited partners. This is the most common way for a few friends or investors to put their money together to buy a rental property or simple business. The risk here is that in a general partnership all partners are personally liable, without limit, for all partnership debts.

Generation-Skipping Transfer (GST) Tax. A transfer tax generally assessed on transfers to grandchildren, great-grandchildren, and so on. Each taxpayer is given a $1 million exclusion from this tax.

Gift. For purposes of taxation, the transfer of property without the donor receiving something of equal value in return. The federal government will assess a transfer tax where the value of the gift exceeds the $10,000 annual exclusion and your $600,000 unified credit equivalent is exhausted. For example, you may make a gift of your LLC interest to a trust for your child.

Gift Tax. A tax that may be due when you give property or other assets away. You are allowed to give away a maximum of $10,000 per person (to any number of people) in any year without the tax applying. Above the $10,000 amount, you have a once-in-a-lifetime exclusion that permits you to give away $600,000 of property to any individuals other than a spouse without paying any gift tax. The gift tax and the estate tax are coordinated (unified) so that the $600,000 exclusion is only available once between them.

Grantor.   A legal term for the person who establishes a trust and transfers assets to it.

Gross Estate.   The total value of the assets you own at death (less liabilities), or that are included in your estate. The value is determined at the date of your death or as of the alternate valuation date, which is six months following the date of death.

Gross Income.   All your earnings from all sources including wages, rents, royalties, dividends, interest, and so forth.

Half-Year Convention.   A term used in accounting. When calculating depreciation on equipment and furniture (personal property), the required method provides one-half year's worth of depreciation deductions in the year you buy or sell the property.

Heirs.   The persons who receive your assets following your death.

Improvements.   Payments for additions or betterments to property that will last more than a year and must thus be added to your investment (capitalized as part of your basis) in the property. Where an LLC makes a capital improvement, it would be subject to these rules and the tax results that flow through to your personal return would be affected accordingly.

Installment Sale.   A sale where taxable gain is recognized over a number of years as payment is received for the property sold. If you are a dealer in property, you can't use the installment method. If you are a dealer, in real estate, for example, but have a single property held as an investment, segregating that different property in an LLC may help support your position with the IRS that the particular property is different from those in which you are a dealer.

Insurance Trust.   An irrevocable trust established to own your insurance policies and thereby prevent them from being included in your estate. Insurance trusts are often used in planning for the tax on interest in closely held businesses and nonliquid assets such as real estate. Restructuring business or investment assets into an LLC will not change this basic planning need.

Interest.   A reference to your ownership of a portion of an LLC. Also known as a Membership Interest.

Investment Interest Limitation.   A limitation on deductions of interest incurred on debt used to carry investment assets. Such interest can only be deducted to the extent of investment income. You are generally prohibited from including gains on the sale of investment assets in this calculation. There is an exception, however, where you make a special election to tax your capital gains at a higher tax rate.

Kiddie Tax.   Unearned income (dividends, rents, interest, and so forth) of a child under age 14. This income will be taxed to the child at the parent's highest tax rate. This tax makes family tax planning much harder.

Lack of Marketability Discount.   One type of discount on the value of an asset. For example, the value of an asset given to a child may be less than its initial or expected value where, because of unusual circumstances, it is not readily salable.

Lease.   A legal contract permitting one party to use property owned by another, usually for the payment of periodic rent. A common use of LLCs is to segregate valuable business assets (patent, trademark, real estate, equipment) in a separate entity, gift the interests in that entity to your children, and have them lease (or license) the right to use the property back to the business.

Limited Liability.   The characteristic of an entity that can be sued, but whose owners generally cannot be held personally liable for debts, or losses of the entity. The classic limited liability entity is the corporation.

Limited Liability Company, or LLC. An entity formed under your state's LLC statute that, like a corporation, has the legal characteristic of limited liability and that also may qualify to be treated for tax purposes as a partnership.

Limited Liability Partnership, or LLP. A partnership that files a certain registration statement with a state's corporate department. An LLP may provide less liability protection for its owners than an LLC. Some states have enacted statutes (laws) permitting these entities so that licensed professionals (doctors, lawyers, accountants, etc.) can obtain some limitation on liability while still having the favorable tax status of a partnership. These entities are generally even newer than LLCs and caution must be exercised. Also, the nuances differ by state, so be sure to consult a local attorney familiar with your state's rules.

Limited Partner. A partner (owner) in a limited partnership who cannot participate in the management of the partnership's business and who is not liable for partnership debts.

Limited Partnership. A partnership with at least one general partner and any number of limited partners.

Liquidation. Termination and winding up of an entity, such as an LLC. A final tax return will have to be filed with the IRS, and with state and local tax authorities. A tax clearance certificate may be necessary from the state. Usually a Certificate of Termination (or similar document) must be filed with the appropriate state agency.

Manager. The individual or entity charged with managing an LLC, making key decisions, and so forth. The Articles of Organization may specify who is to be the Manager. The Operating Agreement should provide details as to the scope of the powers of the Manager, liability for acts, replacement, and so forth. The Manager can be one individual, a group or committee of individuals, or even all Members of the LLC. The selection of the Manager can be important in determining whether the LLC has centralized management, which is an important characteristic in determining whether the LLC can be taxed as a partnership or instead may have to be taxed as a corporation. See also "Centralized Management."

Member. With reference to limited liability companies, an owner of part (or in some states all) of an LLC. A Member in an LLC is analogous to a shareholder in a corporation or a partner in a partnership. Some key characteristics and rights of a Member may be set forth in the LLC's Articles of Organization. An Operating Agreement should be drafted that specifically states a Member's rights, liability, and so forth.

Minority Discount. A discount based on the concept that no person would pay as much for a noncontrolling interest in an asset such as an LLC as for a controlling interest (generally speaking, more than 50%). If you make a gift of an interest in your LLC to your child, the value of the gift must be determined to ascertain whether a gift tax would be due. The gift is generally valued at its fair market value. However, this value may be reduced for a minority discount. See also "Fair Market Value."

Nonrecourse Liability. A liability for which no person is liable. Only the property securing the debt can be used by the lender to satisfy the debt. For example, if your LLC buys real estate, it may be able to secure nonrecourse financing where no Member is personally liable as a guarantor on the debt. If your LLC is taxed as a partnership, the partnership tax allocation rules could have important implications for Members in claiming a tax deduction for interest and other items related to this financing.

One Class of Stock. A reference to the rule that an S corporation generally can have only one class of stock. Differences in the rights of shares that are permitted with S corporations are very limited (e.g., some shares can be voting and others nonvoting). However, liquidation and distribution rights of every share must be identical. While there have been numerous proposals to liberalize these requirements, none have been enacted as of the date of writing this book. Absent liberalization of these rules, an LLC that is taxed as a partnership has substantial advantages over an S corporation in that the Members are permitted great latitude in allocating income, profits, deductions, and so forth. The allocations must, however, meet the requirement of having substantial economic effect.

Operating Agreement. The written contract between all the owners (Members) and generally also those in charge of operating the LLC (Managers). An LLC Operating Agreement is analogous to a corporation's shareholders' agreement and a partnership's partnership agreement. This agreement should address in detail the rights and obligations of Members and Managers. It should contain buyout provisions in the event of the death or disability of a Member. Tax issues should be addressed: naming a Tax Matters Partner and defining his or her rights; allocation of tax benefits; and so forth. It will almost always be a mistake to think that an Operating Agreement can be avoided to save costs.

Ordinary and Necessary Expense. With reference to taxes, a requirement for deductibility. For payments to be deductible, they must be ordinary and necessary expenses of your trade or business. Extravagant or personal expenses will not be deductible. These restrictions will apply to the LLC and thus affect your ability as a Member to claim your share of deductions. Also, if asset protection is a concern, the payment of personal expenses through your LLC, in addition to tax problems, will increase the risk that the limited liability protection afforded by the LLC may be pierced.

Ordinary Income. Income or gain from selling property that is not a capital asset. Ordinary income is taxed at rates of up to 39.6 percent, which is less favorable than capital gains rates of a maximum 28 percent. There is an advantage for taxpayers to realize capital gains rather than ordinary income in many instances.

Organizational Expenses. Costs incurred to set up a business, such as your LLC, that can't be currently deducted. Instead these costs can be written off (amortized) over 60 months beginning with the date your business, partnership or corporation begins to conduct an active business. Be sure to discuss this with your accountant when organizing your LLC.

Partnership. A syndicate, joint venture, group, or other arrangement, in which two or more investors join their money and skills to carry out a business as coowners and to earn a profit. A partnership is generally treated as a flow-through (conduit) so that each partner reports his or her share of partnership income or loss on their personal tax return. The partnership files a Form 1065 as an information report with the IRS but does not pay any tax. An election is available to avoid being taxed as a partnership.

Partnership Interest. The ownership of part of a partnership. Since most LLCs are taxed as partnerships, your ownership of the LLC (your Membership interest) will be treated for tax purposes as a partnership interest.

Passive Income. A type of income. The passive income and loss rules divide income into three types: (1) active (wages, income from an active business); (2) passive (income earned from rental property or as a limited partner investor); and (3) portfolio (dividends and interest on stocks and bonds). Passive losses (tax losses from rental property or from investments made as a limited partner) can only be applied to offset passive income. If you qualify as actively participating in a real estate rental activity, you may be able to deduct up to $25,000 of your passive tax losses against any income without regard to this limitation. Your interest in an LLC will be treated as generating passive or active income depending on the nature of the LLC's business and assets, as well as your involvement.

Passive Loss. Tax losses from rental real estate properties (e.g., as a result of depreciation write-offs) or from investments as a limited partner. Passive losses can generally only be used to offset passive income. If your LLC owns interests in rental real estate, the income or loss generated will be passive for your tax purposes unless you meet the requirement of being an active real estate professional.

Personal Property. Furniture, equipment, and other movable property and assets. Buildings and land are not personal property, they are real property. Real property and tangible personal property are generally subject to probate in the state in which they are located on your death. If you are domiciled (permanently reside) in another state, you can avoid ancillary probate in the state where personal or real property is located by transferring those tangible assets into an LLC since your ownership of an LLC will generally be viewed as an intangible property interest not subject to ancillary probate.

Present Interest. A reference to a gift that the beneficiary can enjoy immediately. A gift must be of present interest to qualify for the annual $10,000 gift tax exclusion. A gift of an interest in an LLC to a child or other donee (and not into a trust) should generally qualify as a gift of a present interest. However, if you as the donor and parent have excessive controls over the LLC and the distribution of income, the IRS may argue that no gift was actually made. For example, if the LLC owns net leased real estate where there is no need for any services, but you take all the LLC income yourself as a salary (to avoid paying distributions to your children who received gifts of LLC interests), the IRS may argue that the gift of the LLC interests to your children was not a gift of a present interest.

Probate. The process of marshalling assets of a deceased person, having the will recognized by the court (often called Surrogate's Court), and having the person designated in the will (personal administrator or executor) officially empowered to act (often by issuance of documents called letters testamentary). Ancillary probate is probate in a state other than the state in which you reside. Ancillary probate, and the attendant fees and time delays can be avoided, in many instances, through use of LLCs.

Pro Rata Share. A simple (from an economic perspective) LLC arrangement in which each Member shares pro rata in the income, expenses, profits, and losses of the LLC. In a more complex arrangement, special allocations of income, expenses, profits, and losses may be used instead.

Qualified Subchapter S Trust (QSST). One type of trust that can own shares in an S corporation. To own shares in an S corporation, a trust must meet specific qualifying requirements. Because an LLC is not subject to these complexities, it can be more flexible to use in an estate-planning context.

Qualified Terminable Interest Property (Q-TIP) Trust. One type of trust that qualifies for the unlimited marital tax exclusion. Therefore, there will be no estate tax on the value of the property transferred to your spouse in a Q-TIP trust on your death. Your spouse must receive all income at least annually until her death. The Q-TIP enables your spouse to obtain income and other benefits, your estate avoids tax, and you can designate who will receive the property remaining in the trust on your spouse's death.

Recourse Liabilities. Debts of an LLC for which individual Members are personally liable. Contrast with Nonrecourse Liabilities.

Registered Agent. A person designated to receive notices directed to an entity. Most entities, LLCs included, specify in the documents they file when formed (Articles of Organization for an LLC) a person upon whom notice should be given (served) in the event of a lawsuit or other matter. This designated person is often called a Registered Agent. If the person named moves to a new address, or is no longer appropriate (e.g., he or she is no longer a Member), be careful to file the appropriate documents to change the Registered Agent and office.

S Corporation. A corporation whose income is generally taxed only to its shareholders, thus avoiding a corporate level tax. An S corporation must meet numerous restrictions to qualify for this favorable tax treatment. An LLC is not subject to these restrictions and when structured to be taxed as a partnership (which most are) can have the same tax benefits of an S corporation with much greater ease and flexibility.

Section 6166 Deferral. A Code provision that permits an estate to defer the estate tax for a period of up to approximately 14 years. Interests in LLCs can qualify for this benefit when the various requirements are met.

Section 2503(c) Trust.   A special trust established for minor children that permits gifts to it to qualify for the annual $10,000 gift tax exclusion even though they are not gifts of a present interest. Gifts of LLC interests can be made outright to a child or in trust for the child for even greater control. Where the gifts are made in trust, the 2503(c) rules can be important.

Shareholders.   Owners of a corporation. This is analogous to owners of an LLC, who are called Members.

Small Business Investment Company.   A company that qualifies for the reinvestment of gain on the sale of securities on a tax-free basis. An LLC does not appear to meet the requirements.

Small Business Stock.   For purposes of taxation, stock that may be eligible for exclusion. Up to one-half of the gain on the sale of certain small business stock may qualify for exclusion from taxation. This benefit can effectively reduce the capital gains cost on qualifying investments to a 14 percent level. An LLC does not appear to meet the requirements for this exclusion.

Sole Proprietorships.   A business run by one person that is owned and operated without any legal entity (no corporation, partnership, or LLC). Advantages of using a sole proprietorship are simplicity, no additional cost and one level of tax. The tremendous disadvantage is that the owner will have unlimited personal liability. An LLC is not an option for a sole proprietor in most states since at least two Members are generally required to form an LLC. The solution may be to make a spouse, child, partner, or business associate a nominal owner (Member).

Tangible Property.   Assets that have physical existence. Real estate, equipment, and furniture are examples of tangible property. Where you own tangible property in a state other than the one in which you permanently reside (where you are domiciled), it will be subject to ancillary probate on your death. An LLC can avoid this.

Taxable Income.   Cash or certain economic benefits that you receive or have control over (constructive receipt), which are subject to tax (because no exclusion is allowed for them).

Tax Basis.   A formula for determining the taxable value of property. The amount invested to purchase property, plus the cost of capital improvements, less depreciation is the adjusted tax basis in that property. For an interest in an LLC, the calculation is more complex. Where the LLC is treated as a partnership for tax purposes, your adjusted tax basis could include the fair market value of property you contributed to the LLC, the amount you paid to purchase the LLC interest, your pro rata share of certain LLC debts, less amounts distributed to you, and so forth. Your adjusted tax basis is the amount used to determine any taxable gain or loss on your sale of the LLC or other asset.

Trust.   Property held and managed by a person (trustee) for the benefit of another (beneficiary). The terms of the trust are generally governed by a contract that the grantor prepares when establishing the trust. LLC interests can be given to a trust for the benefit of your child or any other beneficiary.

Unified Credit.   Permits an individual to gift (during life and death) up to $600,000 of assets to any person or persons without paying any federal estate or gift taxes on this amount. There have been many proposals to increase or decrease this amount.

Uniform Gifts (Transfers) to Minors Act (UGMA or UTMA).   A method to hold property for the benefit of another person, such as your child, which is similar to a trust, but which is governed by state law. It is simpler and much cheaper to establish than a trust and administer, but is far less flexible.

Uniform Limited Liability Company Act (ULLCA).   A uniform act proposed for LLCs. Many states have, or will eventually enact some version of this. Be careful not to assume that any particular state follows the ULLCA in all respects. There are often subtle, if not significant differences between the statutes in different states even where those statutes are based on the same uniform act.

Unrealized Receivables. A receivable that has not yet become actual. In certain cases, the sale of your interest in an LLC will be taxed as ordinary income and not the more favorably taxed capital gains. Where the LLC has realized substantial income (and met other complex and rigid mechanical tests) from unrealized receivables, this may occur. The objective of this tax concept is to prevent you from using an LLC (or other entity) to convert ordinary income (taxed at rates of up to 39.6%) to capital gains (taxed at 28%). For example, if your LLC manufactured widgets to sell in the ordinary course of its business, ordinary income would be realized. However, if just before making the sales you sold all your LLC interests to someone else who would then sell the widgets, you would appear to have capital gains on the sale of your interests (since Membership interests in an LLC are generally a capital asset producing capital gains). However, the widgets may be characterized as unrealized receivables, and you may have to report some or all of the gain on selling your LLC as ordinary income.

Value. The worth attached to something exchanged. For purposes of making a gift of an LLC, you must determine the value of the interest given away. For tax purposes, the fair market value is the value to use.

INDEX